THE PSYCHOLOGY AND TREATMENT
OF THE YOUTHFUL OFFENDER

THE PSYCHOLOGY AND TREATMENT
OF THE YOUTHFUL OFFENDER

By

DAVID E. BRANDT, PH.D.

Associate Professor of Psychology
John Jay College of Criminal Justice
New York, New York

and

S. JACK ZLOTNICK, PH.D.

Associate Professor of Psychology
John Jay College of Criminal Justice
New York, New York

CHARLES C THOMAS • PUBLISHER
Springfield • Illinois • U.S.A.

Published and Distributed Throughout the World by

CHARLES C THOMAS • PUBLISHER

2600 South First Street

Springfield, Illinois 62794-9265

© *1988 by* CHARLES C THOMAS • PUBLISHER

ISBN 0-398-05454-1

Library of Congress Catalog Card Number: 88-1119

With THOMAS BOOKS *careful attention is given to all details of manufacturing
and design. It is the Publisher's desire to present books that are satisfactory as to their
physical qualities and artistic possibilities and appropriate for their particular use.*
THOMAS BOOKS *will be true to those laws of quality that assure a good name
and good will.*

Printed in the United States of America
Q-R-3

Library of Congress Cataloging in Publication Data

Brandt, David E.
   The psychology and treatment of the youthful offender / by David
E. Brandt and S. Jack Zlotnick.
     p. cm.
   Bibliography: p.
   Includes index.
   ISBN 0-398-05454-1
   1. Juvenile delinquents--Psychology. 2. Rehabilitation of
juvenile delinquents. 3. Juvenile delinquency--Prevention.
I. Zlotnick, S. Jack. II. Title.
   [DNLM: 1. Juvenile Delinquency--prevention & control. 2. Juvenile
Delinquency--psychology. 3. Juvenile Delinquency--rehabilitation.
HV 9069 B821p]
HV9069.B73   1988
364.3'6'019--dc19
DNLM/DLC
for Library of Congress
                                             88-1119
                                              CIP

To my wife, Grace, my Mother,
and the Memory of my Father and Grandmother

D.E.B.

and

To my wife, Joan,
and the Memory of my Father and Mother

S.J.Z.

ACKNOWLEDGMENTS

IT IS WITH much gratitude that we wish to acknowledge all those who have made this book a reality, especially the many youths with whom we have worked over the years in rehabilitation programs and community agencies, as well as the students whom we have taught at John Jay College of Criminal Justice and from whom we have learned so much.

We are especially grateful to the staff of the John Jay College Library, especially Antony Simpson, and to Andrew Garoogian of the Brooklyn College Library for their assistance in obtaining research material. We also wish to thank Paula Seidman, the Juvenile Justice Information Specialist at the Juvenile Justice Clearinghouse/NCJRS, Rockville, Maryland, for her responsiveness to questions on a wide range of topics; Joan Zlotnick, for her editing of the manuscript; and Linda VonLumm, for her care in deciphering our handwriting and typing the manuscript. Finally, we are indebted to our wives, Grace and Joan, and our children, Karen and Ari, and Ira and Carrie, for their forebearance and encouragement during the time it took to complete this book.

INTRODUCTION

THE IDEA FOR writing this book resulted from our teaching experiences with a course, not surprisingly entitled "The Psychological Treatment of the Youthful Offender." As both the title of the course and this book suggest, we are not attempting to present a comprehensive assessment of delinquency but rather are focusing our discussion on a number of the basic problems inherent in the areas of delinquency development and its treatment as understood from a psychological perspective.

This does not mean that we have ignored the important historical antecedents that have brought us to this juncture or some of the major problems that exist in the field generally, but, wherever possible, they will be considered in relation to the ways they have intersected with psychological research and formulations. It is these historical antecedents that serve as background for a better understanding of the complexities that have been inherent from the beginning in the discussion of delinquent behavior.

While it is difficult to conceive of any single set of factors that can adequately explain all of the conditions leading to such behavior, we will, nevertheless, highlight some of the salient ones that are suggested by the literature. This leads us, of course, to a consideration of the necessary but nonetheless regrettable omissions we have made. Doubtless, a book on a topic whose literature is as vast as that of delinquency presents a number of logistic and organizational problems concerning what can be included and excluded from the discussion without major sacrifices to the book's coherence or fidelity to the research that has been conducted. We made the decision, for example, to exclude a comprehensive discussion of sociological theory in relation to psychological theory vis-à-vis the topic of delinquency as well as any extensive consideration of alcohol and drug abuse and youth gangs.

Notwithstanding such exclusions, the book focuses on the ways in which delinquent behavior and our psychological understanding of it continue to be in the process of evolving and changing as basic assumptions are challenged and new theories proposed. The first chapter on the history of delinquency traces some of the philosophical, religious, legal, and economic formulations and beliefs that have informed society's conceptualization of the youthful offender. The chapter also describes how psychology entered the discussion vis-à-vis its recognition of adolescence as a distinct phase in the human life cycle and how, over time, that recognition has affected society's treatment of delinquents.

Chapter II explores definitional issues raised in the discussion of delinquency measurement, along with the complexities involved in attempting to accurately report and assess its occurrence from official and unofficial sources. Chapter III examines the contribution that the research on abnormal psychology brings to the subject of antisocial and deviant behavior, raises definitional issues, and questions theoretical assumptions concerning the meaning of abnormal behavior. It also considers the ways in which clinical assessments inform the classification and treatment of abnormal behavior.

Early childhood and adolescent development are the respective subjects of Chapters IV and V, which examine antisocial behavior from a psychodynamic perspective with a recognition of its developmental characteristics. Consideration is given to the youth's life history, with special attention paid to his cognitive-moral development within the early, middle, and late phases of adolescence.

Chapters VI and VII are devoted to a review of some of the psychosocial and biological variables that have been associated with aggressive, antisocial, criminal, and delinquent behavior. Chapter VI reviews behaviorist as well as social learning theories in relation to delinquency and discusses some of the ways in which family characteristics and certain types of psychopathology have been associated with delinquency. Included also is a brief discussion of sociological and psychological theory as regards the role reinforcement plays in delinquent behavior. Chapter VII goes on to assess the biological and genetic theories of human development in relation to antisocial and criminal behavior. Among the studies included for discussion are those suggesting linkages between delinquency and low intelligence, temperament and body type, and chromosomal abnormality. In addition, there is a review of twin studies and adoption studies, which have supported a belief in the genetic linkage to crime and delinquency. It is suggested that the debate between biological and environmental determinants of delinquency poses a false dichotomy based on erroneous assumptions concerning causuality and that the interest of research might be better served by focusing more attention on the interactive aspects of biological and environmental factors rather than studying them as if each operates in a vacuum devoid of the other's influence.

Classification issues as they relate to categorizing delinquents for purposes of treatment are discussed in Chapter VIII. The classification systems described include the Quay System, the I-Level system, DSM-III, and finally Megargee's system based on the use of the MMPI, which the authors suggest may turn out to eventually be the most practical and feasible approach to delinquency classification yet available.

Chapter IX provides the reader with an overview of the research literature that pertains to treating the youthful offender. It includes discussions of the psychodynamic, individual, group, and family treatments, as well as a consideration of behavior modification and "third force" approaches such as Transactional Analysis and Reality Therapy. The chapter also explores problems related to the treatment of young involuntary clients and makes a number of recommendations concerning the initial clinical interview, building and maintaining a therapeutic relationship, transference and countertransference, timing interventions, and overcoming resistance. Issues of confidentiality, race, and techniques that are particularly helpful in working with nonverbal youth are also raised, as is the controversy regarding treatment efficacy and rehabilitation of the youthful offender.

The concluding chapter is devoted to the subject of prediction and prevention. It summarizes many of the factors identified earlier as salient to the etiology of delinquency and describes still other markers for predictive purposes as well as identifies youths whose family background and history make them most vulnerable to delinquency. A number of prevention programs and approaches to prevention are described, and there is a consideration of the various problems that have been targeted in the area of delinquency prevention as well as recommendations on how best to resolve some of these issues. Finally, there is the suggestion that we continue to view delinquency prevention from a mental health perspective as just one form of many maladaptive behaviors that can develop from the combination of negative family and other influences and, further, that mental health practitioners support attempts to arrive at a national policy for youth, with greater resources devoted to primary, secondary, and tertiary prevention in the home, the community, and the school.

CONTENTS

THE PSYCHOLOGY AND TREATMENT
OF THE YOUTHFUL OFFENDER

Chapter I

OVERVIEW AND CHANGING HISTORICAL PERSPECTIVES OF YOUTHFUL OFFENDERS AND THE LAW

IF IT WERE possible to convene all the child savers of the past to share their motivations and aspirations concerning those youths they had hoped to reform, we would undoubtedly not find a clearly evolving historical tapestry of youth reform. What we would encounter instead would be something more akin to a patchwork quilt of designs and configurations held together in some places by religious and philosophical threads, in other areas by social and economic fibers, and in still others by demographic, political, and legal ones. In short, while there might be much interweaving throughout, there would be very little evidence that the threads of science had found their way into the finished product until the beginning of the twentieth century.

While successive groups of reformers felt that they had found the panacea and best approach for rescuing growing numbers of dependent, neglected, incorrigible, and delinquent youth, all would eventually be superseded by still other reformers who would portray their predecessors' efforts as poorly conceived and totally inadequate.

While their motivations at reform were well intentioned, all their work, given the state of knowledge at the time, condemned those efforts to failure. It was not until the advent of psychology that systematic efforts would be undertaken to view youths more appropriately from the standpoint of their nature and needs. This would eventually lead to a social recognition and legitimization of their special status in the human life cycle, thus enhancing the possibility of achieving success in the rehabilitation of delinquent youth.

At the turn of the century in the United States, there were two occurrences which are of interest to our discussion of the psychological treatment of the youthful offender. The first to occur was a legal change in the court's treatment of the youthful offender and the second was a change in the way psychology would come to view this age group.

The state of Illinois passed the Juvenile Court Act in 1899. This act established the first juvenile court and served as a standard for all other states to follow in dealing with juvenile court cases. In establishing the justification for its action, the court declared its need to serve as *parens patriae* for both the protection and the rehabilitation of its charges. In effect, the passing of this act removed from the courts the traditional adversarial roles toward those before it and exchanged them for human service roles. In this manner the court sought to have all concerned arrive at decisions that were first and foremost in "the best interests" of the juvenile. Hearings, henceforth, were to be informal and diagnostic in purpose, and due process guarantees considered necessary for adult criminal trials were to be waived. In brief, the mission of adjudication and punishment where indicated was to be subordinated to that of care and rehabilitation.

While this new "enlightened" judicial spirit was spreading to other states across the nation, another form of enlightenment was unfolding in the area of psychology. It was with the publication in 1904 of G. Stanley Hall's book *Adolescence* that the term "adolescence" took on a pivotal importance and came into prominent use among psychologists and society generally. Juveniles in their teens were now to be viewed as a separate developmental category with very special characteristics and problems that were clearly distinct from those of childhood and adulthood. Recognizing the turbulence of adolescence, Hall stated:

> The teens are emotionally unstable and pathic. It is a natural impulse to experience hot and perfervid psychic states, and it is characterized by emotionalism. (p. 74)

Hall, who was greatly influenced by the Darwinian theory and the anthropological thought so prominent in his time, came to conceive of adolescence as representing the second of three stages in human evolution, which he viewed as being recapitulated by the individual as he grew from childhood to adolescence and finally to adulthood. The corresponding evolutionary stages were savagery, barbarism, and finally civilization.

A segment of Hall's work which was much more readily accepted than his evolutionary model related to his belief that adolescence was a distinct developmental period of great upheaval and adjustment characterized by much conflict and confusion, which Hall referred to as *Sturm and Drang.* This storm and stress, as it was called, resulted from opposing pressures brought on by the maturation process of the adolescent as he continued to develop physically, intellectually and emotionally while concurrently having to deal with and adjust to the growing demands and pressures of the social world in which he found himself.

As a pioneer in the field of adolescent psychology, Hall was one of those who helped set the stage for major developments in the field which would prove as important if not more so than the changes wrought within the legal system. Psychology would henceforth provide a deeper and richer understanding of childhood, adolescence, growth and maturation. It would highlight and specify the interaction between physical, emotional, and intellectual factors in the personality formation of developing youth. It would come to delineate the intra-psychic importance of stage-specific experiences while concurrently examining their role when deficient in deviant, antisocial and even criminal behavior. Finally, psychology would continue to formulate a theoretical basis upon which to establish treatment modalities in order to effect adjustments in adolescents generally and the rehabilitation of the youthful offender specifically.

It would be safe to say that the turn of the century was the time when juveniles generally and those youths in trouble with the law in particular came under increasing scrutiny from both the legal and the psychological community. Yet, while it is true that the first juvenile court law in the United States was enacted in 1899, it should be recognized that this law came into being as a result of historical factors which greatly influenced its enactment. Although children were, until this time, tried with adults in criminal court, a number of courts, notably those in the District of Columbia and Boston, had attempted to establish special hours or sessions to deal with trials in juvenile cases (International Prison Commission, 1904), and there had been, prior to this, a number of other attempts to improve the treatment of delinquent youth in the United States.

It was the Chicago court, however, that in 1899 first legally defined juvenile delinquency when it applied the term to "Any child under the age of sixteen years who violates any law of this state or any city or village ordinance"; in the next legislative session, the definition was expanded to include any youth under the age of sixteen who was "incorrigible, or who knowingly associates with thieves, vicious, or immoral persons, or who is growing up in idleness or crime, or who knowingly patronizes any policy shop or place where any gaming device is or shall be operational" (International Prison Commission, p. 2).

While this legal definition of juvenile delinquency may seem harsh by modern standards, it should be remembered that historically not only had youths been tried in court along with adults but also that often little or no distinction had been made between juvenile and adult offenders. Even when distinctions had been made, the penalties proscribed for youths had been, for the most part, exceedingly severe. This legislation, then, which both defined the term "juvenile delinquency" and provided for the establishment of the first juvenile court in America, must be viewed as a positive step which would ultimately lead to a more equitable treatment of delinquent youths under the law.

Prior to this time then, and, in fact, throughout recorded history, with few exceptions, youths who had violated society's statutes had been dealt with by judicial bodies, however constituted, in a most punitive and severe manner, and at least one scholar indicates that at times youths were subject to even greater penalties than adults would be for certain offenses (Marcus, 1981).

In his research on the subject of delinquency in ancient times, Marcus, whose study is based on information obtained from Cuniform and biblical sources, notes three differences between ancient and modern views:

> In the first place age is not a factor in the determination of a delinquent in the ancient Near East: age is never mentioned in the texts. A minor, for all intents and purposes, was one who was living in his or her parent's house. . . . Responsibility for a minor's behavior rested solely with the parent. Any anti-social act committed by the minor was considered also an offense against the parent who dealt with it accordingly. When proceedings are instituted against a minor . . . it is the parent, not the courts, who institute proceedings. (p. 32)

Truancy was the second category of difference between ancient and modern concepts of delinquency. In the ancient Near East there was no such phenomenon as truancy, since there was no universal education. The third, and for our purposes most important, distinction is that "in ancient times there was no special protection extended to juveniles convicted in criminal cases: the penalty for both an adult and a minor was the same" (p. 33). Moreover, there were times when youths were even more harshly punished than adult offenders; this was the case in offenses against the parent.

Section 195 of the Code of Hammurabi, for example, states that a son who intentionally strikes his father will have his hand cut off. This punishment was known as the mirror punishment, the principle of which Marcus explains as follows:

. . . the part of the body which is instrumental in the offense is considered the guilty party and hence disposed of. In this case it is the hand which is considered guilty and is cut off. (p. 33)

The biblical punishment for this offense is even more severe. Exodus 21:15 proscribes death for the son who intentionally strikes his father or mother. Scholars doubt whether in fact these types of punishments were actually carried out. In the case of biblical punishments, their severity was greatly mitigated by the Talmud, which established procedural obstacles to such penalties, and while there is no explicit statement regarding the age at which criminal responsibility begins, rabbinic law does not appear to have permitted corporeal punishment before puberty or capital punishment before age twenty (Ludwig, 1955). Still, what remains of interest to our discussion is the fact that these severe punishments were proscribed in cases where the offense was against the parent. When the youth assaulted a person other than his parent, the proscribed penalty was less severe. The youth would either be fined or flogged, as under the Code of Hammurabi, or fined, as in the case of ancient Israel.

> Thus we have a situation where striking a non-parent makes one subject to regular criminal law, but striking a parent makes one subject to a "juvenile delinquent" law which carries a more severe penalty. . . . This is precisely the opposite of our modern concept where lack of criminal responsibility by reason of age is a defense, and where one covered by a juvenile delinquent law would receive a less severe sentence than would an adult in a similar case. (Marcus, 1981, p. 34)

Roman law, too, appears to have been exceedingly harsh in its penalties for youthful offenders. The old civil law, which gave fathers the power of life and death over their children, allowed them not only to treat their children and grandchildren as chattel, selling them into slavery at whim, but also to deliver a delinquent child into the bondage of the injured party (Sohm, 1970).

Attempts were made to check such practices by the Twelve Tables (c. 488-451 B.C.E.), which also made distinctions between criminals based on age. While, for example, the death penalty would be imposed on an adult for theft of crops at night, a youth who had not yet attained puberty would, for the same offense, be subject to a fine and a flogging. But having attained puberty, youngsters were no longer entitled to mitigated treatment under Roman law. For those between infancy, which lasted until age seven and was deemed a period of absolute irresponsibility, and puberty, responsibility was determined by how close in age the child was either to infancy or puberty, the nature of the criminal act, and the offender's mental capacity (Ludwig, 1955).

When we examine Anglo-Saxon law we see that it not only specifies the penalties that a youth can be subject to, but that it also makes reference to the age at which the youth is culpable. In the Laws of King Ine (688 C.E.-725 C.E.), it is stated:

> If any one steal so that his wife and his children know it not let him pay LX shilling as 'wite.' (punishment). But if he steal with knowledge of all his household, let him go into slavery. A boy of X years may be privy to a theft . . . (Sanders, 1970, p. 3).

Two hundred years later, the English King Aethelstan (924 C.E.-938 C.E.) proscribed the death penalty for youths above the age of twelve, decreeing that "no thief be spared who may be taken "hand-haebbende" (i.e. with the goods in his hand) above XII years, and above eight pence" (Sanders, p. 3).

In time the laws changed and eventually only those youths under the age of sixteen who resisted arrest or attempted to escape could be executed. In fact, however, there was a distinction between theory and practice, and children as young as eight, ten, and thirteen continued to be executed although thieves under the age of seven were pardoned (Mennel, 1973).

While the seventeenth and eighteenth centuries saw the emergence of such institutional responses to delinquency as Pope Clement XI's Hospital of Saint Michael in Rome, which provided for the care, instruction, and rehabilitation of profligate youth (Sellin, 1930), the treatment of youthful offenders continued for the most part to be severe and frequently not too distinct from that of the adult offender.

It is appropriate at this time to recognize that one of the reasons for this phenomenon was that childhood as a concept that required special considerations and treatment is a rather recent development.

Indifference toward childhood, as reflected by the practice of infanticide, was prevalent in ancient civilizations and persisted in Europe as late as the seventeenth and eighteenth centuries. While such practices eventually declined, the infant mortality rate remained high, with about two-thirds of all children dying before age four (Empey, 1979).

In an attempt to understand the extraordinary nature of family life in general and of parenthood in particular when such high infant mortality rates prevailed, Empey states that:

No parent could retain his or her sanity if he or she became too emotionally involved with such ephemeral creatures as young children.
Aloofness, or the acceptance of God's will, or sending one's children
away from home were three natural solutions to this problem of how to
deal with their deaths. (p. 29)

Still another mode of coping was to allow no distinction between children and adults. Aries (1962), writing about children in the Middle
Ages, points out that

In medieval society the idea of childhood did not exist; this is not to
suggest that children were neglected, forsaken or despised. The idea of
childhood is not to be confused with affection for children; it corre-
sponds to an awareness of the particular nature of childhood . . .
which distinguishes the child from the adult, even the young adult. . .
[In the middle ages] as soon as the child could live without . . . his
mother . . . he belonged to adult society. (p. 128)

What it meant for a child to enter the adult world was that he
dressed, conversed, cursed, drank, engaged in sex and was used sexu-
ally by others, and rarely attended school (pp. 321-322).

If it is true that at one time children beyond infancy were not considered too different from the adults around them, the question that remains to be answered is as follows: What factors contributed to the
emergence of childhood as a concept in the eighteenth century to be succeeded soon after in the nineteenth and twentieth centuries by the
further differentiation of youths into the categories of childhood and
adolescence?

The evidence seems to suggest that a confluence of social, economic,
and political factors, to say nothing of changing philosophical views and
new developments in medicine which greatly reduced the infant mortality rate, ultimately promulgated the concept of childhood. Among the
most critical factors cited by Empey (1978) are the development of children as symbols of innocence and purity (15th and 16th centuries), the
notion of children as guileless, but corruptible (16th and 17th centuries),
the emergence of the nuclear family, and, in the same period, the re-
placement of apprenticeship by schooling (17th and 18th centuries).

By the beginning of the nineteenth century, the development of the
concept of childhood

had resulted in the espousal of a series of nurturance rights for *all* children, even those of the unworthy poor; the right to life, food, clothing,
and shelter, and moral standards to follow. The length of childhood had
also been extended, and age-segregation was more apparent. (Empey,
p. 71)

In the United States, as a result of immigration and massive population shifts, still another development was taking place at this time that would further enhance the concept of childhood. This was an exceedingly high birth rate. Coupled with rapidly declining infant mortality rates, it created a situation where "for the first time . . . education of the young and extended preparation for adult life could be urged upon all classes of society as a rewarding investment" (Grotberg, 1976, p. 425).

With expanding population, immigration, industrialization, and urbanization in nineteenth century America, there was a concomitant increase in the growth of social institutions with increasing bureaucratic responsibility for dealing with the needs of wayward and neglected children, their growing numbers deriving in large measure from broken homes, poverty, dislocation, lack of supervision, and abuse. The plight of such children captured the imagination and pricked the conscience of reformers of that time, thus leading to the refuge movement in America.

While the progressive and benevolent attitude toward the child is generally associated with the reform movement of the nineteenth century, the idealogy underlying this movement had its origin in earlier times. Conflicting as they were, the views of the Puritans and those of such enlightened philosophers as Rousseau contributed to the thinking of the nineteenth century reformers. Whereas the Puritans tried to reform or "save" the children, whom they believed to be innately evil, years later such thinkers as Rousseau were concerned about saving the children, whom they perceived as innately innocent, from the corruption of their environment.

The Puritans' view of children, while theological in origin, was also shaped by the economic necessities of the time. In the latter part of the seventeenth century, life in America was basically agricultural. It was a struggle for survival, and every child's behavior was regulated and subsumed under the common needs of the family through obedience to the parents, whose property he was considered. The child's training and socialization were a matter of necessity, considering the dangers of colonial life, especially if he was eventually to enter the adult world.

This discipline and training were particularly critical in view of the Puritans' concept of the child as innately evil and in need of a rigorous moral upbringing if he was not to bring shame and dishonor upon himself, his family, and his community. Children whose parents failed to raise them properly could be forced to live with another family for purposes of full apprenticeship to an adult social role.

The Puritans were so concerned about the child's morality that they enacted laws to regulate his behavior. In fact, it was in 1646 that the first law pertaining to the child was passed in North America, a law which remained on the books, with some revisions, well into the twentieth century. This was the Massachusetts Stubborn Child Law, which made provisions for punishing juveniles over the age of sixteen who profaned the Sabbath (Powers, 1974, p. 9).

Indeed, the Puritan values continued to have an impact, albeit a diminishing one, on the ways society viewed behavior in general and the behavior of children in particular at the beginning of the nineteenth century. The equation between criminal behavior and sinning was, according to Empey (1979), still very much a part of the social thinking. The affirmation of punishment to both expiate the criminal/sinner and do God's will helped maintain community needs for vengeance and protection.

Slowly, the effects of the philosophy of enlightenment, coupled with the development of the Classical School of Criminology, produced a view that placed greater reliance on human reason and free will as the determinants of human behavior. The Classical School, at once influenced by the new spirit of rationalism and reacting against Europe's criminal justice system, which was "savage . . . unfair, secretive and capricious," employing torture and conducting trials on the presumption of guilt (Brantingham, 1979, p. 37), argued for more rational and humane laws and penalties. Cesare Beccaria, its founder, claimed that human behavior could be shaped through a system of rewards and punishments. Positing his theory on the notion that human behavior is based on hedonistic principles, he argued that if penalties for criminal acts outweighed the pleasure inherent in those acts, then individuals would freely and rationally choose not to engage in such behavior.

As for the philosophers of the enlightenment, they believed that through reason man would be capable of knowing himself as well as improving his condition, and, further, that man was not evil by nature. The newborn child was a *tabla rosa* and, as such, was in a natural state of innocence. Now, when behavior was a problem, instead of attempting to correct the innately evil nature of the child, society's reformers sought to "correct" the environment of the child, namely, the family. If the family could not be reformed so that it would adequately train and discipline its young, then the children would have to be placed in a more disciplined environment, namely, an institution established to care for such children. So we see that while the focus of culpability began to shift from "the wicked child" to his wicked surroundings, the means for reform vis-à-vis sound discipline and the goal of reform — good conduct — remained the same as those in the Puritan era.

Along with this change, there was an increasing lack of confidence on the part of the reformers in the ability of families, especially the poor, whose numbers were growing, to imbue their children with the controls necessary to become industrious and contributing members of society. One method of dealing with this was to invoke the English poor law, which had been transplanted to the colonies, and in earlier times had resulted in the apprenticeship of poor youths.

> In eighteenth century Virginia, for example, officials could bind out as apprentices the children of parents who were poor, not providing "good breeding," neglecting their formal education, not teaching trade, or were idle, dissolute, unchristian or "uncapable." (Rendleman, 1979, p. 63)

Rendleman goes on to point out that this system of separating "undeserving" parents from their children, which had been copied by other colonies and later adopted by the states which enacted legislation toward this end, was viewed by the reformers as a far better alternative to the existing options, namely, for the children of the poor to live in the community poorhouse or almshouse. Children in those houses were exposed to diseases of epidemic proportions, criminal elements, and vagrants. That the system of apprenticing poor youths received widespread support at this time is, according to Rendleman, at least partially explained by the fact that in the nineteenth century, poverty was thought of as a crime:

> . . . vagrant, wayward, delinquent, depraved, dependent, vicious, neglected and perhaps other adjectives were used to describe . . . [both delinquent and poor] children. (p. 66)

The nation was growing and expanding all this time at an unprecedented rate, and the shift was being made from agriculture to manufacturing, from town to city, from home to factory-based production. These factors irrevocably altered family life and had a lasting impact on its structure. The traditional multigenerational family was transmuted as parents and children went out to work in factories, thus changing the existing economic arrangements and roles within the family unit, with the self-sufficient nuclear family replacing the earlier model (Smith et al., 1979a).

The social costs of the dramatic and rapid changes that were occurring throughout the country, especially as they affected the marginal family, the poor, and the child, did not go unnoticed by the reformers of the early nineteenth century, especially those involved with the refuge movement. Pickett (1969) states:

> . . . their activity paved the way for a more humane response to the problems rapidly emerging in the new nation . . . the founding fathers of the Refuge movement felt that the state had a responsibility to the casualties of social and economic change. (p. 20)

There was considerable support for these institutions. One New York City newspaper editor represented the growing sentiment of the public when he wrote:

> If we can clean our streets of the numberless depraved boys and girls that now infest them, and most of whom are frequently tenants of our Bridewell or Penitentiary, a substantial good will be effected and the public relieved of a considerable portion of the taxes raised for these institutions. (p. 59)

The refuges were a major step in the reform movement in at least two ways. First, they were the earliest institutions for dependent and delinquent children that were supported by public funds rather than charities; second, the length of time spent in them by children was a function of administrative judgment. The latter was possible because the refuges represented agencies of the law as well as recognized agencies of reform (Society for the Reformation of Juvenile Delinquents, 1970). It should be noted that the administrators of the refuges were given such discretionary powers, because the time necessary to effect a "cure" for deviance, now equated by some with disease, was a variable dependent upon the administrator's "diagnosis."

Tietelbaum and Harris (1977) suggest that many of the compulsory education laws that were introduced at about this time were also designed to help buttress the family's weakening role in the raising, educating, and socializing of its children. While the compulsory education laws were designed to buttress the declining powers of those families that were still intact, the refuges were established to rescue those youngsters whose families had disintegrated to the point where they were no longer willing or able to provide for their children.

It is evident that the impetus for the refuge movement was a reaction by the reformers to "the indiscriminate institutionalization of children, particularly the practice of sending vagrant and delinquent youths to almshouses and jails where they were confined with adult offenders" (Mennell, 1973, p. 8).

In the mid-nineteenth century, refuges were followed by reformatories, which were believed capable of reforming delinquent youths into law-abiding citizens:

> Reformatories, unlike penitentiaries and jails, theoretically repudiated punishments based on intimidation and repression. They took into account the fact that delinquents were "either physically or mentally below average." . . . [They believed] that proper training can counteract the impositions of poor family life, a corrupt environment, and poverty, while at the same time toughening and preparing delinquents for the struggle ahead. (Platt, 1979, p. 128)

Focusing as they did on the role of heredity and environment on the development of the criminal mentality, those new reformers appear to have anticipated a later development which would take place in the last decades of the nineteenth century, namely, the emergence of the Positive School of Criminology. A reaction against the theoretical and practical failures of the Classical School, it would emphasize the view that human behavior is determined by forces beyond the individual's control. This philosophy would play a role in the development of the juvenile court, as had the earlier establishment of refuges and reformatories, which in their efforts to differentiate between juvenile and adult offenders had significantly shaped the thinking of the juvenile court reformers.

As Haskell and Yablonsky (1978) explain:

> By the end of the nineteenth century as the states provided specialized treatment for children in training schools the criminal courts began to sentence children to schools instead of to prison and to place children on probation for minor offenses. Persons interested in social reform actively sought the establishment of a specialized court for children organized around objectives significantly different from those of the criminal courts. They wanted a court that would understand the child, diagnose his problems and provide treatment that would restore him to a constructive role in the community. The welfare of the child was considered more important than the question of guilt or innocence of an offense. (p. 380)

With the establishment of the juvenile court there was a formal recognition of the legal immaturity of children, and by instituting the concept of *parens patriae* it perpetuated the belief in and concern for the weakening ability of the family to care for its young. The state, in fact, to protect its own interests as well as those of the juveniles, could benevolently intervene to direct the care and custody of youths. In so doing, the juvenile court also gave legal sanction to the stratification of individuals by age.

In truth, the juvenile court and its procedures had evolved from the reform movements of the past even as they were a reaction to them. While former reform movements had established refuges and later reformatories and training schools with the express purpose of separating children from their adult counterparts in order to rehabilitate them, as a result of a confluence of factors, among them declining resources, they had, in fact, done little more than warehouse these youths in quasi-military fashion. Thus, the juvenile court movement, which was the work of latter-day reformers who were concerned about the problems created by the refuges and reformatories, "in fact re-established the ideal of public institution as a rescuer of the delinquent and guarantor of public order" (Smith et al., 1979a, p. 14).

Based then on the doctrine of *parens patriae*, as first enunciated in the English Chancery courts in the fifteenth century, which established the king (or father of his country) as the protector of women and children left destitute as a result of the death or abandonment by their husbands and fathers, the juvenile court assumed the role of benevolent protector of children, acting sometimes as supplement but more often as alternative to the family. Those reformers who established the juvenile court system at the turn of the century thought of it as

> a *child-saving* mission, a rescue operation for the *very young*. In juvenile courts "children were treated as children." Delinquents were of "tender years," or "little ones" whom the court should take "in hand as you would take your own children in hand who had done something wrong." (Rothman, 1979, p. 39)

We can only speculate about the degree to which the early juvenile court movement influenced the growth of the child and adolescent mental health movement and how that movement in turn helped justify the expansion of the juvenile court as a progressive step in the humanitarian approach to delinquent youths. One of the foremost names in the early days of these developments was William Healy, a neurologist indebted to both G. Stanley Hall and Freud. Healy directed the Juvenile Psychopathic Institute of the Chicago juvenile court beginning in 1909, and went on from there to head the Judge Baker Child Guidance Clinic of Boston, which opened in 1917.

Healy viewed delinquent behavior as emanating from emotional conflicts of youthful offenders that derived from repressed instinctual urges and, rather than focusing solely on the negative influences of the youth's environment as a causative agent in delinquency, which was the prevalent approach of that time, he sought significant critical determinants in the youth himself. As Mennel (1973) explains,

Healy always recognized the importance of environmental factors in causing delinquency; he never doubted that social improvements would lessen crime. Nevertheless, his ability to help children depended largely upon his skill as a psychiatrist and he increasingly discussed environment in a familial or personal context and not as a broad social force. . . . Through psychiatric interviews he discovered "potent subconscious mental mechanisms working according to definite laws and . . . types of hidden early experiences which definitely evoke these mental processes that are forerunners of misconduct." (pp. 165-166)

This new direction emphasized the psychological needs of the youthful offender which had to be addressed and led to the establishment of guidance clinics to treat psychologically troubled youth. Bromberg (1965), describing how the advent of child-guidance clinics brought about a new attitude toward crime and punishment, explains that "delinquent boys sent to placement bureaus where social workers studied their needs were placed in foster homes with due care for emotional stresses underlying their delinquencies. . . . In the juvenile court the social worker or probation officer presented the delinquent as a problem that had come to his attention rather than as an indicted criminal" (p. 62).

Juvenile court judges relied heavily on psychological and familial histories of the youths before rendering a decision, and alternatives to institutionalization were actively sought. Often, the youngsters were permitted to remain at home under the supervision of court workers, and the confidentiality of offenders was scrupulously protected. Yet, for all of these and other advances, the juvenile court system was from the outset plagued with problems. Among the most serious were the ambivalence of the court reformers regarding the roles of the court as social agency on the one hand, and as a protector of the social order on the other; the lack of distinction between delinquents committing violent and non-violent crimes and, moreover, between delinquents, dependent, and neglected children; the enormously widespread variations in juvenile justice systems from state to state and even within each state; and, finally, the lack of provision for what is commonly considered due process for juvenile offenders.

Summing up what was achieved by the juvenile justice system in its early decades, Rothman (1979) states:

The record . . . is grim. Probation staffs were invariably undertrained and overworked. Case loads of two hundred or three hundred per office obviously made it impossible for them to carry out their tasks . . . state training schools never did become places of education as opposed to places of punishment. In all, the net result of the juvenile court through its first decades of operation may have been to supplement incarceration, not to substitute for it. (p. 66)

By the nineteen fifties and sixties defects within the juvenile justice system were becoming so evident as to bring it to the forefront of public concern. Contrary to the expectations of the early court reformers, delinquency rates soared, with juveniles committing increasing proportions of serious crimes.

Criticism and pressure for changes in the law was growing from academics, juvenile justice practitioners, and citizens' groups. Their aims were to seek procedural changes, to address the legal fairness of the courts, and to examine the court's failure to make distinctions between violent and non-violent youths. In reaction to this call for change, in 1961 the federal government passed the Juvenile Delinquency and Youth Offenses Control Act, which attempted to initiate a series of changes to better integrate all federal delinquency-related programs as well as to support local economic, social, and educational institutions in their delivery of services to troubled and deprived youths. Shortly thereafter, in 1967, a President's Commission was established to review the existing juvenile justice system and make recommendations for its improvement.

The commission's findings were that resources were not equal to needs and that there were not sufficient trained personnel available to meet the growing demands. The commission also sought to foster greater concern with regard to those youths who had not yet committed crimes and yet were caught up in the same juvenile justice system as those who had.

During this same period of time a number of Supreme Court decisions were rendered: *Kent v. U.S.*, 383 U.S. 541, in 1966; *in re* Gault, 387 U.S. 1, in 1967; and *in re* Winship, 397 U.S. 358, in 1970, which lent legal support to the arguments of a new generation of juvenile court reformers. Respectively, these reforms included the first due process guarantees to juveniles with effective assistance of counsel as regards waiver orders by the courts, the right to counsel and the right to invoke the privilege against self-incrimination as well as to confront and cross-examine witnesses, and finally the requirement that there be proof "beyond a reasonable doubt" before a juvenile could be adjudicated a delinquent for an act which would constitute a crime if committed by an adult.

In these decisions the Supreme Court had all but granted juveniles the same constitutional rights as adults. However, the decision in *McKeiver v. Pennsylvania*, 403 U.S. 528 (1971) reversed this trend by denying youths the right of trial by jury. Another relatively recent development in the juvenile court has been the establishment through statutes of a new category of juveniles most often referred to as status offenders. These youths, variously called PINS (Persons in Need of Supervision), MINS (Minors in Need of Supervision), CHINS (Children in Need of Supervision), or JINS (Juveniles in Need of Supervision), are runaways, truants, and "incorrigibles"—in short, less serious offenders whom the court does not wish to stigmatize by the use of the term "delinquent." Despite apparent gains, some continue to object that such status offender statutes still stigmatize youths, are inequitably enforced, and are unconstitutional (Pennsylvania's Governor's Justice Commission, 1977, p. 71). Some, in fact, have argued that status offenses should be decriminalized.

As Scott (1977) explains:

> Perhaps the greatest controversy surrounding juvenile court is whether or not status offenses should be removed entirely from its jurisdictions. Utah has already done so. Whether status offenses are decriminalized or not, however, there is no question that we have come a long way since the General Laws of Plymouth Colony which provided the death penalty for sixteen offenses including being a "stubborn or rebellious son." (p. 17)

While critics continue to find fault with the juvenile justice system as it is presently constituted, some objecting to its leniency and viewing with skepticism efforts to "rehabilitate" delinquents, others have viewed favorably the reforms of recent years. Regarding the courts, Davis (1980) writes,

> Procedural reforms, while altering the most visible part of the juvenile process — the procedural setting — have not prevented the juvenile court from attaining its basically ameliorative purposes, particularly at the dispositional stage. The protective philosophy has endured, and the juvenile court continues to perform its function of tailoring justice to meet the needs of the child as those are determined by the social service staff. Only by assuring a child of procedural fairness will the court that purports to represent the child's interests impart to him an unjaundiced view of a system of justice that is fair and benevolent. This goal, after all, was one of the original purposes sought to be achieved by application of the principle of *parens patriae.* (p. 1.3)

Another area of controversy at the present time revolves around the role of psychology in the juvenile courts. Some, such as Hakeem (1957), have argued that it has not proven to be beneficial, while others have pointed to the high per capita cost of psychological services in a time of dwindling resources. Responding to these critics, many, including Marohn (1980), have argued that the psychological approach to delinquency must not be abandoned:

> There are many contributing factors to the final common pathway of delinquent behavior. Basic to all of these is the realization that all behavior has psychological meaning and the delinquent act can be understood psychodynamically. From this must flow an attempt to work with delinquent adolescents psychologically and not to minimize or deflect the impact of their psychological problems. Though such an approach may appear costly it is rewarding in its discoveries and accomplishments. (p. 146)

It is obviously the belief of the authors of this book that the role of psychology in dealing with the juvenile delinquent remains critical, and it is with this in mind that we turn to our study of the psychology and treatment of the adolescent offender.

Chapter II

MEASUREMENT OF DELINQUENCY

A S HAS BEEN indicated by some of the earliest documents of recorded history, crime and criminal behavior are subjects which
have been of concern in one form or another since antiquity. With the
development of the physical and natural sciences in the eighteenth and
nineteenth centuries and further advances in science and technology in
the twentieth century, there has been an ever-growing trend to seek
more precision in the documentation of crime as well as a more comprehensive assessment of its meaning.

Among the current problems presented by crime statistics and delinquency reports are those associated with data collection generally,
namely, problems of accuracy and reliability. The possibility of inaccuracy in crime reporting, tabulation, and representativeness leaves
serious questions regarding the validity of the data and the interpretation of their meaning.

Problems in Definition

The first and foremost problem, however, seems to be associated
with the definition of terms, for purposes of this chapter, specifically the
definition of the term "delinquent." The term, whose meaning has been
subject to change over time due in large measure to society's changing
view of delinquent behavior, is at present used by criminal justice personnel in widely varying ways. Such imprecision can have serious consequences, not only in gathering and interpreting data, but in other ways
as well. Consider, for example, what it means to the mental health professional to know that the youth before him has been identified as a delinquent. Due to its connotations, the term can impact significantly on
the client's interview, assessment, and treatment.

21

At least two authors (Gold and Petronio, 1980) imply that many adolescents are actually subject to a unique form of discrimination, since the term "delinquent" is not commonly applied to anyone younger or older than what we now usually consider adolescents, youngsters 13 to 18 years of age. They state:

> In one sense adolescents are most delinquent by definition. Breaking the law before adolescence is attributed to lack of understanding rather than willful deviance; at a later age it is considered a crime. Thus delinquency is an adolescent phenomenon. To state the obvious is not mere pedantry, for the association drawn between adolescence and delinquency has been based largely on official records, which by legal definition must indict adolescents as most delinquent. But there are almost no data that demonstrate that adolescents more often wittingly break the law than children or adults do. (p. 497)

As they explain so aptly at the outset of their essay, "delinquency is presumed to be as endemic to adolescence as acne; the presumption shapes the image of adolescents and shapes the public response to them" (p. 495). Perhaps even more importantly, it also shapes the responses of the professional mental health worker.

To further expand upon the nature of adolescent vulnerability we have only to turn our attention to the realities of how the term "delinquent" is legally defined and how it is used and applied by those in the criminal justice system. To begin with, it should be known that there are approximately 3,000 courts that handle juvenile cases across the country and approximately 16,000 law enforcement agencies, some in counties with just one local sheriff and others in cities with upwards of 27,000 police officers. Even if there were national agreement regarding the definition of delinquency, which there is not, there would still be great disparities in its application, since law enforcement officers among others in the criminal justice system have discretionary powers. Although limited by the seriousness of the offense, such discretionary powers nonetheless constitute a judgment that can result in disparate outcomes, especially in the case of minor offenses. Further, when we examine the statutes, jurisdictions, and outcomes of cases involving juvenile offenders throughout the country, we are left with the disquieting realization that the lack of uniformity in the definition of the terms "delinquency" and "delinquent" often results in consequences which vary across state lines as well as within state lines.

The traditional definition of "delinquent" that is found in most sources refers to a juvenile who has been adjudicated as having committed any act, including the violation of state laws and local ordinances, which, if he were an adult, would result in his being charged with a crime in criminal court. This definition does not adequately recognize those youths who have been adjudicated delinquent whose offenses, if committed by an adult, would not have ended up in the court system. These offenses include truancy, running away from home, and curfew violations, which we now more commonly term status offenses but which in many places are still being defined as delinquency.

The history of this situation and its continuance as a problem suggests how difficult it is to bring about changes which are both judicious and necessary. In their book written over fifty years ago, Reckless and Smith (1932) elaborated on the lack of consensus in definition of the term and, by extension, in the treatment of juvenile delinquents:

> There are regional and sectional differences in the treatment of juvenile delinquents. The decision as to what constitutes juvenile delinquency is a good illustration of the fundamental difficulties of securing adequate statistics at this time. To begin with, the problem of upper age limit of juvenile cases is solved in a variety of ways. The limit varies from sixteen to twenty-one in various states, there being at present no way of enforcing uniform interpretations. Then some courts consider only offenses serious enough to end in commitment to an institution should be called delinquent. (p. 21)

Now, more than fifty years later, when we examine the issue of upper age limit or maximum age at which jurisdiction should be transferred to adult criminal courts, we still find significant variation in both the law and its application. More than ten years ago the National Institute for Juvenile Justice and Delinquency Prevention (1975) reported that

> A majority of state statutes (N = 36) provide for juvenile court jurisdiction until age 18, although several states (N = 5) limit jurisdiction of the juvenile court to those under 16 years of age, and nine states limit original jurisdiction to those under 17 years of age. Several states have different maximum age for young offenders depending on the crime involved. Typically in the latter instance, the juvenile court has jurisdiction up to age 16 in cases involving serious offenses and up to age 18 for all other charges. . . . It should be noted that statutory provisions in all states are accompanied by virtually no commentary or statement of rationale. (p. 9)

The issue of upper age limit was one of many issues assessed by the Task Force for purposes of strengthening and improving the juvenile justice system. The Task Force reported on eight other areas that required attention. They included issues concerning minimum age, age at which jurisdiction attaches, duration of jurisdiction, and waivers. For each area examined, the Task Force provided summaries of the states' practices, analyses of the issues, and finally recommended standards for consideration and possible adoption. It has been 10 years since these recommendations were made, but the disparities among the states continue to exist.

Clearly, the lack of uniformity in state statutes is a critical factor which contributes to the difficulty in ascertaining who will be adjudicated delinquent and who will not. This problem is further compounded by the fact that there is a differential selection process of juvenile offenders for court appearance by those in the criminal justice system most involved with crime in the streets, namely, the police officer.

In a study reported by Goldman (1963), there was an analysis of the arrest records of four communities in Allegheny County, Pennsylvania. These communities were identified as Steel City, Trade City, Mill Town, and Manor Heights. The study also included data based on interviews with police in Pittsburgh and in twenty-two municipalities around that city. One of the conclusions of the study was that there was wide variation in the rates of juvenile arrest: "Arrests from 1,000 population aged ten to seventeen ranged from 12.4 to 49.7 with an average of 32.6 per thousand" (p. 125). In addition, there were a large number of other findings both general and specific that pertain to our discussion. Although they cannot be fully dealt with here, a sampling of the findings includes the following:

> Not all children apprehended in law violation are recorded in the juvenile court . . . .
>
> Among those apprehended by the police, not all are inscribed on police records . . . .
>
> Among those officially registered on police records only a small proportion, 35.4 percent, are referred to juvenile court for official action . . . .
>
> The differential selection of offenders for court by police is determined by the attitudes of the policeman toward the offender, his family, the offense, the juvenile court, his own role as a policeman, and the community attitudes toward delinquency. (pp. 126-129)

One surprising finding was that Manor Heights, the wealthiest of the four communities, had the highest rate of arrest, which was basically for minor offenses that were settled out of court. This may be accounted for in part by the fact that

> the police base their reporting partly on the act of the offender but also on the policeman's idiosyncratic interpretation of this act, and the degree of pressure applied by the community on the police. . . . The

policeman's interpretation of these pressures serves to select or determine
the composition of the sample of those juvenile offenders who will become
officially recognized from among all those known to him. (p. 132)

Goldman goes on to point out that such a selection process, namely,
one determined by "collective pressures and private attitudes, must result in a bias which can have only limited research validity for making
generalizations about the youthful offender" (p. 33). He also indicates
that the police officer's decision regarding the disposition of a given
violation may have significant effects on that juvenile's future behavior,
either decreasing or increasing the probability of his participation in delinquent acts.

In another study of law enforcement personnel reported by Piliavin
and Briar (1964), the findings were that the juvenile's attitude at the
time of this encounter with the police significantly influenced the officer's decision to detain and/or hold him for court. A youth's attitude reflected in his surliness, lack of respect, talking back to the officer or
cursing, as well as other factors such as mode of dress, hairstyle, or resi-
dence in a poor neighborhood, aided in the officer's assessment of the
youth and affected his subsequent decision. The irony here, of course, is
that a devious youth projecting an image which exhibits contrition and
remorse for the actions which caused him to come to the attention of the
policeman in the first place might convince the officer to release him
even though the circumstances in the case might warrant his being
brought to court. Similarly, a less artful youth with a negative attitude
might end up with a court appearance when in fact the circumstances in
his case may call for diverting him away from the courts to a local
agency or youth rehabilitation program.

The earlier studies concerning police discretion and the influence of
juvenile demeanor on case decisions have been supported by a more recent literature search and a survey of case decision making in seven selected jurisdictions by the National Juvenile Justice Assessment Centers
(1979). Referring to all parts of the criminal justice system, including
law enforcement, probation, the courts, and protective services, the
authors state:

It was determined that officials in every system component have almost
unlimited discretionary authority in deciding what "label" is assigned to
juvenile cases and what processing dispositions will be followed in han-
dling juvenile referrals. . . . Law enforcement and court intake agencies make more decisions that affect the lives of children and juveniles
than any other juvenile justice component. (pp. xii-xiii)

As to the ramifications of such findings, they further explain that "once a labeling decision is made by either of these two components, it clearly dictates how the juvenile will be processed in the juvenile justice system" (p. xiii). Finally, the research indicates that "if a juvenile is uncooperative and refuses to make a statement, if his attitude and demeanor is abrasive and negative and if his prior record shows any pattern of delinquent and incorrigible behavior, then officials in every system component are more likely to classify the juvenile as a delinquent/juvenile offender in spite of any other information considered about the incident" (p. xvi).

As these and other studies demonstrate, it is no simple matter to come to grips with the measurement, magnitude, and meaning of delinquency. Great care should be given in making generalizations about the origins and the nature of those identified as delinquents. In his review of the literature concerning the definition of the terms "delinquent" and "delinquent behavior," Weiner (1982) states:

> . . . delinquency is difficult to define and measure. . . . In the first place . . . it may involve a single delinquent act, a single episode of delinquent acts, occasional but repetitive acts or a continually delinquent way of life. Second, delinquent acts may range in severity from major crimes . . . to minor offenses. . . . Third, only some of the young people who commit delinquent acts are caught; of those . . . only some are arrested; of those . . . only some come to trial . . . of those tried only some are adjudicated delinquent. (p. 391)

Weiner goes on to conclude that

> . . . global references to "juvenile delinquents" as if these youngsters constitute some homogenous group should be viewed with skepticism. Delinquency can be uniformly defined according to what acts it consists of, regardless of who does them or why, delinquents, on the other hand, are a markedly heterogeneous group from a psychological point of view. (p. 391)

It should be evident then to psychologists working with delinquent youth that their task is far from simple. What the practitioner must be alert to is that generalizations about the personality, perception, development, and motivation of a particular delinquent youth, as with adolescents generally, is inappropriate, for it fails to recognize how multifaceted and multidetermined delinquent behavior really is. Our present knowledge about the legal vagaries and vicissitudes by which a youth can become identified as delinquent should impel us to seek out a classification system that is more conceptually consistent with the realities of what we know about delinquency. Such a classification system will be explored elsewhere in this text. The remainder to this chapter, however, will be devoted to a further analysis of the existing official and unofficial data on delinquents and the problems associated with their use.

Data Collection

Added to the problem of definition are problems related to the gathering, reporting, and interpreting of delinquency data. There are two types of juvenile crime statistics which are gathered nationally: official and unofficial statistics. The official statistics come from police and court reports, while the unofficial statistics are derived from a tabulation of self-report studies and crime victim surveys. The official data is provided by the Uniform Crime Reports and the Juvenile Court Statistics. Of the two, the former reports arrest and crime data sent by police departments to the FBI on a monthly basis and the latter, crime statistics filed each year by the juvenile courts with the National Center for Juvenile Justice.

The National Commission on the Causes and Prevention of Violence (1969) indicates that the Uniform Crime Reports (UCR) provide better estimates of actual delinquency than do the court cases reported to the National Center for Juvenile Justice. Regarding the courts' data, the commission states that "they are inherently less useful than police data in profiling the levels and trends of crime" (p. 14). It is of interest to note at this point that while the commission suggests that the Uniform Crime Reports provide better estimates, a number of more recent studies and reports (Gold and Reimer, 1975; O'Malley, et al., 1965; U.S Department of Justice, 1980) indicate that official data compared to unofficial self-report studies grossly underestimate the magnitude of non-serious delinquency among youth under the age of 18. The belief is that approximately 80-90 percent of these youth at least one time or another have committed an offense for which they could have been arrested. Yet, it also seems clear that official records are assumed to be accurate for the purposes of estimating serious/violent adolescent criminality.

Inconsistencies continue to abound in the debate concerning governmental efforts to collect accurate delinquency data. Smith et al. (1979b) report that

> . . . while self-report studies always report more offenses per capita than do official statistics, it is widely believed that respondents conceal

their delinquency acts. While victimization studies turn up more crimes than are reported to the police, they also report that victims of some offenses fail to report crimes to the interviewer even though they reported them to the police. (p. 261)

The authors go on to explain that the difficulty of collecting accurate data is compounded by still other factors:

Worse yet, the relations between delinquency and other variables seem to vary when different measures of delinquent behavior are used. Thus, while in most cases the existence of several variables enables researchers to increase the precision and reliability of measurements, in the case of delinquency the existence of several measures has largely led to conflicting conclusions. (p. 261)

And finally, a Justice Department study group, headed by officials from its Bureau of Justice and the FBI, was recently quoted (Burham, 1985) as saying that the Federal Bureau of Investigation's crime statistics were seriously flawed and recommending that substantial changes be made in how data was collected and published. Among the problems identified were the following:

The accuracy of Uniform Crime Reports is thought to vary from state to state and by jurisdiction within a state. . . . Besides under-reporting, errors are said to result from misclassification, lack of uniformity in applying definitions and for on-line agencies, data entry errors. (p. B19)

While the ongoing controversy continues concerning the accuracy of available statistics and their limitations, we can, nevertheless, proceed to use the existing data, if not to assess the exact number of criminal offenses committed by youths, then at least to gain some insight into the approximate scope and nature of juvenile crime. We will continue by examining the data from the recognized major source of such statistics, namely, the Uniform Crime Reports.

The Uniform Crime Reports

The Uniform Crime Reports, using provisional estimates supplied by the Bureau of the Census, show the 1984 U.S. population to be 236,156,000, of which 27 percent, or 63,762,120, were under 18 years of age, and 29 percent, or 18,524,000, were between the ages of 13 and 17 years.

It is further estimated that in 1984 law enforcement agencies made 11.9 million arrests, with 10.8 percent of those arrests for violent crimes and 89.2 for property crimes. The report states:

The estimated 11.9 million Crime Index offenses occurring in 1984 represented a 2-percent decline from 1983. Marking the third consecutive year of decline. . . . It was 11 percent below the 1980 level but 5 percent higher than in 1975. . . .

Overall violent crime was up 1 percent in 1984 as compared to 1983 [and] . . . the number of property crimes in 1984 was down 2 percent from the 1983 volume. . . .

Considering 5 and 10-year time frames, the 1984 violent and property crime totals each showed declines from the 1980 figures, 5 and 12 percent, respectively. Both categories, however, registered increases as compared to 1975. Violent crime was up 22 percent and property crime 3 percent. (p. 41)

As to where most of the crime occurred in 1984, the Uniform Crime Reports show that while the arrest rate for the total estimated United States population was 4,951 per 100,000 inhabitants, it was highest in cities of 250,000 or more residents, where the rate was 7,526 per 100,000. The next highest rate was found in suburban counties, which recorded 3,866 per 100,000, followed by rural counties, which had 3,078 criminal infractions per 100,000 (p. 161).

Elsewhere in the report arrest data by age, sex, race, and ethnicity are presented in tables for comparative purposes. These tables provide an added perspective by which to view and assess crime trends over the years, yet represent data from fewer law enforcement agencies covering smaller populations than do other tables in the report. This is explained by the fact that only those reporting agencies which have submitted comparable data to the UCR for given periods are included. Both the number of participating agencies and populations served are indicated in each of the tables.

The Uniform Crime Reports' 1984 figures (see Table 1, Total Arrests of Persons Under 15, 18, 21, and 25 Years of Age) indicate that the total arrests recorded for persons of all ages were 8,921,708, of which 1,537,688 were persons under 18 years of age. While those under 18 years of age constituted 17.2 percent of all persons arrested in 1984, 524,760 of those arrests were of youths under 15 years of age, representing 34 percent of this total youth population and 5.9 percent of all arrests made in 1984.

Of the Crime Index or Part I offenses which the FBI reports and which include homicides, forcible rape, robbery, aggravated assault, burglary, larceny-theft, motor vehicle theft, and arson, 13 percent of the arrestees were under 15 years of age and 31 percent were under the age of 18.

TABLE 1

Total Arrests of Persons Under 15, 18, 21 and 25 Years of Age, 1984
[9,879 agencies; 1984 estimated population 179,871,000]

Offense charged	Total all ages	Number of persons arrested				Percent of total all ages			
		Under 15	Under 18	Under 21	Under 25	Under 15	Under 18	Under 21	Under 25
TOTAL	8,921,708	524,760	1,537,688	2,868,066	4,507,344	5.9	17.2	32.1	50.5
Murder and nonnegligent manslaughter	13,676	138	1,004	2,918	5,649	1.0	7.3	21.3	41.3
Forcible rape	28,336	1,481	4,397	8,214	13,264	5.2	15.5	29.0	46.8
Robbery	108,614	7,206	27,795	50,603	72,682	6.6	25.6	46.6	66.9
Aggravated assault	231,620	9,966	31,148	60,808	103,643	4.3	13.4	26.3	44.7
Burglary	334,399	49,704	127,708	195,201	248,346	14.9	38.2	58.4	74.3
Larceny-theft	1,009,743	156,595	338,785	488,668	627,122	15.5	33.6	48.4	62.1
Motor vehicle theft	93,285	8,504	33,838	52,204	67,177	9.1	36.3	56.0	72.0
Arson	14,675	4,091	6,244	7,728	9,388	27.9	42.5	52.7	64.0
Violent crime[1]	382,246	18,791	64,344	122,543	195,238	4.9	16.8	32.1	51.1
Property crime[2]	1,452,102	218,894	506,575	743,801	952,033	15.1	34.9	51.2	65.6
Crime Index total[3]	1,834,348	237,685	570,919	866,344	1,147,271	13.0	31.1	47.2	62.5
Other assaults	408,389	26,014	66,880	117,588	196,109	6.4	16.4	28.8	48.0
Forgery and counterfeiting	63,359	1,206	6,179	15,982	29,522	1.9	9.8	25.2	46.6
Fraud	203,175	7,850	16,997	35,194	72,013	3.9	8.4	17.3	35.4
Embezzlement	6,290	65	455	1,414	2,643	1.0	7.2	22.5	42.0
Stolen property; buying, receiving, possessing	95,527	6,665	22,989	42,014	59,462	7.0	24.1	44.0	62.2

TABLE 1

(*Continued*)

Offense charged	Total all ages	Number of persons arrested				Percent of total all ages			
		Under 15	Under 18	Under 21	Under 25	Under 15	Under 18	Under 21	Under 25
Vandalism	189,524	46,016	87,135	115,304	141,026	24.3	46.0	60.8	74.4
Weapons; carrying, possessing, etc.	137,909	5,769	20,657	41,540	67,418	4.2	15.0	30.1	48.9
Prostitution and commercialized vice	88,337	261	2,375	15,856	44,410	.3	2.7	17.9	50.3
Sex offenses (except forcible rape and prostitution)	75,709	6,401	13,409	20,693	31,553	8.5	17.7	27.3	41.7
Drug abuse violations	562,255	11,407	67,211	169,709	308,175	2.0	12.0	30.2	54.8
Gambling	27,377	104	671	2,372	5,810	.4	2.5	8.7	21.2
Offenses against family and children	32,877	690	1,577	4,820	10,204	2.1	4.8	14.7	31.0
Driving under the influence	1,346,586	457	18,563	157,078	432,939	(⁴)	1.4	11.7	32.2
Liquor laws	383,234	8,476	101,904	247,084	297,755	2.2	26.6	64.5	77.7
Drunkenness	886,434	2,704	23,582	108,760	261,504	.3	2.7	12.3	29.5
Disorderly conduct	514,403	22,111	73,552	161,474	272,385	4.3	14.3	31.4	53.0
Vagrancy	22,640	582	2,044	5,674	9,352	2.6	9.0	25.1	41.3
All other offenses (except traffic)	1,845,398	70,453	256,575	552,982	928,602	3.8	13.9	30.0	50.3
Suspicion	16,419	927	2,496	4,666	7,673	5.6	15.2	28.4	46.7
Curfew and loitering law violations	67,243	18,905	67,243	67,243	67,243	28.1	100.0	100.0	100.0
Runaways	114,275	50,012	114,275	114,275	114,275	43.8	100.0	100.0	100.0

[1] Violent crimes are offenses of murder, forcible rape, robbery, and aggravated assault.
[2] Property crimes are offenses of burglary, larceny-theft, motor vehicle theft, and arson.
[3] Includes arson.
[4] Less than one-tenth of 1 percent.

Of the violent crimes, youths under 18 years of age were reported responsible for 7.3 percent of the homicides, 15.5 percent of the forcible rapes, 25.6 percent of the robberies, and 13.4 percent of the aggravated assaults.

Of crimes against property, youths under 18 years of age were reported responsible for 38.2 percent of the burglaries, 33.6 percent of the larceny-thefts, 36.3 percent of the motor vehicle thefts, and 42.5 percent of the arsons.

In terms of arrest trends for the 5-year period 1980-1984 (see Table 2, Total Arrest Trends, 1980-1984), we find that total arrests were up 11.2 percent, while arrests of youths under 18 years of age dropped 11 percent. Total Crime Index arrests were down 1.4 percent, while they declined 17.3 percent for those under 18 years of age. Finally, arrests for some crimes were up significantly for those under 18 years of age. Those crimes include forcible rape, up 24.9 percent; other assaults, up 1.6 percent; fraud, up 209.6 percent; weapons possession, up 5.5 percent; and sex offenses (excluding rape and prostitution), up 36.6 percent.

However, when we compare arrest trends of those under 18 years of age over the past two years (1983-1984), we find that while the Crime Index total is down 1.7 percent, five of the eight crime arrests included in the index are trending up (see Table 3, Total Arrest Trends, 1983-1984). These include forcible rape, up 11.4 percent; aggravated assault, up 4.2 percent; larceny-theft, up 8 percent; motor vehicle theft, up 4.6 percent; and arson, up 7.4 percent.

What is even more striking than these statistics is the rise in the figures and the percentage changes reported for arrests among those under 15 years of age. While 1984 saw an overall rise of 0.6 percent for those under 18 years of age, it witnessed a more dramatic (5%) increase among those under 15. And while a 1.7 percent decline was recorded for serious crimes among the former group, a 2 percent rise was seen among the latter. It would appear, at least in the period from 1983-1984, that serious crime arrest was becoming more prominent among the younger age groups in the delinquent population.

Table 3 further indicates that in 1984 all violent crimes committed by those under 15 years of age, with the exception of robbery, were on the increase as were all property crimes, with the exception of burglary. Among violent crimes, there were reported increases in forcible rape (26.8%), homicide (11.5%), and aggravated assault (10.6%), and among property crimes there were increases in larceny-theft (4.1%), motor vehicle theft (10.9%), and arson (11.5%).

TABLE 2

Total Arrest Trends, 1980-1984

[6,134 agencies; 1984 estimated population 141,692,000]

Offense charged	Number of persons arrested								
	Total all ages			Under 18 years of age			18 years of age and over		
	1980	1984	Percent change	1980	1984	Percent change	1980	1984	Percent change
TOTAL	6,399,061	7,113,041	+11.2	1,409,768	1,255,121	−11.0	4,989,293	5,857,920	+17.4
Murder and nonnegligent manslaughter	12,052	11,230	−6.8	1,083	819	−24.4	10,969	10,411	−5.1
Forcible rape	19,592	23,091	+17.9	2,925	3,654	+24.9	16,667	19,437	+16.6
Robbery	99,044	94,415	−4.7	30,848	24,861	−19.4	68,196	69,554	+2.0
Aggravated assault	174,053	187,751	+7.9	27,498	25,406	−7.6	146,555	162,345	+10.8
Burglary	329,760	272,241	−17.4	151,726	103,700	−31.7	178,034	168,541	−5.3
Larceny-theft	769,276	809,698	+5.3	300,912	274,261	−8.9	468,364	535,437	+14.3
Motor vehicle theft	90,637	76,511	−15.6	41,790	27,636	−33.9	48,847	48,875	+.1
Arson	12,793	11,847	−7.4	5,783	5,126	−11.4	7,010	6,721	−.1
Violent crime[1]	304,741	316,487	+3.9	62,354	54,740	−12.2	242,387	261,747	+8.0
Property crime[2]	1,202,466	1,170,297	−2.7	500,211	410,723	−17.9	702,255	759,574	+8.2
Crime Index total[3]	1,507,207	1,486,784	−1.4	562,565	465,463	−17.3	944,642	1,021,321	+8.1
Other assaults	277,494	315,096	+13.6	53,640	54,517	+1.6	223,854	260,579	+16.4
Forgery and counterfeiting	46,478	50,881	+9.5	6,070	4,925	−18.9	40,408	45,956	+13.7
Fraud	150,909	167,826	+11.2	5,285	16,365	+209.6	145,624	151,461	+4.0
Embezzlement	4,786	5,409	+13.0	669	387	−42.2	4,117	5,022	+22.0
Stolen property; buying, receiving, possessing	83,766	82,645	−1.3	25,863	19,798	−23.5	57,903	62,847	+8.5

TABLE 2
(Continued)

| Offense charged | Total all ages | | | Number of persons arrested | | | | | |
| | | | | Under 18 years of age | | | 18 years of age and over | | |
	1980	1984	Percent change	1980	1984	Percent change	1980	1984	Percent change
Vandalism	156,650	152,902	−2.4	80,813	71,149	−12.0	75,837	81,753	+7.8
Weapons; carrying, possessing, etc.	102,073	111,274	+9.0	16,492	17,397	+5.5	85,581	93,877	+9.7
Prostitution and commercialized vice	53,665	69,114	+28.8	1,941	1,776	−8.5	51,724	67,338	+30.2
Sex offenses (except forcible rape and prostitution)	42,738	61,001	+42.7	8,184	11,178	+36.6	34,554	49,823	+44.2
Drug abuse violations	351,101	460,356	+31.1	68,961	55,253	−19.9	282,140	405,103	+43.6
Gambling	26,021	24,236	−6.9	822	583	−29.1	25,199	23,653	−6.1
Offenses against family and children	22,743	23,014	+1.2	1,086	929	−14.5	21,657	22,085	+2.0
Driving under the influence	833,450	1,053,360	+26.4	18,377	14,373	−21.8	815,073	1,038,987	+27.5
Liquor laws	284,071	301,288	+6.1	97,326	80,380	−17.4	186,745	220,908	+18.3
Drunkenness	741,395	705,060	−4.9	30,599	18,020	−41.1	710,796	687,040	−3.3
Disorderly conduct	402,881	410,180	+1.8	73,595	60,272	−18.1	329,286	349,908	+6.3
Vagrancy	16,429	18,428	+12.2	3,135	1,677	−46.5	13,294	16,751	+26.0
All other offenses (except traffic)	1,156,347	1,468,362	+27.0	215,488	214,854	−.3	940,859	1,253,508	+33.2
Suspicion (not included in totals)	8,614	8,459	−1.8	1,696	1,516	−10.6	6,918	6,943	+.4
Curfew and loitering law violations	46,282	57,666	+24.6	46,282	57,666	+24.6	....	....	....
Runaways	92,575	88,159	−4.8	92,575	88,159	−4.8	....	....	....

[1] Violent crimes are offenses of murder, forcible rape, robbery, and aggravated assault.
[2] Property crimes are offenses of burglary, larceny-theft, motor vehicle theft, and arson.
[3] Includes arson.

TABLE 3

Total Arrest Trends, 1983-1984

[8658 agencies; 1984 estimated population 162,547,000]

Offense charged	Number of persons arrested											
	Total all ages			Under 15 years of age			Under 18 years of age			18 years of age and over		
	1983	1984	Percent change	1983	1984	Percent change	1983	1984	Percent change	1983	1984	Percent change
TOTAL	8,204,726	8,222,720	+.2	465,032	488,380	+5.0	1,418,984	1,427,857	+.6	6,785,742	6,794,863	+.1
Murder and nonnegligent manslaughter	13,036	12,418	-4.7	113	126	+11.5	995	932	-6.3	12,041	11,486	-4.6
Forcible rape	24,133	26,048	+7.9	1,096	1,390	+26.8	3,652	4,067	+11.4	20,481	21,981	+7.3
Robbery	104,733	98,941	-5.5	7,116	6,691	-6.0	28,042	25,789	-8.0	76,691	73,152	-4.6
Aggravated assault	206,434	211,259	+2.3	8,295	9,173	+10.6	27,402	28,564	+4.2	179,032	182,695	+2.0
Burglary	330,037	304,293	-7.8	48,399	45,587	-6.0	129,488	116,837	-9.8	200,549	187,456	-6.5
Larceny-theft	948,570	933,320	-1.6	140,227	146,027	+4.1	312,027	314,545	+.8	636,543	618,775	-2.8
Motor vehicle theft	82,862	85,139	+2.7	7,091	7,865	+10.9	29,560	30,930	+4.6	53,302	54,209	+1.7
Arson	13,912	13,538	-2.7	3,437	3,832	+11.5	5,402	5,802	+7.4	8,510	7,736	-9.1
Violent crime[1]	348,336	348,666	+.1	16,620	17,380	+4.6	60,091	59,352	-1.2	288,245	289,314	+.4
Property crime[2]	1,375,381	1,336,290	-2.8	199,154	203,211	+2.0	476,477	468,114	-1.8	898,904	868,176	-3.4
Crime Index total[3]	1,723,717	1,684,956	-2.2	215,774	220,591	+2.2	536,568	527,466	-1.7	1,187,149	1,157,490	-2.5
Other assaults	345,673	376,401	+8.9	21,950	24,181	+10.2	57,806	61,942	+7.2	287,867	314,459	+9.2
Forgery and counterfeiting	58,949	58,612	-.6	1,006	1,131	+12.4	5,628	5,807	+3.2	53,321	52,805	-1.0
Fraud	188,807	187,542	-.7	8,754	7,804	-10.9	19,470	16,692	-14.3	169,337	170,850	+.9
Embezzlement	5,462	5,665	+3.7	64	63	-1.6	381	415	+8.9	5,081	5,250	+3.3
Stolen property; buying, receiving, possessing	90,345	87,919	-2.7	6,500	6,140	-5.5	22,061	21,207	-3.9	68,284	66,712	-2.3

TABLE 3
(Continued)

Offense charged	Total all ages			Under 15 years of age			Under 18 years of age			18 years of age and over		
	1983	1984	Percent change	1983	1984	Percent change	1983	1984	Percent change	1983	1984	Percent change
Vandalism	167,706	175,070	+4.4	39,327	42,719	+8.6	75,744	80,816	+6.7	91,962	94,254	+2.5
Weapons; carrying, possessing, etc.	125,811	126,564	+.6	4,841	5,365	+10.8	17,683	18,996	+7.4	108,128	107,568	−.5
Prostitution and commercialized vice	90,285	82,165	−9.0	190	229	+20.5	2,119	2,166	+2.2	88,166	79,999	−9.3
Sex offenses (except forcible rape and prostitution)	60,912	70,069	+15.0	4,571	5,973	+30.7	10,111	12,479	+23.4	50,801	57,590	+13.4
Drug abuse violations	474,779	505,451	+6.5	9,662	10,618	+9.9	57,754	61,161	+5.9	417,025	444,290	+6.5
Gambling	27,494	24,431	−11.1	86	97	+12.8	664	582	−12.3	26,830	23,849	−11.1
Offenses against family and children	28,510	28,051	−1.6	409	617	+50.9	1,020	1,401	+37.4	27,490	26,650	−3.1
Driving under the influence	1,248,689	1,235,953	−1.0	422	349	−17.3	19,196	16,968	−11.6	1,229,493	1,218,985	−.9
Liquor laws	348,045	346,934	−.3	7,527	7,895	+4.9	94,253	94,183	−.1	253,792	252,751	−.4
Drunkenness	876,768	835,313	−4.7	2,526	2,491	−1.4	25,424	21,648	−14.9	851,344	813,665	−4.4
Disorderly conduct	471,391	476,947	+1.2	19,425	20,835	+7.3	69,830	69,052	−1.1	401,561	407,895	+1.6
Vagrancy	22,411	21,187	−5.5	557	537	−3.6	2,236	1,890	−15.5	20,175	19,297	−.4
All other offenses (except traffic)	1,691,081	1,722,930	+1.9	62,430	65,983	+5.7	243,145	242,426	−.3	1,447,936	1,480,504	+2.2
Suspicion (not included in totals)	11,112	11,300	+1.7	762	871	+14.3	2,262	2,325	+2.8	8,850	8,975	+1.4
Curfew and loitering law violations	60,974	64,330	+5.5	16,815	18,094	+7.6	60,974	64,330	+5.5	.....	.....	.....
Runaways	96,917	106,230	+9.6	42,196	46,668	+10.6	96,917	106,230	+9.6	.....	.....	.....

[1] Violent crimes are offenses of murder, forcible rape, robbery, and aggravated assault.
[2] Property crimes are offenses of burglary, larceny-theft, motor vehicle theft, and arson.
[3] Includes arson.

The Relationship Between the UCR and Other Studies

The phenomenon of rising participation of the younger age groups in violent crimes appears to be supported by findings of the birth cohort studies conducted by Wolfgang (1972) and Shannon (1976). Wolfgang studied the incidence and nature of delinquency among two cohorts of Philadelphia males, one born in 1945 and the other in 1958, both of whom attended school in that city between the ages of 10 and 17, and turned 18 in 1963 and 1976, respectively.

Wolfgang (1983) found that

> . . . boys who were born in 1958 and reached their eighteenth birthday in 1976 composed a more violent cohort than their urban brothers did, who were born in 1945 and who turned eighteen in 1963. . . . The more recent group is more delinquent in general and has engaged in more injurious behavior. (p. 84)

He also discovered that the more recent cohort "are more violently recidivistic and commit more index offenses before reaching age 18. They start their injury offenses earlier (age 13 as compared to 14) and continue longer" (p. 84).

In another birth cohort study conducted in Racine, Wisconsin, Shannon (1981) researched three birth cohorts (1942, 1949, and 1955) totalling 6,127 persons, of whom 4,079 lived in that city from approximately age 6 until the time the data was collected for the last cohort in 1976. Shannon's findings indicated that while the overall rates of police contact did not increase from cohort to cohort, the rates for the more serious Part I offenses, including assault, burglary, theft, and robbery, did increase. These more serious offenses and others more than doubled between the first and third cohort for those youths between 6 and 17 years of age. Shannon also found that the male youthful offenders who were 15 years of age comprised the group with the highest frequency of police contact for serious offenses.

In his review of trends in violent juvenile crime covering the period from 1960 to 1979, Empey (1982), while not differentiating between younger and older delinquents, indicated that arrests for these offenses have increased by 233 percent and that

> despite signs that the rate of arrest for violent crime has moderated in recent years, the data suggest that young people are considerably more violent today than they were 20 years ago. (p. 91)

While it is certainly clear that delinquent youth are more violent than they were in 1960, data covering the more recent period (1975-1984) indicate that there has actually been a 28 percent decline (UCR, 1984) in serious crime among those under 18 years of age. Yet, as stated earlier, it may be that we are beginning to see an upturn in violent crime among those under 15 years of age. At present it is too early to tell whether this is a trend or simply an anomaly. We will know more in the months and years ahead. In any case, when the discussion turns to the unofficial data, we will find researchers whose studies do not support the belief in a rising violent crime rate among those under the age of 18.

It should be noted that while the data shows that there were 1,537,688 juvenile arrests in 1984, we should not conclude that this constituted the actual number of youths arrested. It is known that those arrest reports also cite offenses committed by repeat offenders who have been arrested more than once and in some cases many times.

In a study by Shannon (1976) of a city in the Midwest, it was demonstrated that 75 percent of the felonies committed by juveniles were committed by 5 percent of the youths under 18 years of age and that less than 14 percent committed all felonies in the group. Others who have found similar results are Wolfgang et al. (1972).

As regards gender differences, while women represent a majority (51%) of the population in the United States, there are five males arrested for every female, and males account for 83 percent of all arrests, 79 percent of those for index crimes, 89 percent of those for violent crimes, and 77 percent of those for property crimes.

As would be expected, male juveniles are arrested more often for serious crimes than are female juveniles. Arrests of girls under 18 years of age made up only 6.1 percent of the total number of arrests for the eight most serious index crimes; boys accounted for 25 percent of that total. Arrests of girls under 18 years of age for violent crimes constituted less than 2 percent of the total arrests for such crimes, while arrests of males under 18 constituted nearly 15 percent of the total arrests. Young male offenders are 8 times more likely to be arrested for violent crimes and 4 times more likely to be arrested for property crimes than females.

Apart from prostitution, girls are arrested more often than boys for committing only one other offense, namely, running away from home. The case has been made by Empey (1982) that these statistics reflect society's double standard concerning the belief that girls need more supervision than boys do.

A number of researchers have called for a closer assessment of the possible linkages between age, gender, race, and crime in order to examine the overrepresentation of black youth in violent crimes. Chilton and Galvin (1985) state:

> Race was usually ignored or discussed only in connection with discrimination within components of the system of justice. This neglect has been similar in some ways to the neglect . . . of age and gender patterns in crime. . . . Just as age patterns can be clues to the source of some crime and delinquency, and gender differences can provide clues . . . regarding some forms of crime . . . racial differences in criminal involvement — especially if examined in connection with age and sex data — should provide additional clues to the source of some crime. If we continue to assume that there are no differences in criminal involvement by race, or act as if the differences are spurious or illusory, we will be poorly equipped to understand or respond to contemporary urban crime trends. (pp. 6-7)

In 1984 blacks constituted approximately 12 percent of the United States population, whereas they represented approximately 25 percent of the total arrests. When the racial composition of the cohort under 18 years of age is examined we find that white youths constitute 75.2 percent, black youths 23.1 percent, and all others (Alaskan Native, Asian Pacific Islander, and American Indian) 1.8 percent of arrestees (see Table 4, Total Arrests: Distribution by Race, 1984). As regards the ethnic composition of that same cohort, 11.9 percent are Hispanic and 88.1 percent non-Hispanic.

Of considerable interest is the nature of the crimes for which the juveniles are being arrested. As with the differences found between the types of crimes committed by young males and females, there are significant differences between the crimes committed by young white offenders and their black counterparts.

Of significance is the nature of crimes for which the youths are being arrested. When examining the total crime index figures we find that 69.6 percent of the arrestees are white youths and 28.4 percent are black youths. Further, the majority (72.7%) of white youths are arrested for property crimes, whereas the majority of black youth arrests (53.7%) are for violent crimes. In 1984 over 80 percent of the white youth arrested were arrested for arson, forgery, vandalism, vagrancy, and running away from home, and over 90 percent were arrested for drunkenness, driving under the influence of alcohol, and liquor law violations. The profile of black youth arrests shows more than 50 percent were arrested for violent crimes and gambling, while more than 40 percent were arrested for fraud and prostitution.

TABLE 4

Total Arrests, Distribution by Race, 1984

[9,851 agencies; 1984 estimated population 179,374,000]

Offense charged	Total arrests					Percent distribution[1]				
	Total	White	Black	American Indian or Alaskan Native	Asian or Pacific Islander	Total	White	Black	American Indian or Alaskan Native	Asian or Pacific Islander
TOTAL	8,890,662	6,528,686	2,216,299	89,873	55,804	100.0	73.4	24.9	1.0	.6
Murder and nonnegligent manslaughter	13,656	7,339	6,133	91	93	100.0	53.7	44.9	.7	.7
Forcible rape	28,297	14,929	13,013	208	147	100.0	52.8	46.0	.7	.5
Robbery	108,534	40,693	66,725	472	644	100.0	37.5	61.5	.4	.6
Aggravated assault	231,403	140,053	88,213	1,926	1,211	100.0	60.5	38.1	.8	.5
Burglary	333,854	234,423	95,187	2,556	1,688	100.0	70.2	28.5	.8	.5
Larceny-theft	1,008,105	681,959	305,935	10,845	9,366	100.0	67.6	30.3	1.1	.9
Motor vehicle theft	93,187	63,464	28,169	856	698	100.0	68.1	30.2	.9	.7
Arson	14,647	11,369	3,068	116	94	100.0	77.6	20.9	.8	.6
Violent crime[2]	381,890	203,014	174,084	2,697	2,095	100.0	53.2	45.6	.7	.5
Property crime[3]	1,449,793	991,215	432,359	14,373	11,846	100.0	68.4	29.8	1.0	.8
Crime Index total[4]	1,831,683	1,194,229	606,443	17,070	13,941	100.0	65.2	33.1	.9	.8
Other assaults	407,841	274,770	126,494	3,946	2,631	100.0	67.4	31.0	1.0	.6
Forgery and counterfeiting	63,215	43,083	19,596	334	202	100.0	68.2	31.0	.5	.3
Fraud	202,875	141,865	59,328	682	1,000	100.0	69.9	29.2	.3	.5
Embezzlement	6,287	4,664	1,545	27	51	100.0	74.2	24.6	.4	.8
Stolen property; buying, receiving, possessing	95,284	59,840	34,551	501	392	100.0	62.8	36.3	.5	.4

TABLE 4

(Continued)

Offense charged	Total arrests					Percent distribution[1]				
	Total	White	Black	American Indian or Alaskan Native	Asian or Pacific Islander	Total	White	Black	American Indian or Alaskan Native	Asian or Pacific Islander
Vandalism	189,326	153,370	33,297	1,591	1,068	100.0	81.0	17.6	.8	.6
Weapons; carrying, possessing, etc.	137,789	89,057	47,243	630	859	100.0	64.6	34.3	.5	.6
Prostitution and commercialized vice	88,308	49,294	37,776	391	847	100.0	55.8	42.8	.4	1.0
Sex offenses (except forcible rape and prostitution)	75,589	60,816	13,726	627	420	100.0	80.5	18.2	.8	.6
Drug abuse violations	560,729	392,904	162,979	2,056	2,790	100.0	70.1	29.1	.4	.5
Gambling	27,370	11,900	14,315	25	1,130	100.0	43.5	51.3	.1	4.1
Offenses against family and children	32,587	23,407	8,857	245	78	100.0	71.8	27.2	.8	.2
Driving under the influence	1,330,495	1,195,305	116,163	12,691	6,336	100.0	89.8	8.7	1.0	.5
Liquor laws	382,078	334,161	38,177	7,690	2,050	100.0	87.5	10.0	2.0	.5
Drunkenness	883,878	718,748	145,199	18,502	1,429	100.0	81.3	16.4	2.1	.2
Disorderly conduct	513,496	358,488	146,457	6,579	1,972	100.0	69.8	28.5	1.3	.4
Vagrancy	22,621	14,354	7,605	431	231	100.0	63.5	33.6	1.9	1.0
All other offenses (except traffic)	1,841,681	1,255,685	555,583	14,351	16,062	100.0	68.2	30.2	.8	.9
Suspicion	16,398	7,991	8,130	14	263	100.0	48.7	49.6	.1	1.6
Curfew and loitering law violations	67,073	47,225	18,778	423	647	100.0	70.4	28.0	.6	1.0
Runaways	114,059	97,530	14,057	1,067	1,405	100.0	85.5	12.3	.9	1.2

See footnotes at end of table.

A birth cohort study conducted by Hamparian et al. (1978) in Columbus, Ohio also found an overrepresentation of minority youth in violent crimes. Studying 1,138 Columbus youths who were born between 1957 and 1960 and had been arrested for violent crimes prior to 1976, they discovered that the youths were predominantly male, black, and economically disadvantaged, with the overwhelming majority coming from families whose income was below the median income for the county. In addition, these youths had a history of interpersonal problems at home and behavioral problems both at school and on the job.

While the data on minority group youth indicate a greater propensity for involvement in violent crime than their white counterparts, other data indicate that young black males also have the greatest propensity to be the victims of violent crimes, that they have higher rates of birth than the general population, and have been overrepresented in that portion of the "baby boom" population's age group to which most crimes are attributed. To these explanatory factors might be added those summarized by Mann (1984), who argues that differentials in black-white arrest data might also be influenced by

> differential law enforcement practices rooted in the hostile reciprocal relationship between blacks and other minorities and the police; the effect of recent urbanization on minorities; economic and other crime-provoking social discrimination and the alleged high prevalence and intensity of various criminogenic factors among minority groups. (p. 50)

As implied by Mann, there are many relevant variables that are not factored into the UCR statistics. Indeed, we have seen thus far that the Uniform Crime Reports provide information on such variables as the offender's age, sex, race, and place of crime. While we can identify the typical offender as a young urban male (much more often white if the crime is a property crime and black a majority of the time if the crime is a violent one), the remainder of the delinquent profile is less complete and therefore less meaningful.

If the UCR were to provide other biographic and demographic data, including variables that relate to the offender's prior police record (number and types of previous arrests and convictions), family background (size, composition, income, and record of child abuse and neglect), education (level completed, school-related problems and reported truancy), employment history (type of work, length of employment, difficulties on the job), and gang affiliation (degree of involvement and status), our basis for interpretation might be strengthened.

While it is true that we can supplement the data with information gathered from the birth cohort studies (which we have already mentioned) and the unofficial data sources (which we are about to discuss), our ability to generalize and interpret from the official data remains somewhat limited.

Other Data Sources

The major portion of the discussion has centered on official delinquency statistics. Another way in which information is gathered is through unofficial data, the use of self-report studies, in which the measurement of the crime data is supplied by the offenders themselves. Whether it be through mail distribution of questionnaires or through confidential personal (face-to-face) interviews in the respondents' homes, the purpose of this National Youth Survey is to gain information not available from arrest records, as a majority of these offenders have never had any formal contact with the police or any other part of the criminal justice system. To arrive at what has been termed the rate of "hidden delinquency," the self-report questionnaire items include all of the Uniform Crime Reports' Part I offenses except homicide and 60 percent of Part II offenses, as well as other offenses. For example, the questionnaire might ask the respondent how often he has stolen or tried to steal something worth more than 50 dollars or whether he has ever carried a hidden weapon other than a pocket knife.

Self-report studies at times confirm and at other times challenge the official data. For example, in his review of the research findings of the self-report studies on the issue of gender and delinquency, Bartollas (1985) concluded that girls commit more delinquent acts than official accounts of delinquency report they do, while confirming the official findings that boys break the law more frequently than girls and commit more serious crimes than their female counterparts.

As to the issue of black-white differences in delinquency rates, Gold and Reimer (1975) and Hirschi (1969) found that the self-report studies indicated far fewer distinctions than those reported by the Uniform Crime Reports. In fact, Gold and Reimer found that the reported rates of delinquency were very similar for the less serious offenses, whereas they were somewhat higher among black youths for more serious offenses.

On the other hand, Elliot and Ageton (1980), examining self-report data with respect to black-white differences, did find race differences that were much closer to the official statistics, especially in the area of serious property offenses. They state,

> The findings . . . indicate that race and class differences are more extreme at the high end of the frequency continuum, that part of the delinquency continuum where police contacts are most likely. In fact, at this end of the frequency continuum, self-report and official correlates of delinquency behavior are relatively similar. While we do not deny the existence of official processing biases, it does appear that official correlates of delinquency also reflect real differences in the frequency and seriousness of delinquent acts. (p. 98)

Essentially, Elliot and Ageton argue that the exhibited racial differences occur because there are a greater number of high-rate repeat offenders among black youths whose chronic delinquent activity inflates the figures.

The reasons for the significantly greater delinquent involvement among a small cohort of young, urban, male black offenders might perhaps be explained in social psychological terms. Such influential factors as growing up in urban poverty with severe ghetto unemployment, broken families, substandard housing, poor schools, and discrimination could lead to growing levels of anxiety, frustration, and violence, especially among those youth who are the most vulnerable. Such youths are more often those with the fewest social skills, weakest academic achievement, fewest economic resources, and poorest employment prospects who nevertheless have need for developing a sense of identity, independence, and material satisfaction.

As with the external factors that they must contend with, there are also significant internal ones brought on by puberty and physical development, along with the accompanying psychological and emotional changes, which exert significant influence on their behavior.

It is suggested that while these youths have a need to experience a sense of independence from adult authority, their vulnerability would limit the forms and means of expressing that autonomy. It could be further argued that, more than most, they would be attracted to role models and peers with similar backgrounds who also perceive their situation as bleak and their futures as limited and who have already chosen to express their independence from the adult world in antisocial delinquent activity. Such role models and peers serve as examples to others who are vulnerable by offering them rewards, including acceptance, recognition, status, and the possibility of social and/or material gain through a delinquent life-style. The resulting sense of negative identity that develops might further enhance the possibility that members in this, the most vulnerable group of all, will go on to become the chronic offenders that we find reported in the birth cohort studies.

While this view partially explains why the most vulnerable of black youth become chronic offenders, it fails to fully explain why the great majority of black youth with similar backgrounds do not become delinquent but rather enter prosocial and law-abiding life-styles. The reasons for these differences may have more to do with the latter's resilience, positive sense of identity, and psychological strengths that help them resist the negative pressures and temptations they encounter. These and other psychological factors which might explain differential vulnerability to juvenile delinquency will be discussed elsewhere in this text. For now, however, we will turn our attention once again to delinquency data, more specifically to the problems inherent in the methodology of self-report studies.

While self-report studies do provide information on the broader scope of adolescent involvement in delinquent behavior than is otherwise available through official reports, they have, nevertheless, been found wanting because of their methodology. Smith et al. (1979b), in their summary of some of the criticism leveled against self-report studies for accepting respondents' statements as accurate indices of delinquency, state:

> . . . the respondent may lie to appear less delinquent, he can lie to appear more delinquent, or he can simply refuse to take the whole exercise seriously. Another major problem is that the respondent can report only what he can recall. (p. 270)

Finally, they point out that delinquents are known to have a lower level of reading ability than non-delinquents and are likely to have greater difficulty reading and answering the questionnaires than their non-delinquent counterparts. Such a problem is of no small consequence when we consider that the mailed questionnaire is the principal method used in this research procedure.

A third major source of statistics regarding the nature and scope of crime comes from the National Crime Survey constructed by the U.S. Bureau of the Census for the Bureau of Justice Statistics. The information from this survey is gathered through interviews conducted in a representative sample of households and businesses throughout the nation concerning the estimated rate and number of victimizations experienced by the interviewee.

These interviews are conducted in a systematic and detailed fashion and deal with all aspects of the offense and the offender, including the victim's own perception of the criminal's age, sex, and race.

At least one researcher recently reviewed the juvenile crime data of the National Crime Survey from 1973 to 1980 and concluded that the data did not support the contention that serious juvenile crime had risen dramatically during that period. Laub (1983) states:

> Our data show that the rate of juvenile offending in personal crimes
> . . in urban areas, and in places with 1,000,000 or more inhabitants,
> has remained stable, or has declined. . . . To be sure, juvenile involve-
> ment in crimes of rape, robbery, assaults, and larceny is substantial.
> However, the NCS data are not consistent with the growing national
> alarm regarding serious national crime. (672)

The victimization data seems then to be in conflict with the figures reported by the Uniform Crime Reports, with the UCR showing higher rates of increase for all index crimes for the period 1971-1981. A probable explanation for the reported differences is that the UCR and NCS examine different aspects of crime and its trends, using different methodologies and serving different purposes. For example, the Uniform Crime Reports count crimes committed against all people, while the National Crime Survey counts only those crimes committed against persons age 12 or older and their households. Further, the UCR counts only crimes coming to the attention of the police, whereas the NCR obtains data on reported and unreported crime. Based on its semi-annual interviews with 129,000 randomly selected people, the Bureau of Justice Statistics reported that in 1983 there were 37.1 million crimes committed, of which only 35 percent were actually reported to the police.

Summarizing the Bureau's findings, the *New York Times* reported that

> . . . nearly 70 percent of motor thefts are reported while less than half
> of rapes and other violent crimes are reported. . . . Only 48 percent of
> six million violent crimes such as rape, robbery and assault were re-
> ported to police. . . . Women and blacks were more likely than white
> men to tell the police they were victims of violent crimes. . . . Teen-
> agers and undereducated adults were less likely to report crimes. (p. B
> 15)

The article reports that the most frequently given reason for not reporting crimes was that the victims felt that the incident was not important enough. For violent crimes, the most frequent reason, given by 28 percent of the respondents, was that it was "a private or personal matter."

In their summary of the victimization data, Klaus et al. (1983) found that while young urban black males have the highest violent crime rates, they are also more likely to be victims of violent crime than whites or members of other racial groups, and that people with low incomes have the highest violent victimization rates of all.

In an earlier critical view of the literature, Smith et al. (1979b) identify a number of the difficulties associated with the unofficial data (NCS), which include findings concerning overreporting of offenses in victim surveys, underreporting of offenses not included in the survey, and the fact that higher income victims report victimization more readily than do lower income victims. They further explain that it is generally only where the victim saw the offender, as in contact crimes, that such factors as age, race, sex, and relation to the victim can be ascertained and adult offenders distiguished from youthful offenders.

Summing up the strengths and weaknesses of such studies, they state,

> Victimization surveys have their problems. But they do provide an avenue of access to the pool of crime not reported to the police and they have the capability of eliciting information about the offense that is not available by other means. (p. 278)

While the debate concerning the validity of the crime measures continues, there has been at the same time an ongoing controversy regarding the practical use to which the data is put. For example, while idealogues from both the political right and left accept the findings that the overall current rate of juvenile crime for those under 18 years of age and younger is declining, the explanations for this decrease and the perceived implications for policymaking have been far from uniform. While those from the political right claim that the reduction in juvenile crime has been brought about by "get tough" policies and the push for even more stringent measures to combat delinquency, e.g. more incarceration and adjudication in adult courts, others would agree with Hufstedler (1984), who argues that

> . . . hard liners cannot take credit for the drop in youth crime. The answer lies in demographic changes that have dramatically affected many elements in our lives. "The age cohort that will reach 18 years old in this decade, is 15 percent fewer than in the last decade. Within the next ten years, there will be 20 percent fewer youngsters in this age cohort." (p. 419)

Nevertheless, neither those on the political right nor left are sanguine about the future. The concern for youth crime continues to grow in our society due in large measure to the fact that juveniles commit much more crime than might be predicted from their proportion in the population. Another reason for this growing concern is that while there has been a reduction in the age cohort that is most criminogenic in terms of number of offenses (which explains the decline in the number of offenses), the severity of those crimes has not declined.

While using statistics to support her argument, Hufstedler does not neglect to describe the difficulties involved in using such measurements:

> Criminal statistics generally, and juvenile statistics in particular, are both suspect and misleading. As anyone familiar with these systems understands, we do not have any uniform methods or criteria for collecting data. (p. 419)

Conclusions

For all of the problems associated with the collection and interpretation of delinquency statistics, there are certain aspects of the data that we feel somewhat confident represent an accurate reflection of the situation as it presently exists. First, the overwhelming majority of adolescents have committed an offense at some time in their lives that would have characterized them as delinquent. Most have not gone beyond this one-time offense, and, of those who have, most have committed offenses of a minor nature. It seems accurate to say that for the majority of such youthful offenders, time itself is a curative and that as they mature they grow out of delinquent life-styles.

The data supports the following findings as well: that urban crime and delinquency are highest; that young males continue to outnumber young females in the commission of crime; that minority males are overrepresented in juvenile crime, especially when it involves violence; that a small percent of delinquent youth are chronic offenders and are most responsible for the criminal activity among their peers; and, finally, that while the amount of youth crime appears to be trending down, serious offenses among younger juveniles (under 15 years of age) appears, over the short term (1983-1984), to be trending up.

As we conclude our discussion of delinquency data and measurement we find that definitional problems, the complexity of behavior, and at times contradictory findings of the data sources leave us with a number of unresolved issues concerning the magnitude and interpretation of delinquency statistics. Nevertheless, as psychologists and mental health practitioners whose major focus is on the individual, we have come to accept, perhaps better than most, uncertainty and contradictions in much of human motivation and behavior, whether it be prosocial or antisocial, law abiding or criminal. Finally, a recognition of these ambiguities, especially as they pertain to the youthful offender, should alert us to be wary of labels and appearances in our efforts to explore antisocial and criminal behavior, assess personality, evaluate motivation for behavioral change, and lastly develop and implement a treatment plan that helps facilitate such change.

Chapter III

ABNORMAL PSYCHOLOGY AND
DELINQUENCY

U NDERSTANDING the basic principles and concepts of abnormal
psychology is of particular relevance to the assessment, classification and treatment of juvenile delinquents, since the psychology of delinquency falls within the domain of deviant or abnormal behavior. In this chapter we will outline some of the basic issues in abnormal psychology that we feel are of conceptual importance to a psychological understanding of delinquency. While in this chapter we will not focus on delinquency per se, the issues which are raised here will provide the background for a fuller appreciation of the material in the following chapters.

We have already discussed, in Chapter II, some of the problems relating to the definition of delinquency. It is axiomatic that before we can work with a problem we have to define what the problem is. The difficulties in definition are not limited to the concept of delinquency; in fact, they extend to all areas of abnormal psychology. Popular misrepresentations of those labelled as "mentally ill" might include "psychotic killers," "depraved child molesters," and "raving lunatics." The extreme ranges of a given population, because they draw so much attention to themselves, come to define the total population. These misrepresentations, familiar to social psychologists, are referred to as "stereotypes." According to this way of thinking, the typical juvenile delinquent is likely to be perceived as a young tough male wearing a denim jacket with "Savage Skulls" painted on the back and carrying a heavy chain, when in fact such individuals constitute only a small percentage of those defined as juvenile delinquents. As we have noted earlier, the issue is not academic, since it affects the response of many individuals such as teachers, lawyers, judges, the police, and even legislators who come into contact with those labelled delinquent.

In fact, as Coleman et al. (1984) point out, sharp dividing lines between "normal" and "abnormal" behavior simply do not exist. For the most part, individuals do not fall into discrete categories; they exist along a continuum, exhibiting a range of behavior. Furthermore they may, depending on the circumstances of their lives and the degree of stress present, move from one point in the continuum to another. For example, a "well-behaved" adolescent may begin to exhibit "delinquent" behavior because of family stress generated by parental conflict and divorce.

In addition, being labelled "disturbed" or "troubled," whether or not the label is accurate, creates its own problems. Rosenhan (1973) found that individuals who faked symptoms of mental illness to gain admission into a psychiatric hospital were later unable to convince the staff that they were in fact quite sane. Rosenhan further noted that many behaviors exhibited by inmates in psychiatric institutions tend to be viewed as abnormal by the staff whether the behavior is abnormal or not. In another study, Termerlin (1970) had mental health professionals observe an interview with a normal individual who, as part of the experiment, had been deliberately labelled by a prominent psychiatrist as "psychotic." Those professionals and non-professionals who observed the interview tended to label the person interviewed as disturbed despite the fact that he acted in a perfectly reasonable manner during the interview. The observers labelled him as disturbed simply because a respected professional had diagnosed him as such. In other words, expectations and settings may play a more important role than reality in judgments of normality, even for professionals. Often, the burden of proof lies with the individual, not the professional.

Adolescents may be particularly vulnerable to these misjudgments. A. Freud (1958) has pointed out that because of the unstable behavior caused by the developmental stresses associated with adolescence, it is frequently difficult to distinguish normality from pathology during adolescence. Anthony (1967) has suggested that adults, based on their unconscious fantasies, may tend to stereotype adolescents as dangerous or disturbed. An adolescent labelled as a troublemaker by a teacher or as a delinquent by the court may be continued to be perceived in that way even though the accusation may have been inaccurate or the behavior in question proven to be transitory.

Offer and Sabshin (1966) and others have pointed out that the terms "normal" and "abnormal" can be understood from different conceptual points of view, including deviations from social or cultural norms, personal unhappiness, maladaptive behavior, statistical deviations, and deviation from an ideal standard of mental health. While each approach has merit, the authors point out that, except in extreme cases, normality is a relativistic as opposed to an absolute concept. For example, an adolescent may be diagnosed as having a conduct disorder because he or she consistently violates social norms. From a personal point of view, the adolescent may not experience any particular unhappiness. Furthermore, the behavior in question may be relatively adaptive for that individual. In other words, neither norm violation nor statistical rarity can necessarily be equated with pathology. This is particularly true for adolescents who, under the pressure of normal developmental forces, are struggling for self-definition and are likely to behave in either eccentric or apparently antisocial ways as a part of a normal exploration of life-styles.

This is not to say that in many instances norm violations or statistically rare behavior is not generated by psychopathology but rather that we cannot automatically assume that it is. In fact, the value of understanding the conceptual and operational difficulties involved in labelling behavior as normal or abnormal is that it requires us to look further than the manifest behavior and examine it in the broader and deeper context of the individual's history, life, and milieu.

In this section we will present a brief overview of some of the major theoretical assumptions regarding the causes of abnormal behavior. It is important to bear in mind that while these assumptions relate to abnormal psychology, they are part of a general psychology which seeks to explain both normal and abnormal behavior. Hence, a theory which attempts to explain abnormal behavior in adolescents is an extension of a theory which explains adolescent behavior in a broader context.

Psychologists do not believe behavior occurs randomly. They assume there is a cause for every behavior and a stimulus for every response, whether or not that stimulus or cause is immediately apparent. Causative factors of behavior may be divided into three broad categories: those which are biological in nature, those which may be considered environmental (that is, part of the physical or social environment of the individual), and those which are psychological, i.e. predispositions for the individual to act in particular ways based on their personality structure,

learning and experiences. While we discuss each of these areas sepa-
rately, we are not suggesting that such factors operate independently of
each other. Rather, our basic assumption is that behavior is multiply determined and is the end result of the interaction of biological, environmental, and psychological factors. Therefore, in understanding a
phenomenon as complex as delinquency, all of these variables need to be
investigated.

Biological Determinants

It is a given fact that the physical status of an individual will affect his
functioning. A person may not be able to perform a complex physical
task as well when tired as when rested. A child becomes more cranky
when hungry than fed and so on. In many instances, however, the biological determinant is not necessarily observable and can only be inferred indirectly.

One of the more fundamental biological determinants of behavior is
the individual's genetic makeup. For example, an extra X chromosome
on the twenty-third pair in males results in Kleinfelter's syndrome.
These individuals are thought by some to be apparently at higher risk
for developing delinquency (Wright et al., 1979). In most instances,
however, it is difficult to relate the functioning of a single gene to a particular behavior and it is assumed that most behaviors have a poly-
genetic influence, in which the resulting behavior is caused by many
genes acting together either additively or interactively. Evidence for
genetic disorders in these instances cannot be made directly but rather is
inferred through the family histories of these individuals. More specifically, this is done by comparing concordance rates of first-degree rela-
tives and also those of monozygotic and dizygotic twins. For example,
the concordance rate for schizophrenia is significantly higher among
monozygotic twins than dizygotic twins. Nonetheless, workers in this
field speak in terms of genetic predispositions towards disorders rather
than genetic causes (Gottesman and Shields, 1973). In fact, the diathesis
stress theory is one which assumes that it is an interaction between
genetic predisposition and life stress which results in disorder (Rosenthal, 1970).

In addition to specific genetic factors, the neurological status of the
individual from birth through old age can have a significant effect on behavior. Developmental studies by Chess et al. (1965) and other researchers have noted that up to 10 percent of infants are born with "difficult

temperaments." These children may cry more, be predominantly negative and have difficulty with change. Many of these children may have adjustment problems later in life. Children diagnosed as having attention-deficit disorders, with or without associated hyperactivity, may be, at least temporarily, suffering from some form of neurological impairment. Later in life a wide range of behavior disorders, including emotional liability, impaired impulse control, delusions, and impaired intellectual functioning, may be associated with neurological impairment. (For a complete description of these disorders, see the Third Edition of the *Diagnostic and Statistical Manual of Mental Disorders* of the American Psychiatric Association, 1980).

Neurochemical imbalances have also been suggested as causative factors in some psychiatric disorders. For example, Snyder et al. (1974) have pointed out that increased levels of dopamine may be related to schizophrenic symptoms. Akiskal and McKinney (1975) suggest that decreases in catecholamines or indolamines play an important role in depression. Nonetheless, they also emphasize the role of developmental events and stress, in addition to biochemical factors, related to depression.

The psychological changes resulting from excessive use of drugs or alcohol can also generate severely maladaptive behavior. For example, acute or chronic alcohol intoxication is associated with delirium, dementia, hallucinations, and severe mood changes. In addition, alcohol abuse is frequently associated with violent death and crimes of violence (Tittle et al., 1978; Leventhal, 1984).

Other drugs associated with disturbed behavior include barbiturates, amphetamines, and phencyclidine (PCP). In addition to agitation, violence, and emotional liability, chronic abuse of psychoactive drugs is associated with a reduced ability to function on a daily basis, personality changes, physiological deterioration, and physical dependence or addiction. Drug abuse among adolescents is particularly harmful, in that it interferes with the achievement of normal developmental tasks as well as exacerbating the normal emotional liability associated with this stage of life, to say nothing of the involvement in delinquent behavior.

It is, of course, important to bear in mind that drug abuse is frequently associated with underlying psychopathology and social pathology. Pathology is often masked by the drug effects and cannot be seen clearly until the individual is detoxified. Therefore, drug abuse presents a dual problem: first, it causes difficulties because of the physiological responses to the drug; and, second, it is a symptom of psychological distress.

Finally, we should note that any factors which alter normal physiological functioning such as lack of sleep, malnutrition, and chronic pain may generate or exacerbate maladaptive behavior. We will discuss the relationship of various biological factors to delinquency in Chapter VII.

Psychological Determinants

In addition to the biological and environmental factors discussed above, much of our behavior is dependent upon our experience and learning as opposed to pure instinct. Experiences are stored in the central nervous system and predispose the person to respond to various stimuli configurations in particular ways.

For example, behavioral psychologists assume that all behavior including maladaptive behavior is learned. In the classic (although recently disputed) experiment by Watson and Raynor (1920), a young child was conditioned to fear a white rat (a conditioned response) by pairing the rat (the conditioned stimulus) with a loud noise (the unconditioned stimulus). The authors conclude that many of the phobias in psychopathology are actually "conditioned emotional reactions." In a similar, although more complex vein, social learning theory suggests that behavior and personality development are a function of the individual's exposure to particular models of behavior and the observations of the consequences. Hence, a young boy observing an adolescent boy being positively reinforced for behavior is likely to engage in the same type of antisocial behavior at some future point.

Classical psychodynamic theories assume that the behavior of the individual is motivated by unconscious conflicts. These conflicts are assumed to be formed in early childhood as the child attempts to reconcile his or her sexual and aggressive instincts with the demands of reality and the morality of society. The form or content of these conflicts depends upon the child's early experiences and the nature of the instinct at the time the conflict is generated. While they are no longer functional or adaptive, these conflicts are assumed to determine the behavior of the child and adult and are the ultimate cause of pathological behavior. For example, an individual who had difficulty reconciling angry feelings towards his father as a small boy may, as an adolescent, displace those aggressive feelings onto authority figures.

What these theories of pathology hold in common is their deterministic assumptions, that is, a given set of circumstances or experiences will predispose the individual to behave in a particular way. In that sense they imply that the behavior lies outside the control of the individual. On the other hand, other theoretical schools see the individual as a more active participant in the control of his or her behavior. For example, the mechanistic views of early behaviorists have been amplified by cognitive theorists. These writers suggest that the person does not passively receive or respond to various stimuli but rather interprets them on the basis of existing congitive schemes and then decides how to act on them. Psychopathology from this point of view results from cognitive structures which lead to erroneous perceptions of self, other individuals, and other aspects of reality. These structures are then seen as responsible for depression (Beck et al., 1979) and other disorders such as agoraphobia, obsessive-compulsive patterns and eating disorders (Guidano and Liotti, 1983). In fact, Samenow (1984) argues that much of delinquent behavior can be explained by that fact that these individuals think differently about themselves and society than non-delinquent individuals.

In a similar vein, the instinct-induced conflict model of the early psychoanalysts has been expanded on by the ego psychologists. Hartmann (1958) suggested a "conflict-free ego sphere for that ensemble of functions which at any given time exert their effects outside the region of mental conflict." While not negating prior analytic assumptions, this represented an important theoretical addition, in that it assumed that the control for at least some behavior was determined not only by conflict, instinct, and the environment but by the individual himself.

The implication of these theorists in explaining at least certain forms of deviant behavior is quite significant, in that it assumes that the individual, not necessarily determinants beyond his control, is responsible for his or her behavior. It certainly raises the important question of the degree to which the adolescent is responsible, despite adverse social or family factors for his delinquency.

Classification

The purpose of classification is to order or categorize objects or phenomena according to particular variables. By doing so we can reduce an unmanageably large number of objects or events to a smaller number of categories which allows for greater ease of study and communication. It is important to bear in mind that the categories which constitute a system of classification, while they may be logical, are arbitrary. For example, we may classify objects by color, size, or shape and be entirely consistent in our categorizing; which variable we choose to sort by depends upon which proves most useful for our system. Secondly, we must realize that in classifying an object we also lose a certain amount of information about any given member of the class. If we sort objects by color, the information about shape and size is lost. This is particularly troublesome when categorizing people, since the uniqueness and important information about each person is lost. One way around this problem is to devise more complex systems of classification, e.g. by adding more variables or categories. However, if the system becomes too complex, it begins to lose its value. In the end, any system of classification involves a compromise of some sort. What is important is to be aware of the nature and implications of the compromise.

The current system of psychiatric classification is the *Diagnostic and Statistical Manual of Mental Disorders,* referred to as the DSM-III. (American Psychiatric Association, 1980). What makes this latest revision unique is that it is multi-axial, that is it takes into account not only the individual's psychiatric diagnosis (Axis I) but other factors as well, such as personality or developmental problems (Axis II), medical or physical problems (Axis III), degree of psychosocial stress (Axis IV), and highest level of functioning over the past year (Axis V). Thus, a more complete statement can be made about an individual than stating, for example, that she is suffering from a phobic disorder.

The list of Axis I disorders is of interest because consistent variables do not exist across categories but only within categories. For example, the first category listed is "Disorders Usually First Evident in Infancy, Childhood or Adolescence," i.e. disorders are categorized on the basis of a developmental period of life. The second category listed is "Organic Mental Disorders." These are categorized on the basis of a known or assumed physical basis for the disordered behaviors. "Anxiety Disorders," on the other hand, are categorized only on the basis of observed behavior and no implications are made as to the cause of the disorder; it is purely a descriptive statement.

In other Axis I categories the kind of information provided by the diagnosis is different. This is not necessarily bad but rather reflects the state of the art. It is simply not possible to establish a system based on causes, such that we can say that category A disorders are based on poor parenting, category B on biochemical disorders, category C on social causes, etc. Certainly, this would be helpful in terms of treatment, but we have not yet arrived at the point of being able to do so.

While there have been numerous criticisms of the current diagnostic system (Rosenhan, 1975), it does have the advantage of operationalizing the definitions of various psychiatric disorders, so that at the very least, if the stated diagnostic criteria are followed, one can be clear about what is being communicated, notwithstanding the usefulness of the communication.

Another important issue with regards to the multi-axial system is that it begins to take into account the fact that behavior is multidetermined and that one cannot understand an individual simply along a single dimension. In fact, one of the failures of classification systems for delinquents has been the tendency for them to be described along only one dimension. (A discussion of problems relating to the classification of delinquents can be found in Chapter VIII.)

Also of importance to the problems of diagnosis are the concepts of reliability and validity. Reliability refers to the degree to which a statement made is found to be consistent. With regards to diagnosis we are concerned with temporal and interjudge reliability. Temporal reliability refers to the degree to which a statement made at one point in time will remain true over a period of time. For example, if on the basis of certain information and using a particular diagnostic system we diagnose a male adolescent as exhibiting an undersocialized aggressive conduct disorder, would we make that same diagnostic statement a week later, given the same information, or would we perhaps diagnose him as suffering from some form of schizophrenia? In other words, if the diagnostic system generates the same diagnostic statement over time, then we can say that it has a high degree of temporal reliability. Interjudge reliability refers to the degree that two independent observers using the same criteria will come to the same diagnostic conclusion. Will three professionals judging the adolescent come up with the same statement, or will they draw three different conclusions? Finally, validity is concerned with the degree to which a diagnostic system or test measures what it purports to measure. If a test is designed to measure the individual's potential for aggressive behavior but in fact is measuring the individual's level of social anxiety, then that instrument or system is not valid.

Issues of validity and reliability must be taken into account when any diagnostic statement is made. Frequently, statements are accepted because they appear to be valid, that is, they have face validity only, but fail to hold up under more rigorous examination.

There are several methods by which a diagnosis may be made. Interviews are the most common. A clinical interview may be totally unstructured or highly structured when the interviewer has very specific questions in mind. The chief advantage of the interview is that it allows the psychologist or other mental health worker to follow up on areas that may be raised spontaneously during the interview. The major drawback is that the conclusions drawn by the interviewer are subjective and may reflect the personal bias of the clinician.

Psychological tests are another widely used technique for making diagnostic statements. There are primarily two types: objective and projective tests. Among the objective techniques are the intelligence tests, like the Wechsler Scales, and self-report personality inventories, such as the Minnesota Multiphasic Personality Inventory. These are scored or interpreted on the basis of published norms and standards; hence, the term "objective." However, while objectivity may contribute to reliability and validity, it is not to be equated with them.

Projective tests such as the Rorschach and Thematic Apperception Test present the subject with ambiguous situations to respond to. These responses or projections of the inner dynamic onto the ambiguous external reality are then interpreted by the examiner based on his or her knowledge of and experience with the test. While these tests do allow the subjects a wider range of responses, as in the clinical interview, they tend to be less reliable and/or valid measures of personality (Nunnally 1978). In fact, Meehl (1954) has pointed out that clinical diagnostic statements made on a statistical (i.e. more objective) basis tend overall to be more accurate than clinical intuition.

Treatment and Prevention

When someone feels or behaves in ways that cause discomfort to himself or others, some form of psychotherapeutic intervention may be indicated. Broadly speaking, the goals of psychotherapy would include a reduction of psychopathology, a reduction of psychological pain and suffering, increased pleasure and experiencing, improved self-perception and, certainly important in the case of delinquents, an improved relationship with the external world (Maher, 1967). The specific goals will vary depending upon the nature of the problem and the type of treatment applied.

Treatment techniques can be divided into two major categories: psychological, which rely primarily on verbal interaction, and biological, which alter the physical status of the individual in some way, most commonly through the use of psychoactive drugs. The form of intervention chosen depends largely on the assumptions made by the therapist as to the cause of the problematic behavior or feelings. (Frequently, these assumptions reflect the therapist's training and bias as much as the "actual" cause of the problem.) Thus, if one assumes that an adolescent engages in delinquent behavior because of faulty psychosexual development, then psychoanalytic treatment might be indicated; if it was assumed to be due to faulty learning, then behavior modification would be used; if it was believed to be due to some neurochemical imbalance, then medication might be prescribed.

There is a wide range of psychological treatments presently in use. These include psychodynamic, behavioral, cognitive, and humanistic-existential therapies. In addition to individual therapy techniques, marital, family, and group treatments have been developed which place greater emphasis on interactional aspects of behavior. While these treatments are based on divergent theoretical points of view, they are all based on the general assumption that the individual's difficulties lie within a less than "optimal" psychological makeup and that by talking to the person it is possible to alter the way he feels, behaves, or perceives his situation in the world. This form of treatment has its origins in the work on conversion hysteria conducted by Charcot in the late nineteenth century. He was able to demonstrate that hysteria was caused by the patient's psychology and not by a neurological lesion (Meissner, 1982). These findings stimulated Freud (along with Breuer) to develop a theory of psychopathology and indeed a metapsychology which became known as psychoanalytic theory upon which psychoanalysis was based. While it has undergone numerous theoretical changes since its inception, it remains based on the assumption that experiences in early childhood leave unconscious residuals which effect personality and generate pathology later in life. A "cure" is effected by listening and talking to the patient in order to help him gain greater insight into the history and dynamics of his personality and problems. Indeed, most modern therapies in one way or another are based on this model, even though they may be at great variance with the more traditional assumptions of Freudian theory.

Behavior therapy, as distinguished from the psychodynamic assumptions noted above, is based on the premise that maladaptive behaviors or feelings are a class of learned behaviors and may be modified by various learning techniques. They focus to a much greater extent on the modification of the observable behavior and the contingencies associated with it as opposed to unobservable dynamics. For psychodynamic therapists, a cure occurs when the underlying cause of the behavior is understood and eliminated. For the behaviorist, the "cure" constitutes the modification of the behavior itself. Somewhat of an integration of the two has recently developed in cognitive therapy which focuses both on internal cognitive processes as well as on observable behaviors (Guidano and Liotti, 1983).

In addition, all forms of therapy rely on a relationship between therapist and patient. In dynamic therapies this relationship may become a central focus of the treatment and is referred to as "transference." While not emphasized to the same degree in other forms of therapy, it is assumed the therapist will interact with the patient in such a way as to maximize the patient's trust and motivation to change. In fact, it appears that the relationship between patient and therapist, along with the patient's motivation to change, may be of greater importance to the outcome of therapy than the actual theoretical model on which the therapy is based.

The effectiveness of psychotherapy has been questioned for some time. Eysenck (1952) suggested that being on a waiting list for psychotherapy was as helpful in terms of symptom remission as actually receiving the treatment. However, measuring the effectiveness of a process as complex as psychotherapy is difficult, and the standards and techniques vary from one study to another. In addition, some forms of therapy may be more effective for particular individuals with particular problems than others. An effective system of matching patient and problem with therapist and technique has not yet been devised. Nonetheless, more recent evaluation studies suggest that regardless of the particular treatment intervention used, about 70 percent to 80 percent of patients show some improvement (Bergin and Lamberg, 1978).

Biological treatment interventions primarily involve the use of drugs. In most, but not all, instances the aim is symptomatic relief as opposed to eliminating an underlying cause. The drugs used fall into five major categories: antipsychotic, antidepressant, antimanic, antianxiety, and stimulants.

Antipsychotic drugs such as the phenothiazines (e.g. Thorazine) are used primarily to alleviate the symptoms associated with schizophrenia. While they help to suppress extreme agitation, delusions, and hallucinations, the underlying psychotic organization remains. Nonetheless, they may make the patient more manageable and in many instances allow him to function within the community. However, long-term use may result in Parkinsonian-like side effects known as tardive dyskinesia. Drugs used for treating depression include the tricyclics (e.g. Tofranil) and the MAO inhibiters (e.g. Nardil). These drugs increase the concentration of serotonin and norepiniphrine (both excitatory neurotransmitters) and therefore may alter the underlying biological basis for some endogenous depression (Akiskal, 1975). In this respect, they differ from the antipsychotic drugs which alleviate symptoms but leave the underlying process untouched. One other treatment used for depression is electroconvulsive therapy. This technique involves passing a high-voltage, low-amperage current through the patient's central nervous system. The current produces loss of consciousness and convulsive seizures. The convulsions are lessened by the administration of a muscle relaxant. While useful in the treatment of major depressions, this therapy may have apparently dangerous side effects (Breggin, 1979) and is not widely used.

Bi-polar affective disorders (particularly the manic aspect) have responded well to lithium carbonate. This drug prevents recurrent manic-depressive episodes and like some antidepressant medication does more than suppress symptoms. Patients who respond positively to this drug are able to function normally. The drug is quite toxic, however, and blood levels must be monitored carefully.

Antianxiety agents (propanediols and benzodiazepams), also known as minor tranquilizers, are widely prescribed for the alleviation of anxiety and tension. In fact, Valium and Librium have been the drugs most commonly prescribed by physicians. While these drugs are effective in reducing anxiety, they do not effect either the situational or psychological basis for the anxiety. Hence, in most instances they fall into the "band-aid" category of drugs. Long-term use causes dependence; side effects include lethargy and drowsiness.

Lastly, a group of drugs, primarily amphetamines, which are stimulants, are paradoxically used to control hyperactivity and distractibility in children. While these drugs may be effective with many children, allowing them to function in school, careful diagnosis is required so that children who are normally active and distractible or who are this way due to other factors are not medicated unnecessarily.

There are many ethical issues regarding treatment, particularly as it relates to those individuals who are not given the right to refuse treatment. This would include those declared mentally incompetent by the court and children and adolescents. Szaz (1963) has suggested that involuntary commitment and/or treatment is a violation of the patient's civil rights. On the other hand, others have suggested that the needs of society are more important than rights of the adolescent or child. Should a delinquent adolescent have the right to refuse treatment which may reduce his delinquent behavior? If not, who becomes the client, the adolescent or society? Under what circumstances do the values or needs of society take precedence over the rights of the individual? These are clearly important questions, despite the fact that they are more concerned with values than theory. Certainly, they are of great relevance to the treatment of delinquents.

A last, but important aspect of abnormal psychology is that of prevention of mental illness. Cowen (1967) stated that

> Our greatest failing lies in the imbalanced emphasis that has been placed in the treatment of evident, often times florid, pathology as opposed to efforts directed at stemming the flow of disorder. This failing has been magnified by the circumscribed reach of existing methods as well as their limited effectiveness. There is greater hope that the flow of disorder may be slowed down through the modification of influential social systems which shape human development rather than through one to one clinical intervention. (p. 445)

Prevention programs may typically work with larger social systems such as schools (Zax and Cowen, 1967) and neighborhoods to identify individuals or families who may be at risk for developing difficulties at some later point. Such programs may in the long run prove to be more effective in dealing with problems such as delinquency than treatment techniques that attempt to alter already established maladaptive or antisocial behavior.

Chapter IV

EARLY CHILDHOOD FACTORS
AND DELINQUENCY

W E HAVE pointed out that adolescents commit violent and property crimes disproportionate to their numbers in the population.
It is our point of view that juvenile delinquency is to a large degree a developmental phenomenon and as such an examination of some of the
major issues in developmental psychology, particularly as they may relate to understanding antisocial behavior during adolescence, would be
in order.

Developmental psychology refers to the changes in behavior which
occur over time as a result of the complex interaction between biological
and environmental factors and the ways in which these interactions are
organized within and emerge from the individual. The word "interaction" is of key importance. We do not take the position that delinquency
is generated by either biological or environmental factors alone, but
rather that it develops as a result of inherited predispositions and temperaments and the ways in which these factors are shaped by the individual's physical and psychosocial environment.

There is no single theory which can adequately explain all aspects of
development. Rather, theories tend to focus on specific issues such as the
development of cognition, independence, sexuality, socialization, etc. In
addition, theories vary along two other dimensions. One is the degree to
which they explain development as a continuous or discontinuous phenomenon. Continuous models describe development as emerging in a
quantitative manner as a gradually increasing elaboration of preexisting
functions. Bandura and Walters' (1963) Social Learning Theory is an
example of this approach to understanding development. They state,
". . . social learning theories would predict marked changes in behavior

only as a result of abrupt alterations in social training and other relevant biological or environmental variables which rarely occur in the social learning histories of most individuals in the pre-adult years" (p. 25).

In contrast, discontinuous theories of development stress qualitative changes in behavior from one developmental period to another. These theories are often referred to as stage theories. A stage is an arbitrary temporal division of a period in the life cycle. Thus, Piaget (1969) divides cognitive development into sensory-motor, preoperational, concrete operations, and formal operations stages. Each of these stages describes the way the developing individual utilizes particular modes of cognitive organization to understand the world. There are certain correlaries associated with the concept of stages. The first is that development occurs in fixed sequences. Stage one will always precede stage two and so on. Stage theories also imply developmental discontinuity because they assume that qualitatively different processes emerge from preceding stages and that they reflect reorganization processes involved in the preceding stages. Hence, the way in which a child in the sensory-motor stage organizes and understands information is different qualitatively than the way in which the child functioning on the level of concrete operations organizes information.

In addition, there are certain normative expectations associated with each stage or developmental period. These are frequently referred to as developmental tasks. For example, during the sensory-motor period it is expected that the child will come to understand that objects continue to exist despite the fact that they cannot be seen, while during the concrete operations stage it is expected that the child will understand that the volume of liquid remains constant despite changes in its shape (Piaget 1969).

What must, of course, be kept in mind is that development occurs within the context of an environment and that the development of any aspect of behavior cannot be understood without considering environmental influences. Clearly, one could not consider the development of a child without discussing the influences of his or her family, school, neighborhood, cultural setting, etc. Nonetheless, theories of development vary on the amount of weight they give to environmental factors. For example, psychodynamic theories place greater emphasis on the role of internal forces (both biological and psychological) on development than learning theories, which emphasize the importance of the reinforcing and punishing aspects of the environment. It is likely that both theoretical approaches have merit. We will begin by discussing psychodynamic approaches to understanding the development of antisocial behavior in children and adolescents and then, in the following chapters, examine the role of psychosocial and biological factors.

Psychodynamic Theory

Of all the psychological conceptualizations of delinquency, psychodynamic theories, based on the assumption of the presence of an unconscious and the centrality of biological instincts, differ most markedly from sociological approaches, in that they assume that the prime determinants of delinquent behavior lie within the individual as opposed to within his or her environment. Delinquency is understood as a symptom of faulty development in early childhood and/or as a product of the adolescent's inability to integrate the increased sexual and aggressive drives associated with the onset of puberty. One of the earliest workers in this field, Aichhorn (1935), stated that "symptoms of delinquency and the fundamental problems underlying delinquency are constantly confused . . . a delinquent act is founded on the same mechanism which we regularly find in the neurotic symptom" (p. 39).

Psychodynamic theory explains a symptom as the expression of an unconscious conflict or wish, which cannot be adequately denied by the individual's ego. Therefore, in order to understand the delinquent and his or her behavior, one must be able to understand the unconscious dynamics which underlie the behavior. Typically, this would necessitate a rather thorough understanding of the individual's personal history with particular emphasis on the ways in which the individual has integrated and/or expressed both sexual and aggressive drives. While a full-blown analytic investigation of each individual is rarely practical or even useful, the questions raised about any individual from this perspective can provide the clinician with valuable insights regarding the delinquent's motivation for the behavior in question. In other words, it is not necessary to see the individual four times a week for a year in order to utilize this approach. Its value lies in its theoretical richness which can allow the clinician to generate useful hypotheses regarding the understanding of the delinquent's behavior. In this chapter we will examine some of the major psychodynamic formulations of delinquent behavior and suggest ways in which these may be utilized in an overall evaluation of the delinquent.

Aggression and Acting Out

In order to understand this perspective more thoroughly, we first need to turn our attention to two basic concepts. These are the analytic formulations of the aggressive instinct and the concept of "acting out."

Of all the manifestations of delinquency, the most disturbing are those involving crimes of violence in which the expression of aggression appears to be a predominant motivation for the crime. Psychodynamic theories vary in their explanation of violence and aggression. The chief difference between them lies in the degree to which they understand aggression to be either innate or a function of the development of the individual.

While his theory underwent a number of modifications in the course of his lifetime, Freud (1940) ultimately concluded that man was motivated by two basic instincts: a sexual instinct (Eros) and a death instinct (Thantos). "The aim of the first of these basic instincts is to establish ever greater unities and to preserve them thus—in short, to bind together; the aim of the second, on the contrary, is to undo connections and so to destroy things" (p. 20). These instincts were basic biological givens in Freud's theory and as such were perceived to be fundamental determinants of behavior and perhaps, more importantly, a fundamental aspect of human nature. Freud believed that these instincts were either fused or modified by each other so that "a surplus of sexual aggressiveness will change a lover into a sexual murderer, while a sharp diminution in the aggressive factor will lead to shyness or impotence" (p. 21).

Later analytic theorists rejected Freud's notion that aggression was an instinct, believing instead that its expression was more a function, particularly in its most destructive aspects, of development and experience as opposed to an inevitable aspect of human behavior. For example, Fromm (1973) distinguished between benign aggression, which enables the individual to protect himself against threats, and malignant or destructive aggression. Fromm felt that the latter was generated by the conditions under which man lives rather than the presence of a destructive instinct. The distinction between an aggressive "instinct," which is a biological innate process and bound to be expressed, and an aggressive "drive," which is modifiable by experience, is by no means clear. Kutash (1978), despite his attempts to distinguish between the two, uses the terms interchangeably. The issue of whether or not man biologically possesses a destructive instinct seems open to interpretation and question. However, one basis for agreement seems to lie in the fact that instincts in man, including aggression, can be modified by environmental and experiential factors. For example, Hartmann et al. (1949) have suggested that aggressive instincts in man are subject to both ego and superego control and may be modified by displacement, repression, sublimation or fusion with sexual instincts. These modifications of the drive are dependent upon the individual's ego and superego functioning. In the healthy individual, adequate ego functioning assures that the aggression is expressed in an adaptive rather than a destructive manner. For example, aggression may be expressed in socially acceptable assertiveness or competitiveness or in the striving for a goal. Kutash refers to this as aggression in the service of the ego. Destructive or hostile aggression, on the other hand, occurs with much greater frequency in those individuals suffering from some form of psychopathology, which by definition implies inadequate ego functioning caused by developmental, physiological, or environmental factors. Thus, in their present state, psychodynamic theories rely more on ego functioning rather than on the expression of destructive aggressive instincts to explain aggressive and violent behavior.

The psychodynamic concept of acting out has clear relevance for the description and understanding of delinquent behavior. While a precise definition of the term "acting out" is not agreed upon (Rexford, 1966), it generally refers to the individual's tendency to express in action, rather than in language or fantasy, an impulse or some derivative of that impulse. Further, in its usage, it usually connotes socially or developmentally negative or maladaptive behavior and is frequently used in explaining delinquency in adolescents. In fact, Freud first used the term to describe the behavior of an adolescent patient with whom he was working (Dora) who abruptly terminated treatment with him. Thus, she "acted out" with him what had been done to her, specifically, being deserted by men.

In an extensive review of the literature on acting out, Rexford suggests that the term refers to a purposeful activity of the ego, which can be described in terms of predispositional, developmental and adaptive factors. In other words, the behavior needs to be understood in terms of the individual's history, psychological status, and needs. Various authors have focused on different aspects of this process. While Freud initially saw it as a defense against remembering what was painful, later theoreticians saw not only memory but also instincts being expressed in action. Fenichel (1954) felt it was a process by which the individual unconsciously relieved inner tensions.

Blos (1966) pointed out that it was necessary to differentiate between three different aspects of acting out. These were (1) the predisposition of the individual to act out, (2) the actual behavior, and finally (3) the function it serves. Considerable attention has been given to predispositions towards acting out by several writers, who describe the development of the delinquent personality. These writers have addressed themselves to the ways in which, during early childhood, the individual fails to integrate or master inherent tendencies to express through behavior that which would be best expressed through words, fantasy, or optimally through sublimation. In other words, the young child has to learn to say that he feels angry at his younger sibling rather than hitting him. Many authors have seen the predisposition towards acting out as resulting from the development of a faulty character structure during the first six years of life. Both Rexford and Blos have pointed out that there is a need to differentiate between the actual behavior and the underlying causes, which may be quite complex. In this respect it follows many other psychoanalytic conceptualizations which differentiate between behavior and the motivation for that behavior and assume the origins of the behavior to be based on internal rather than external factors. Finally, Blos has suggested that in some instances acting out behavior may reflect a normal developmental process during adolescence and in fact may serve an adaptive function, i.e. it may allow the individual symbolically to recreate and master situations which generated unreasonable anxiety as a child. For instance, an adolescent who felt unreasonably intimidated by his father as a child may angrily confront his high school teachers and thus master his anxiety of authority figures. In this context the behavior, which may or may not be antisocial, would still be considered personally adaptive.

Both aggression and acting out need to be understood within a developmental context. Therefore, we will next turn our attention to how developmental factors may result in delinquent behavior.

Pregenital Development

A two-year-old who forcefully takes a toy from a playmate's hand is not considered a delinquent; a sixteen-year-old who steals his friend's bicycle is. The difference lies not so much in the behavior as much as in the differences in behavioral expectations for the two- and the sixteen-year-old. Society tolerates, even if it does not condone, antisocial behavior in small children. However, it neither accepts nor condones such behavior in the adolescent. In other words, behavior is usually understood, among other variables, within the context of the individual's chronological age.

Psychoanalytic theory has made some important contributions in this area, particularly as it relates to the socialization and development of both sexual and aggressive behavior. In this section we will address some of the major factors seen as important from this theoretical perspective and which lead to normal or delinquent behavior.

A basic assumption of these theorists is that all children are born "delinquent." August Aichhorn (1936), one of the first to apply psychodynamic theory to the understanding of delinquency, stated that

> Every child is at first an asocial being in that he demands direct primitive instinctual satisfaction without regard for the world around him. . . . The task of upbringing is to lead the child from this asocial to a social state. (p. 4)

In other words, given that all are born with aggressive instincts, all have the propensity to express these instincts in an antisocial manner until these instincts are modified in the course of development. Friedlander (1947), in an extensive and basically still current exposition of the psychodynamics of delinquency, says the following: "It cannot be sufficiently emphasized that all workers dealing with delinquents in any capacity ought to be aware of the fact that the antisocial urges they meet within the delinquent are *normal* (italics added) manifestations of the instinctive life of the small child, and the preoccupations of delinquents with their desires and pleasures is equally manifest in the toddler" (p. 27). The failure to modify these instincts in the small child may manifest itself as delinquent behavior in the adolescent.

Aggression is modified in the child through his relationship to his parents and through the development of the ego and superego. Post-Freudian writers such as Winnicott (1965) and Mahler (1975) emphasized the importance of the early or preoedipal (the first three to four years) relationship with parents on later development. These authors focused on the ways in which the child's sense of self and reality gradually emerge through both a growing identification and differentiation from primary caretakers and the ways in which these caretakers transmit security, love, and reality to the child. Thus, the child's ability to feel safe and trusting is a function of the parents' ability to provide an environment in which the child feels protected, not only from external threats, but from his own impulses as well.

Friedlander (1947) has suggested that even before the child can intellectually or morally understand the need for socially acceptable behavior, the only motivation for modifying his behavior (that is, controlling his impulses) may be the wish to please his mother so as not to lose her love. Consequently, the mother has great influence over the child in terms of modifying antisocial behaviors such as temper tantrums or aggressive behavior directed toward siblings or other children. If the mother's influence is used in a rational and consistent manner, it will lead to early and age-appropriate modification of instincts which would otherwise generate antisocial behavior in and out of the family setting.

It is clear, therefore, that during these formative years, mothers play a critical role and that problems existing within the personality of the mother may create problems for the child. For example, Rexford and van Amerngen (1957) found that mothers with unmet dependency needs of their own generated impulsive behavior in their own children. These mothers, because they themselves did not experience sufficient love as children, could not provide a sufficiently satisfying emotional environment for their children and were unable to set limits. Similarly, Malone (1966) noted that mothers' own feelings of deprivation and narcissistic needs can make it difficult for them to give to their children in consistent ways, leaving their children either frustrated or overindulged. Kaufman and McKay (1956) found that infantile types of depression (anaclitic), resulting from a physical or emotional deprivation, seem to be a major predisposing and necessary factor in delinquency. Myerson (1975) noted that if the emotional contact between mother and child is good, delinquency or acting out behavior is rarely an outcome. Further, numerous studies have pointed out that parents who abuse their own children (frequently, adolescent parents) were typically abused or unloved as children.

Thus, one consistent finding has been that children who regularly act in an antisocial manner frequently come from families in which parents were unable to give consistent love, set consistent limits, and provide the child with a clear sense of reality in terms of others and in terms of themselves. Children from such families tend to act in antisocial ways during adolescence because of the absence of parents who themselves are in control and can set limits. Further, poor self-esteem may result from inconsistent caretaking, and there may be a failure to perceive others in the world in a realistic manner due to the child's inability to integrate aggressive and sexual instincts in an appropriate way. These children are more likely to exhibit antisocial behavior during the primary grades and demonstrate chronically delinquent behavior during their adolescence. Apparently, there is some truth to the old saw, "As the twig is bent so grows the tree."

As with earlier stages of development, the satisfactory resolution of the oedipal stage aids in social adaptation. Blos (1957, 1965) has noted oedipal factors, representing struggles against authority figures, are prevalent in male delinquents. In its traditional sense this developmental phase contains aggressive feelings directed against the parent, which, if not properly resolved, may be displaced onto other authority figures such as teachers, adults in general, and other children. Obviously, the child's relationship with his parents as well as his ability to master his own impulses will have a significant effect on the outcome of this phase of development.

It should also be noted that it is at this point, around five years of age, that an internalized and integrated superego becomes an important factor in the control of impulses and the child's sense of morality becomes an important aspect of his or her personality. The superego represents the internalization of the parent's morality and it is this structure, along with the ego, that allows the child to act appropriately in the absence of the parent. The way in which the superego develops depends in part on the types of role models parents present to the child.

So far, we have discussed how both normal and abnormal developmental and/or instinctual factors may contribute to delinquent behavior. We can now turn our attention to the ways in which these factors interact with the structural concepts of the id, ego, and superego to generate antisocial behavior.

Since one of the major functions of the ego is the inhibition of instinctual impulses originating in the id, it is clear that ego weaknesses in this area might well lead to delinquent behavior. As noted above, it is not assumed that the ego of the small child is capable of such control, but we do expect that the ego of the adolescent should be. From a descriptive standpoint, we can assume that delinquency may result from a failure of ego development, more specifically, from a failure to move from the pleasure to the reality principle.

Aichhorn (1936) felt that only part of the ego of the delinquent succeeds in making the transition from the pleasure principle to the reality principle. Similarly, Friedlander (1947, 1949) believed that the ego of the delinquent is still governed by the pleasure principle, so that when instinctive urges arise reality ceases to exist. In fact, it is this ego "weakness" in the child, along with a lack of an independent superego, which both Aichhorn and Friedlander referred to as a "latent delinquent character structure." Aichhorn stated that:

> . . . the child remains asocial or else behaves as if he had become social without having made an actual adjustment to the demands of society. This means that he has not repudiated completely his instinctual wishes but has suppressed them so they lurk in the background awaiting an opportunity to break through to satisfaction. This state we call 'latent delinquency'; it can become 'manifest' on provocation. (p. 4)

It would appear that an individual with this type of character structure would be much more likely to act out impulsive antisocial behavior during adolescence, given the relatively greater strength of aggressive instincts during this stage of development and the effects these drives have on adaptive ego functions (Berman, 1984).

However, others have cautioned against a unidimensional perspective of ego disturbance. Redl (1951, 1966, 1970) has stated that it is important to distinguish between various ego functions, noting that while the ego of the delinquent may be "weak" in regard to impulse control, it may in fact be strong in its ability to enlist allies, find temptations, manipulate others, etc. Aichhorn implied this when he suggested that only part of the ego of the delinquent has developed ability to accurately adapt to reality while another part has failed to adapt to social norms. More recently, Keith (1984) has suggested that no matter what the developmental factors in the adolescent's background, the common pathway leading to antisocial behavior is the presence of a "sluice" within the ego, an acting-out mechanism, which allows for the expression of unacceptable impulses.

It appears that while ego deficits are of value in explaining some delinquent behavior, they do not explain the behavior in totality. In fact, we may frequently run across delinquent adolescents whose ego functions, e.g. reality testing and impulse control, seem perfectly intact. These individuals may choose to behave antisocially. Therefore, we need to look further for our understanding of this behavior.

A. Freud (1965) believed that the developmental advance to the reality principle did not guarantee socialization. Factors such as identification, imitation, and introjection also played an important role in this regard. This would then bring us to the concept of the ego ideal and the superego. Both are based on identifications with role models presented to the child which become internalized into behavioral expectations and goals. The superego is conceptualized as a regulatory structure in the personality which is more specifically determined by the child's identification with parental morality and later the behavioral standards of the community. Aichhorn and others have noted that delinquency may be caused by faulty identification with parental morality or an inability to identify with such norms due to a failure to become sufficiently attached to these parental role models. However, even the presence of a superego will not guarantee the identification with the content of specific community laws. It assures only the acceptance and internalization of a governing norm in general but not the acceptance of any law or rule in particular. In other words, we tend to think about thieves as being immoral (stealing representing immoral behavior), yet we can also accept the premise that there is honor among thieves (honor representing morality).

In fact, the delinquent superego may be based on an identification with antisocial norms of the parent or the community in which the child was raised. Johnson (1944) suggested that a child may unconsciously be encouraged by the parent to act out the parent's own unconscious forbidden impulses. In these instances, it is not, strictly speaking, the child's superego which is not functioning but rather that of the parent. Certainly, we can also think of instances in which the directive to behave in an antisocial way is delivered in a very deliberate way as well, such as in the case of an identification with a criminal father, as witnessed by the findings of Lewis in criminality among the parents of delinquents (Lewis, 1981).

Ironically, a highly developed superego may lead to delinquent behavior in another way. Freud (1916) suggested that the presence of an unconscious sense of guilt generated by earlier infantile wishes may lead to criminal behavior:

> In many criminals, especially youthful ones, it is possible to detect a very powerful sense of guilt which existed before the crime, and is therefore not its result but its motive. It is as if it were a relief to be able to fasten this unconscious sense of guilt on to something real and immediate. (p. 76)

Finally, we should note that in the course of development, adolescents often detach themselves from those parental identifications on which the superego is based. This may create, temporarily at least, a moral vacuum which can leave the adolescent vulnerable to more delinquent identifications with peers or others. The area of ego and superego functioning in the delinquent is complex. We cannot simply assume that the ego or superego of the delinquent is deficient. We would do better to specify the areas of deficiency and understand the developmental aspects of those deficiencies.

Cognitive-Moral Development

Related in some ways to the concept of the superego (Nass, 1966), the development of morality in early and middle childhood has been addressed most extensively by Kohlberg (1976, 1979). In addition to drawing on the idea that the child's morality develops on the basis of identification with the morality of parents, Kohlberg also drew from the concepts and methods of Piaget (1932). While a detailed presentation of Piaget's theory is beyond the scope of this book, Piaget assumed that knowledge of the world resulted from the child's interaction with his environment. These interactions had the effect of gradually altering the child's perception and understanding of reality, such that it became increasingly less egocentric and more abstract. (See Piaget [1969] or Flavell [1963] for a more detailed discussion.) Kohlberg, like Piaget, assumed that the child's moral development followed from his cognitive development. However, he expanded on Piaget's conceptualization by postulating three levels, each divided into two substages, of moral development which he called the preconventional, conventional, and postconventional. The preconventional level, associated with childhood, is characterized by moral reasoning concerned with the external consequences of behavior, e.g. being punished for poor behavior (Stage 1) or gaining rewards for behaving properly (Stage 2). This preconventional level of morality, which is basically egocentric, is typical of children from the ages of 4 to 10. Conventional moral reasoning is less egocentric and concerned with gaining the approval of others (Stage 3) and the maintenance of social order and respect for authority (Stage 4). While this level is characteristic of late childhood and early adolescence, most adults continue to function at this stage (Kohlberg, 1979). Moral reasoning at the postconventional level is characterized by a more abstract sense of right and wrong based on democratic principles accepted by law (Stage 5) or a morality of individual conscience (Stage 6), which may at times conflict with the law as in instances of civil disobedience as practiced by Ghandi or Martin Luther King. However, a relatively small percentage of individuals reach the postconventional level of moral reasoning.

While adolescent moral reasoning becomes less egocentric, the adolescent is more concerned with gaining social approval (Stage 3) than he is with the maintenance of social order (Stage 4). (Approximately, 90 percent of adolescents function at Stage 3.) Hence, based as it is on the need for social approval, this type of morality is more likely to lead to conforming to peer group norms, for example, smoking marijuana, than to broader social norms. Therefore, adolescents may feel they are acting morally despite the fact that they are violating broader social norms.

A reasonable question to ask then is whether or not delinquent adolescents are less moral than their non-delinquent peers. While it would seem by definition the delinquents would be less moral, the findings in this area are equivocal. Some writers such as Hall (1984) have suggested that adolescents are "morally blind." Edelman and Goldstein (1981) concluded that delinquents were less moral as a group; on the other hand, Jurkovic (1980) and Gold and Petrino (1980) found no consistent relationship between delinquent behavior and moral development. Jurkovic concludes:

> Delinquency as a legal classification clearly does not imply a premature arrest in moral development. Just as the youngsters differ in their personality and behavioral style, so do they differ in their level of moral judgment. Thus acquisition of conventional concepts in no way prevents delinquency, although dysocial behaviors may have a qualitatively different meaning to conventional than preconventional adolescents. (p. 716)

On the other hand, he does suggest that individuals at a preconventional level may be at a higher risk for delinquency, whereas those at a conventional level may or may not be.

These inconsistencies may be found for a number of reasons. First of all, there is no consistent relationship between moral thinking and moral behavior (Hoffman, 1980). As we noted earlier, psychoanalytic writers have found no consistent relationship between superego development and whether or not an individual will follow the laws of the community. Secondly, the level of moral reasoning used may vary according to the situation (Sprinthall and Collins, 1984). Thirdly, since there is a relationship between levels of cognitive development and levels of moral reasoning and since many delinquents have been found to function at lower intellectual levels, the problem may not be so much lower morality as much as the lack of intellectual capacity to reason at higher levels. Finally, what is moral for adolescents varies with the cultural setting in which they find themselves. Classification systems take this factor into account. For example, DSM-III has subcategories of socialized versus unsocialized conduct disorders, and Quay (1979) has a category for sub-cultural delinquents. Thus, these categories reflect the fact that an individual may be acting morally within one context but immorally within a larger context.

Summary and Conclusions

One of the major conclusions to be drawn from this theoretical approach is that the potential for the expression of antisocial behavior exists in all children and adolescents. This rests on the assumption hi of the presence of a biologically inherited aggressive instinct, which unless modified by experience and development, will be acted out in a destructive manner.

Thus, psychodynamic theory requires that we examine those developmental factors which will either modify, inhibit or facilitate the expression of instincts. These factors include the child's earliest interactions with his parents, especially the nature of the affectionate mother-child bond, and the ways in which the parents set or failed to set limits on inappropriate behavior and also includes the kinds of role models the parents presented to the child.

In addition, the relationship with the parent promotes the development of the psychic structures, the ego and the superego. These structures ultimately allow the child to behave in ways consistent with social expectations in the absence of the parent or other authority figures. Deficits in ego or superego development and/or functioning increase the probability of the occurrence of antisocial behavior during childhood or adolescence. These deficiencies in childhood have been referred to as a "latent delinquent character structure." Nonetheless, it is important to bear in mind that the ego of the delinquent may be deficient in only certain areas, e.g. impulse control, but function well in other areas such as reality testing.

Because of the increased stress on the ego and the superego associated with puberty, due primarily to the increased quantity of sexual and aggressive instincts and because of the increasing detachment from parental authority, there is a greater likelihood for acting out of antisocial behavior during adolescence. In fact, according to some authors, "normal" acting out during this developmental stage cannot always be distinguished from true pathology. Some acting out may, in fact, serve developmentally useful functions. Nonetheless, the frequency and severity of the delinquent behavior differentiates normal adolescent hi-jinx and rebellion from more serious and problematical behavior, including crimes of violence.

As presented, psychodynamic theory allows us to understand delinquent behavior in terms of the child's development and the functioning of those psychic structures (the ego and superego) responsible for the control of behavior. This continues to remind us that the causes of delinquency are multifaceted and that the understanding of the behavior rests on the understanding of its causes. Finally, it helps us to distinguish between delinquency caused by developmental and/or psychic pathology, social pathology, or developmental stress.

Chapter V

ADOLESCENT DEVELOPMENT

WE HAVE discussed some of the ways in which factors during the early years of childhood can contribute to a predisposition toward delinquent behavior. We will now examine the ways in which adolescent development itself can contribute to delinquency. To a large degree, this would depend on how one would define delinquency. If the definition were to include all status offenders, then just about all adolescents could be labelled delinquents. Our concern here is with those adolescents whose behavior reflects a continuous pattern of serious offenses.

An important question to be addressed is the degree to which the biological, social, and psychological changes associated with adolescence may be related to delinquency. As we will explain below, some authors (e.g. Hall, 1904; A. Freud, 1958; Blos, 1962) argue that adolescence, because of the developmental demands involved, is inherently stressful and thus generates rebellion and behavior which is indistinguishable from psychopathology. Others (e.g. Mead, 1928; Offer, 1969) have argued that this need not necessarily be the case and that real pathology, social or otherwise, is, in fact, distinguishable from normal adolescent behavior. Indeed, some have suggested that adolescence as a developmental stage and its concomitant behaviors are a cultural invention (Stone and Church, 1957).

These controversies notwithstanding, adolescence in our culture involves change and adaptation to both biological and social demands. Whether an individual experiences these demands as stressful or not depends on a number of cultural, familial, and ontogenetic factors. One important variable in this regard is whether or not adolescence is a continuous or discontinuous developmental period. That is, does it, in fact,

involve a major reorganization of preexisting processes, or is it an elaboration of already existing processes? While developmental discontinuity
is more likely to generate more stress at transitional life stages, there is
also the question as to whether this discontinuity is inherent in development or whether, as Benedict (1938) suggests, it is created by the culture.

The major developmental tasks of this stage of life include the integration of a stable sexual identity and the capacity for heterosexual relationships, the establishment of a new body image, the giving up of
childhood attachments to parents, the establishment of adult object relations, and gaining a sense of identity (which includes self-definition,
purpose, and values).

It has been suggested by many psychoanalytic writers that these very
important and difficult developmental tasks, along with a significant increase in sexual and aggressive instincts, will inevitably create some disturbance in functioning. A. Freud (1958) has theorized that the dynamic
balance and stability achieved during the latency period

> does not allow for the quantitative increase in drive activity nor the
> changes in drive quality which are both inseparable from puberty.
> Consequently it [the pregenital organization] has to be abandoned to
> allow adult sexuality to be integrated into the individual's personality.
> The so-called adolescent upheavals are no more than external indica-
> tions that such internal adjustments are in progress. (p. 263)

Consequently, she feels that it is difficult in many instances to distinguish between normal developmental upsets during adolescence and
true pathology. This implies that some degree of acting out, rebelliousness, and emotional instability may be as much a part of adolescent development as temper tantrums are in toddlers.

Similarly, Erikson (1968) feels that adolescence is a time of normal
developmental "crisis." It is a period where a searching for self-definition
and purpose may lead to temporary feelings of isolation and alienation
from both self and society. Erikson has suggested that there is a period of
time, a "psychosocial moratorium," during which this search for identity
is carried out. During this moratorium the young person is allowed, by
society, the freedom to explore various roles and different ways of being
in the world without being forced to be committed to any one of them. It
appears, in addition, to help the adolescent with the process of emotional separation from parents. Often, the roles which are tried out are
antithetical to those which the adolescent was exposed as a child. Thus,
one of the outcomes during this period of time may be delinquency.

Erikson has the following to say regarding delinquency during this period.

> For much of juvenile delinquency, especially in its organized form, must be considered to be an attempt at the creation of a psychosocial moratorium. In fact, I would assume that some delinquency has been a relatively institutionalized moratorium for a long time in parts of our society, and that it forces itself on our awareness now only because it proves too attractive and compelling for too many youngsters at once. (p. 157)

Normal adolescent defense mechanisms include rebellion and anger as a means of defending against childhood sexual and dependency ties to the parents. Acting out during adolescence becomes a way of mastering past anxieties and as a way of assimilating preverbal memories and impulses. However, since these mechanisms are also essential components of delinquency, we are led to conclude that delinquency may well be an expectable aspect of adolescent behavior. For example, Aarons (1970) feels that "[e]very adolescent is a delinquent at least in fantasies attendant upon rebellion against original love objects." Myerson (1975) and Varchevker and Muir (1975) see delinquency both as a defense against earlier childhood attachments through rebellion and also as an attempt to establish a separate identity. Erikson (1968) has used the term "negative identity" to describe a state in which the individual defines themselves "based on all those identifications and roles which, at critical stages of development, has been presented to them as most undesirable or dangerous . . ." (p. 174). He feels that many delinquents hold such an identity as a (hopefully) transitory way of defining themselves during their search for a more meaningful identity. In other words, in the process of development the adolescent detaches him or herself from those role models which kept antisocial or delinquent behavior in check and is left with a partial moral vacuum.

We should note, however, that the presence of pathology or delinquency during adolescence is not universally accepted. Recent psychological studies also have found that not all adolescents experience crisis, turmoil, rebellion, etc. (Offer and Offer, 1975; Masterson, 1967). With regards to delinquency, the differences between these two points of view may lie more in terms of how they are being operationally defined than the actual manifest behaviors. For example, Offer & Offer (1975) found that in their groups of normal subjects there were, in fact, instances of violent and delinquent behavior during the early stages of adolescence. However, during the high school years these "normal" adolescents differed from other adolescents studied by Offer (1979), in that they did not become chronic delinquents. It is the chronic delinquents who are much more likely to draw the attention of society and be adjudicated by the courts. The more transitory delinquent is less likely to be noticed.

It would seem then that if adolescence creates a developmental stress, which may lead to delinquency, it does so for a short period of time in the early stages of adolescence. Chronic delinquency and recidivism may then represent a developmental stress interacting with a pathological process. In other words, predisposing factors from earlier developmental stages and/or psychopathology may exacerbate the difficulties of adolescent development and increase the probability of chronic delinquent behavior.

We should again remember Aichhorn's belief that one must distinguish between the underlying reasons for delinquency and the delinquent behavior. It would seem important to be able to distinguish between delinquency based on a temporary developmental stress and one based on more serious psychological difficulties. It is the latter which is of greater concern, since it is both more chronic and more disruptive to society.

Early Adolescence

Blos (1962) depicts the passage through adolescence as occurring in six phases which he suggests describe the essential psychological transformations that occur between childhood and adulthood. These phases are: latency, preadolescence, early adolescence, adolescence proper, late adolescence, and postadolescence.

Blos views the latency period (approximately 6-10 years of age) as important, because it "furnishes the child with equipment, in terms of ego development which prepares him for the encounter with the drive increment of puberty" (p. 53). The developmental tasks of this stage include: adequate intellectual development such that good judgment can be exercised and distinctions made between reality and fantasy; the establishment of reasonable social relationships and social understanding; the development of appropriate physical independence and mastery over the environment; and resistance to regression under everyday stress and the ability to manage with less assistance from the outside world. The point is made clearly that an adequate adjustment to adolescence is made best by those individuals who have made an adequate adjustment to the issues of childhood.

The preadolescent stage (10-12 years of age), generated by increases in hormonal activity, results in increased levels of physical activity as well as an increased denial of impending sexuality. Boys are likely to show an exaggerated disinterest in and dislike of girls, whereas girls may deny femininity by becoming tomboys. Blos does not suggest additional developmental tasks at this stage; however, the individual's capacity to adequately sublimate the physical energies associated with this age would seem to be important.

Since Blos defines adolescence as the "sum total of all attempts at adjustment to the stage of puberty, to the new set of inner and outer — endogenous and exogenous — conditions which confront the individual" (p. 11), we will first discuss some of the biological and psychological issues connected with puberty itself before discussing other factors associated with the psychology of early adolescence.

Puberty refers to the changes associated with achieving adult physical status both in terms of primary and secondary sexual characteristics. While often generally perceived to be a discrete event, in fact the development of reproductive capacity is set in place at conception. In other words, puberty represents a rapid change in maturation rather than the development of a new system. The change in rate is apparently initiated by a decrease in the sensitivity of the hypothalmus to sexual hormones. This decreased sensitivity causes the hypothalmus to stimulate the anterior pituitary gland to increase its output of gonadotropic hormones. These hormones in turn stimulate the testes in males and ovaries in females to produce testosterone and estrogens, respectively. These hormones, along with increases in adrenal hormones, account for the physical changes associated with puberty. In addition, in females, the fluctuating hormonal levels associated with menses occur. The pubertal spurt ordinarily begins two years earlier for girls (approximately 11 years of age) than boys (approximately 13 years of age).

Of some interest in this area is the possible relationship between increased testosterone levels in males and aggressive behavior. Mattson (1981) suggests that while some positive correlation between aggression and testosterone has been found, one cannot conclude that a direct cause-and-effect relationship exists. Gold and Petrino (1980) found no relationship between physical maturation and self-reported delinquent behavior. Nonetheless, rapidly rising levels of testosterone and associated physical changes may increase the vulnerability of adolescent males already psychosocially and psychiatrically predisposed to aggressive and antisocial behavior.

The parallel issue for females would be the relationship between the menstrual cycle and delinquent behavior. In a recent review of the literature relating to this issue, Mann (1984) found that while there were a number of studies which found a relationship between menstruation and aberrant behavior in females, methodological problems associated with these studies preclude drawing any conclusions regarding the relationship between menses and delinquent behavior. However, the premenstrual tension experienced by some women may increase the likelihood of antisocial behavior in those females already predisposed to act that way by developmental and social factors.

The development of secondary sexual characteristics in adolescents has been described in detail by Tanner (1972). He describes five sequential stages relating to the development of the genitals, breasts (in females), pubic hair, and rate of growth. Among the chief differences between male and females are that males generally are taller, heavier, and stronger, due to a greater ratio of muscle to fat, than females. As noted above, the process begins and ends earlier for females than males.

The psychological adaptation to the physical changes associated with puberty is a major developmental task of early adolescence. Among the more important factors to be dealt with are body changes and responses to sexuality. The outward changes associated with puberty draw obvious attention and create a preoccupation with self-image. Self-esteem in adolescence is very much tied in with how one's body compares with one's peers. Significant deviation from normal development may leave the adolescent feeling isolated, often with concomitant feelings of shame, anxiety and embarrassment. Boys who remain behind their contemporaries in physical development are at a distinct disadvantage in areas of sports and heterosexual relationships. Psychological difficulties associated with delays may continue into adulthood. While similar difficulties exist for girls, they do so in an opposite manner. Girls who develop early are reportedly socially less successful than average or late maturing girls (Weatherly, 1964). Of interest is that few, if any, studies have related deviations in pubertal development to delinquent behavior.

Early Adolescence Disengagement

If we accept the notion of at least some physical and social discontinuity, then early adolescence (13-15 years) is perhaps the most difficult of the adolescent periods, since it involves adjustment to all three spheres of influence, i.e. physical, social, and psychosocial. Even Offer

(1969) who argues against the concept of adolescent turmoil found that the subjects in his study noted that the greatest amount of turmoil was seen between ages 12 and 14 and that the most difficulties in everyday relationships occurred in the pre-high-school years. Educators tend to separate these young people (at least in larger educational settings) both from older adolescents, who are in high school, and younger children, who are in grammar school, by placing them in junior high schools or middle schools. If the adolescent has been described as not having either the status of an adult or child, then the early adolescent, at least from the point of our culture, is even more disenfranchised, since he doesn't even have the status allotted to older adolescents. While older adolescents may be seen as growing more accustomed to their own sexuality and independence, young adolescents are forced to react to these developmental issues without much experience. Perhaps it is in part for this reason that the Uniform Crime Statistics (mentioned earlier) have shown a dramatic increase in the rate of crimes committed by individuals falling within this age range.

Chief among the developmental tasks of this stage is the need to begin to establish intimate relationships outside of the family. While the child is tied both emotionally and physically to the family, the problem facing the young adolescent is how to begin to undo those ties while simultaneously integrating the physiological changes associated with puberty. Freud (1949) claimed that one of the most difficult tasks associated with puberty was the "detachment from parental authority." Blos, among other psychoanalytic writers, suggested that the increased sexual drive associated with puberty brings about a reemergence of oedipal conflicts, which due to superego prohibitions causes the young adolescent to flee, at least psychologically, the family nest. A. Freud (1958) suggested that adolescents make use of a number of defense mechanisms in order to shield themselves against the emotional attachments of childhood. These include: (1) reversal of affect (reaction formation) i.e. turning love into hate, dependence into revolt, and respect into derision; (2) displacement, which involves the transferring of feelings of love, admiration, and dependence for parents to others such as peers rock stars, etc. (frequently, these new figures of attachment will represent values and ideals which are diametrically opposed to those of the family); and (3) withdrawal of libido to the self (increased narcissism), which may lead to temporary feelings of grandiosity and omnipotence frequently typical of young adolescents. It is important to bear in mind that while the young adolescent's conscious feeling is of detachment and independence, he or she still remains unconsciously attached to parental figures.

As reliance on parents begins to diminish, peers become increasingly important for identification, sources of information, and direction. The nature of the peer group that the adolescent identifies with is likely to have significant influence on his or her behavior, and its value may be antithetical to those of the parents. That delinquency is typically a peer group and/or gang phenomenon is well documented (Thrasher, 1936; Cohen, 1955). One might in fact think about the young adolescent as having both an individual and group ego. This decreased attachment may also lead to either rebellion against parental norms and/or a detachment from parental values (Spiegel, 1951). In other words, the child's internalized values or superego are no longer dependent upon attachment and identification with parents. This process can make the adolescent vulnerable to greater influence by delinquent peers, particularly in those neighborhoods where there are relatively high levels of criminal activity. This susceptibility to peer influence is also reinforced by the adolescent's marginal social status (Lewin, 1939).

As noted above, Offer (1969) concluded that most adolescents do not exhibit much turmoil or rebelliousness. He suggested that it is important to distinguish rebelliousness from attempts at emancipation from parents. Further, he found that the "rebelliousness" observed only lasted a few years, primarily during the pre-high-school years, and that it was not necessarily associated with delinquency. It may be concluded that some of the early rebellion in adolescence has to do with a transition from childhood roles that has to be made by the child while concomitant adjustments are made by the parents. It is clear that such a process can generate stress in both the young adolescent and his or family. In fact, it should be remembered that much of adolescent development takes place within the context of the adolescent's family and that difficulties may not only arise within the adolescent but also in the families' response to the adolescent. Brandt and Silverman (1985) pointed out that the personality of the mother can have significant impact on how the adolescent manages the process of developing psychological separation. Further, Anthony (1969) suggested that adults may react to adolescents based on their own conscious or unconscious fantasies or needs regarding adolescence. Hence, in understanding the behavior of a given adolescent, it is important to take into account the dynamics of all family members.

Middle Adolescence

The essential issues facing the young adolescent, those of sexuality and emotional autonomy, continue to be refined during adolescence proper and late adolescence. Blos (1962, 1979) suggests that the developmental task of adolescence proper (the middle phase of adolescence) includes further emotional disengagement from the parents via a definitive resolution of the oedipal complex and the establishment of heterosexuality. For males this may involve a struggle against passivity such that he

> . . . turns to overcompensatory devices which make him appear belligerently affirmative of his male powers and prerogatives. Furthermore he turns to male group or gang affiliations which . . . initiate the adolescent into a collective code of maleness. (1962, p. 109)

In addition, somatic maturation, which peaks during the middle of adolescence, increases not only sexual but also aggressive drives. Aggression may manifest itself in quarrelsomeness and dreams of murder and suicide. Aggression may be turned against the self, others, or the physical environment.

It is of considerable interest to note that there is a sharp increase in the rate of delinquency at this period of life. In 1980 individuals between 15 and 19 years old committed property crimes at four times their per capita representation in the population and violent crimes at approximately three times their per capita representation. Even taking into account the fact that these exact proportions may shift from year to year, there is a rather striking relationship between the developmental phenomena associated with the middle stage of adolescence, particularly as regards the adolescent male's assertion of his newly developed strength and aggression, and delinquency. Gold and Reimer (1975) found a monotonic relationship between age and the rate of self-reported delinquency in 13- to 18-year-olds. They further noted a sharp increase in both frequency and seriousness of delinquency at age 15. On the basis of these findings, Gold and Petrino (1980) concluded that

> These data confirm that violative behavior increases significantly from early to late adolescence. They do not indicate whether there is a decline in delinquency generally as adolescents become adults, but they do testify that the commission of serious crimes is most prevalent at age 15 and begins to decline after that. So delinquent behavior is associated with adolescence. Although its frequency may or may not be higher in adolescence than adulthood, its gravity seems to be greatest at middle adolescence. (p. 505)

Apparently something is going on during middle adolescence which makes it considerably different from other periods, since there is no other age group which shows a sharp increase in rate or such per capita frequency of antisocial behavior.

So far we have discussed the effects of sexual maturation (puberty) and sexual disengagement (the final resolution of the oedipal complex) on adolescent behavior. Two additional developmental tasks are the dissolving of anaclitic ties to the parents or individuation and the establishment of a sense of self or identity. Both of these are developmental tasks of the middle to late adolescent stages.

In fact, the process of emotional disengagement is one that begins early in life. Mahler et al. (1975) have described the ways in which the infant begins to detach from its mother. She refers to this as the separation-individuation phase of development, which

> "lasts from about 5 months to 2½ years, and moves along two separate but intertwining tracks: the one separation, leading to intrapsychic awareness of separateness, and the other of individuation, leading to the acquisition of a distinct and unique individuality." (p. 292)

The achievement of this sense of individuality, according to Mahler, is dependent upon two factors. One is the internalization of a consistent image of a "good" (and presumably protective) mother, the other, a mental representation of the self as distinct and separate from others. While this results in the child's ability to feel secure in the physical absence of the parents, the child, nonetheless, remains emotionally dependent on them.

Individuation during adolescence, on the other hand, requires that the individual give up these internalized parental images in order to attain a sense of self. Blos (1967), writing about what he refers to as the second individuation process of adolescence, suggests that

> Adolescence individuation is the reflection of those structural changes [ego and superego] that accompany the emotional disengagement from internalized infantile objects. (p. 163)

There appear to be a number of conceptual similarities between Mahler's concept of individuation and Erikson's (1968) concept of ego identity (Brandt, 1977). Erikson sees the achievement of a sense of identity as the normative developmental "crisis" of adolescence. It is achieved, he suggests, through "the selective repudiation and mutual assimilation of childhood identifications and their absorption in a new configuration . . ." (p. 159). In other words, there appears to be some agreement on the fact that the achievement of a sense of identity requires that the adolescent divest himself or herself of the attachments and identifications of childhood.

This process, however, can create psychological vulnerability which may generate delinquent behavior, particularly in those individuals already predisposed by their own preadolescent history to inadequate impulse control. First of all, the struggle for autonomy may involve a certain degree of negativism. What is of interest is that there appear to be behavioral parallels between the young child's early struggle for autonomy and those of the adolescent. Mahler describes the toddler's behavior in her study in the following way:

> We see a lot of active resistance to the demands of adults, a great need and a wish (often still unrealistic) for autonomy (independence). Recurrent mild or moderate negativism, which seems to be essential for the development of a sense of identity is characteristic of this subphase. (p. 116)

As we noted above, Erikson (1968) refers to a negative identity status in which adolescents choose a way of being in the world which is deliberately opposite of what is expected of them. In other words, the definition of self in this instance is based on opposition. They choose

> "an identity perversely based on all those identifications and roles which, at critical states of development, had been presented to them as most undesirable or dangerous and yet as most real." (p. 197)

Drawing from the work of Erikson, Marcia (1966, 1980) has identified four ego identity states in adolescence: (1) *identity achievement* — those who have gone through a decision-making process and have achieved a level of personal direction based on going through that process (usually referred to as an identity crisis); (2) *foreclosure* — who are committed to choices made for them by parents or others and have avoided going through an identity crisis; (3) *identity diffusion* — who have no set personal directions or ideologies and may or may not be in the midst of a crisis; and (4) *moratorium* — who are struggling with personal and occupational choices and are in the middle of a crisis.

The latter two states tend to be more characteristic of the mid-adolescent period. While there is little written regarding the relationship between ego identity states and delinquent behavior, Erikson (1965) has suggested that the high rate of recidivism among some delinquent adolescents, particularly those with no commitments (identity diffusion), may be caused by the fact that they found themselves in close contact with other antisocial individuals and thus have temporarily "absorbed" a delinquent identity. Further, most research in the area suggests that individuals falling into the identity diffused or moratorium categories tend to have less stable personality characteristics and more ambivalent relationships with parents and are more challenging of authority.

It would seem then that many of the developmental issues facing the middle adolescents have the effect of at least temporarily alienating them from the values and individuals they were attached to as children. Further, this process may also involve a certain amount of negativism and rebellion. This certainly is not true for the great majority of adolescents, but, given the relatively high rate of delinquency for individuals within this age group, it would appear to play a major role in delinquent behavior.

Late Adolescence

Issues regarding identity continue to face the older adolescent and in fact may "overtax the integrative capacity of the individual and result in adaptive failure, ego deformations, defensive maneuvers, and severe psychopathology" (Blos, 1962, p. 130). Nonetheless, it remains a time of consolidation. A more harmonious personality structure emerges in which there is reduced conflict between id, ego, and superego. "Now the individual is able to conduct various daily interactions with the social and physical environment and satisfy basic needs within socially prescribed boundaries" (Muuss, 1982, p. 118).

Ego development moves into what Loevinger (1976) describes as the conscientious stage in which group values are replaced by individual standards. The late adolescent is, thus, less influenced by peer groups than is the younger adolescent and is beginning to see himself or herself as a more autonomous individual (although perhaps still rather doubtfully) and operating on his or her own value system.

While delinquency rates for this age group remain quite high, the more stable personality characteristics of this group are paralleled by a decline in the seriousness of delinquent offenses (Gold and Petronio, 1980) and the fact that frequency of first offenses for this age group is much lower than for younger adolescents. This may also be accounted for by the fact that the older adolescent is more likely to be treated as an adult offender by the courts. Hence, the adolescent's awareness of the punitive consequences of antisocial behavior may serve as more of a deterrent.

Still another way of looking at the relationship between the developmental phenomena of adolescence and delinquency is to examine the degree to which adolescent delinquents become adult offenders. One might expect that as the psychological and social stresses associated with adolescence pass, the tendency to engage in antisocial behavior should decrease. There is in fact some evidence that this is the case, although it depends on the type of delinquent. In a follow-up of his early cohort study (Wolfgang et al. 1972; Wolfgang, 1983) 61 percent of juvenile offenders were found to avoid arrest as adults. However, of those with only one or two offenses (non chronic offenders) 72 percent had no further arrests as adults. Similarly, Robbins (1966) found that it was only those individuals who had committed a large number of offenses as adolescents who became adult offenders. So while most adult offenders have arrest records as adolescents, it does not follow that most adolescents with arrest records will become adult criminals. The important caveat here is that the chronic offender is likely to remain such.

We might conclude this chapter by restating some important facts. First, adolescents commit crime at a rate disproportionate to their numbers in the population. Secondly, there are, at least in our culture, developmental stresses associated with adolescence, which often include a major psychological reorganization and a temporary alienation from family and social values and controls. We are not suggesting that the normal physiological and psychosocial processes associated with adolescence cause delinquent behavior (the large majority of adolescents do not become delinquents) but rather that they seem to provide fertile ground from which delinquent behavior may grow. Whether it does or not seems to depend not only on the processes themselves but rather the history of the individuals' preadolescent period and on the social and familial environment in which adolescents find themselves. To borrow a term from Lewis (1981), these developmental processes create "vulnerabilities to delinquency" in those individuals psychologically less able to deal with this time of life.

Chapter VI

PSYCHOSOCIAL FACTORS AND DELINQUENCY

IN THIS CHAPTER we will examine a variety of theoretical approaches to understanding delinquent behavior. Unlike the psychodynamic theories presented in the previous chapter, these theories rely more heavily on behavioristic concepts including classical and instrumental conditioning as well as learning by imitation. In addition, we will look at some of the ways in which family factors and certain forms of psychopathology have been associated with delinquency.

While psychodynamic theory suggests that delinquent behavior is a product of unconscious dynamics, behavioral approaches suggest that delinquency results from the patterns of reinforcement and punishment and the types of social models the individual has been exposed to. One of the chief strengths of these approaches is that they have a greater experimental base than do the psychoanalytic approaches. On the other hand they do not provide as much in the way of clinical detail, nor do they focus on the process of development to the same degree.

Eysenck (1981) suggests, as do a number of writers, that socialized behavior needs to be learned. However, he hypothesizes that socialization develops, not through cognitive processes, but rather by means of classical (Pavlovian) conditioning. Children are punished for antisocial behavior and so come to associate this behavior with "pain/fear/anxiety." In this model the antisocial behavior is the conditioned stimulus, punishment the unconditioned stimulus, and anxiety or fear the unconditioned response. Further, he postulates that children who are well socialized are more easily conditioned than children who behave more antisocially. He assumes that differences in conditionability are inherited and that criminality can be understood as an interaction between this predisposition and socialization. This does not mean that all children who are less conditionable become antisocial; rather, it suggests that these children need to be subjected to a greater degree of socialization or conditioning in order to learn to behave in acceptable ways. Biological predisposition to behavior will be discussed at length in the following chapter. However, it is worth noting here that while studies do in fact indicate that criminality may be related to pedigree in some way, there is, in fact, no evidence that it is of necessity related to inherited tendencies toward conditionability as Eysenck suggests.

Wilson and Herrnstein (1985) have recently postulated that individuals are free to choose whether to commit or not commit a crime. The choice made is dependent upon the consequences associated with either committing or not committing the crime. In other words, committing a crime is associated with certain rewards (e.g. monetary) and punishments (e.g. getting caught). Similarly, not committing a crime is associated with rewards (e.g. enhanced self-respect) and punishments such as loss of status among peers. The authors speculate that the tendency to commit or not depends on the ratio of gains minus losses associated with committing the crime to gains minus losses associated with not committing the crime.

In addition they introduce time and uncertainty as additional variables. For example, an adolescent will not steal a car if he feels he is likely to get caught in the process, since the immediate losses associated with the theft (getting caught) are greater than the gains (status among peers). However, in many instances the losses associated with crime are perceived to be less immediate (e.g. the adolescent thinks "I may get caught in the long run, but probably not this time") and the rewards immediate (e.g. immediate status enhancement from peers). In addition, the rewards associated with not committing a crime may be perceived as distant (e.g. the adolescent may reason "If I don't commit this crime, in the long run I'll be a better person for it.").

Religious doctrine states that if you resist temptation you will go to heaven. But the pleasures associated with temptation are immediate, whereas those associated with heaven are much more temporally distant and, hence, less effective as a controlling factor. This is particularly true for adolescents, who perceive time differently and are far more impulsive than adults.

What can have an immediate effect, however, is conscience. Conscience, Wilson and Herrnstein (1985) argue, is a conditioned reflex, a feeling which has become associated with an aversive situation or stimulus. Taking a point of view very similar to Eysenck's, they state

> Persons deficient in conscience may turn out to be persons who for various reasons resist classical conditioning—they do not internalize rules as easily as do others. Persons who, even with a strong conscience, commit crimes anyway may be persons who have difficulty imagining the future consequences of present action or who are so impulsive as to discount very heavily even those consequences they can foresee, and hence will resist the instrumental conditioning that might lead them to choose non crime over crime. (p. 49)

This may be particularly true for adolescents, whom we have described as being under developmental stress and may thus be less able or willing to control impulses and who in the process of searching for their own sets of values may find themselves in something of a temporary moral vacuum.

Social Learning Theory

Social learning theory is of particular relevance to understanding delinquency because of its analysis of aggressive behavior (Bandura and Walters, 1959, 1963; Bandura, 1973, 1976, 1978, 1979). The theory consists of four parts, relating to the acquisition, instigation, maintenance, and self-regulation of aggressive behavior. It is a theory that relies on the modification of traditional behaviorism as well as cognitive psychology. It emphasizes that aggressive behavior is a set of learned responses to specific situations as opposed to one which is innate or instinctive as psychodynamic and ethological theories suggest. Thus, Bandura (1979) states:

> In the social learning view people are endowed with neurophysiological mechanisms that enable them to behave aggressively, but the activation of these mechanisms depends upon appropriate stimulation and is subject to cognitive control. (p. 201)

He goes on to explain:

> According to the instinct doctrine organisms are innately endowed with an aggressive drive that automatically builds up and must be discharged periodically. Despite intensive study, researchers have been unable to find an autonomous drive of this sort. (p. 209)

(One has to wonder whether in fact Bandura is not creating somewhat of a straw man here, since few behavioral scientists, including the sociobiologists, would take the extreme position that aggressive behavior is not modified by experience or the environment in some way.)

According to social learning theory, behavior (aggressive or otherwise) is learned or acquired through observing or imitating the behavior of others. The acquisition of a response is not seen as necessarily dependent upon the reinforcement of successive approximations or trial-and-error learning. Bandura correctly points out that learning to drive a car (or steal one for that matter) solely on the basis of trial-and-error procedures would have disastrous consequences. Bandura and Walters (1963) further point out that the applications of learning theory to deviant behavior are flawed because they rely on animal studies or human learning in a one-person situation. They suggest that since we are interested in behavior which is defined as "socially deviant," we should also look for its acquisition in "dyadic and group situations."

Social learning theory makes a distinction between the acquisition of a response and its performance. Acquisition is dependent upon imitation, whereas the performance of the behavior is dependent upon motivational factors. From this theoretical perspective, reinforcement provides motivation and information as opposed to functioning as a "mechanistic response shaper." Thus, it places learning and performance into a cognitive framework as opposed to more traditional Skinnerian approaches which explain behavior on the basis of the immediate consequence of the response.

In support of these assumptions, Bandura and Walters (1963) report a series of experiments. In one experiment a group of children was exposed to a model behaving aggressively toward an inflated doll, a second group saw a model who inhibited any aggressive behavior, and a control group observed no model. The children's aggressive behavior towards the doll was then observed with the models absent. Children who observed the aggressive model displayed the greatest number of aggressive responses toward the doll, and those who observed the non-aggressive model displayed the least amount of aggressive behavior.

In another experiment designed to test the effects of vicarious reinforcement or punishment (i.e. the response consequences to the model), one group observed a film of a model behaving aggressively followed by the model being punished for this behavior. A second group observed a film of a model rewarded by praise after behaving aggressively, and a control group with no exposure to the model. After watching the films, children were observed in a situation similar to the models. The group who observed the aggression rewarded behaved in a significantly more aggressive manner than the group who observed the model being punished. There were no significant differences between the control group and the model punished group. The effect is not limited to aggressive behavior alone. Walters et al. (1963) showed kindergarten children films in which the model was rewarded or punished for playing with "forbidden" toys. Children who observed the model rewarded were more likely to play with these toys when left on their own after seeing the film despite the fact that they were told not to than were those children who observed the model punished.

Bandura (1978) concludes:

> People can acquire, retain and possess the capability to act aggressively, but the learning may rarely be expressed if the behavior has no functional value for them or if it is negatively sanctioned. Should appropriate inducements arise in the future, individuals may put into practice what they have learned. (p. 34)

There are clearly numerous opportunities to observe aggressive or deviant behavior in real life. It can be observed at home, on television, in peer groups, etc. The implications for understanding the origins of delinquent behavior are obvious. Social learning theory thus has many conceptual similarities to theories which relate delinquency to family discord and to some sociological theories as well. We will return to these issues below.

Aggressive behavior, once acquired, may be instigated by either aversive stimulation or cognitively mediated motivation (i.e. anticipated positive or negative consequences). Examples of aversive instigators include physical assaults, verbal threats and insults, reductions in the conditions of life, and thwarted goal-directed behavior. While each of these categories has been experimentally demonstrated to result in aggressive behavior, they do not do so reflexively. Instead, the theory suggests, aversive stimulation leads to a state of emotional arousal which may lead to a number of different types of responses depending upon how the individual appraises the state of arousal and the ways in which he or she have learned to cope with aversive situations. In other words, some people may react to aversive conditions by responding aggressively, others may withdraw or somatize their anger, while still others may engage in constructive problem-solving behavior. It is Bandura's (1979) contention that

> The overall evidence regarding the different forms of aversive instigators supports the conclusion that aversive antecedents, though they vary in their activating potential, they are facilitative rather than necessary or sufficient conditions for aggression. (p. 214)

This distinguishes social learning theory from psychological and sociological theories which explain aggressive behavior as resulting from a single variable such as frustration or frustrating social situations (Miller, 1941). There is experimental evidence to support this idea. For example, Davitz (1952) found that whether or not young children responded aggressively to being frustrated in a play situation was a function of the type of games they were taught to play prior to being prohibited from eating candy or watching a movie. In other words, adolescents do not become delinquent simply because they have been frustrated or because they have aggressive instincts. They become delinquent because they have been exposed to deviant models and believe that behaving in a similar way will be beneficial to them.

In addition to being instigated by aversive conditions, aggression or other forms of socially deviant behavior may occur as a result of anticipated positive consequences or expected rewards. These would include such things as money or enhanced self-esteem or status. An adolescent may engage another in a fight because doing so would increase his status among his peers. Aggressive behavior may also result from observing others behaving aggressively such as in a gang fight. In extreme instances aggression may be stimulated by the delusional systems of psychotic individuals.

Maintenance and Self-Regulation

Along more traditional behavioristic lines, Bandura states that aggression is strongly influenced by its consequences. The positive consequences of such behavior include tangible reinforcers such as money or increased social status. In other instances, aggressive behavior may result in the reduction of aversive consequences. Fighting back or indeed instigating aggression may prevent the individual from future humiliating or painful experiences such as being picked on by the class bully.

Bandura (1978) differs from behaviorists, in that he does not believe that individuals simply react to or are controlled by the environmental consequences of their behavior. While a full discussion of his metapsychology is beyond the scope of this chapter, he states the following:

> Most external influences affect behavior through intermediary cognitive processes. . . . By altering their immediate environment, by creating cognitive self inducements, and by arranging conditional incentives for themselves, people can exercise some control over their own behavior. An act therefore includes among its determinants self produced influences. (p. 345)

Further, he postulates a self-system that provides standards against which behavior is judged, evaluated, and regulated. (This sounds suspiciously like the Freudian concepts of ego and superego, but Bandura denies that this is the case.) Thus, depending on how individuals perceive and evaluate their behavior, they may either reward or punish themselves for aggressive behavior. However, in this instance self-regulated incentives are conceptualized as motivators, which precede behavior, as opposed to reinforcers, which strengthen behavior as consequences. Therefore, individuals will reprimand themselves for behaving aggressively if they judge the behavior to be reprehensible and refrain from behaving in ways that result in self-censure. On the other hand, if aggressive behavior is positively valued by individuals they are considerably more likely to engage in such behavior. One of the logical conclusions to be drawn from this analysis is that aggressive and/or chronic delinquents may not only derive external rewards from their behavior but also may derive considerable self-satisfaction or internal rewards.

Relationship of Psychological to Sociological Theory

At this point we would like to examine, albeit in a limited way, some of the similarities that exist between selected theories of sociology and psychology regarding juvenile delinquency. The value of this lies in the fact that it may assist in a greater cross-disciplinary understanding of the issues involved and enlarge our conceptual framework.

One sociological theory proposed by Hirschi (1969), called social control theory, assumes delinquency exists because it has not been prevented. In other words, deviance is taken for granted and it is conformity to social norms that needs to be explained. According to this theory, conformity is the result of the effective use of social controls, such as the police.

Containment theory (Reckless, 1970) is an extension of social control theory. It postulates that individuals are pushed by either internal impulses and/or pulled by a "bad" environment to deviate. What prevents deviant behavior are either "inner or outer controls." Good inner controls refer to such factors as "ego strength" or a good self-concept. Outer controls would include family, school, positive social structure, etc. Control and containment theory are conceptually similar to psychodynamic theory, since both assume an inherent tendency to deviate. Both also assume that this tendency needs to be controlled in order for the adolescent to behave in a socially acceptable manner.

Sutherland's differential association theory (Sutherland and Cressy, 1970) presents an alternate point of view. He assumes that criminal behavior is learned, by communication, in the course of interacting with others. What is learned are the techniques, attitudes, motivations and rationalizations (collectively referred to as "definitions") associated with delinquent behavior. The more the adolescent is exposed to such definitions, the greater the likelihood he will engage in such behavior. Akers (1979), a sociologist, has integrated learning theory with differential association theory. He suggests that deviant behavior is learned according to the principles of instrumental conditioning (i.e. the probability of a response occurring is a function of the consequences of making that response) and that it is learned in both social and non-social situations so long as it is reinforced. Further, he assumes that the strength of deviant behavior is a direct function of the amount, frequency, and probability of its reinforcement. Hence, Sutherland's and Akers's theories are conceptually similar to those of Bandura, Wilson and Herrnstein, and other behavioral models.

The differences among sociological theories are similar to those among psychological theories. The differences lie in whether they assume individuals are inherently antisocial or whether they learn to be that way. This is the old "nature versus nurture" (or learned versus instinctive behavior) argument and it's not a particularly useful argument for enhancing our understanding of the issues relating to delinquency. Theories which emphasize one point of view at the expense of the other must do so only by avoiding large amounts of evidence which suggest the opposite of what they postulate.

Family Factors and Psychopathology

One way in which families have been conceptualized is as a system in which each member of the family has some impact and/or effect on the other. Sometimes these effects may be positive and growth enhancing and in other instances negative and pathogenic. In addition, families serve as alter egos for children, as models, providing discipline, encouragement, support, reinforcement, etc. The system is also temporally dynamic. The nature of the child's interaction changes as his needs change during the course of the child's development. For example, while maternal protectiveness is of utmost importance during infancy and early childhood, it may prove to be destructive during adolescence (Brandt and Silverman, 1985). Certainly, one consistent finding is that the more the family either fails to or is unable to provide the child with adequate nurturance, modeling, discipline, etc., the greater the likelihood that the child will behave in ways that reflect that deficiency. This may include anything from depression to delinquency. It is also clear that children are much more vulnerable to family difficulties early in life when they need the greatest amount of support. It would seem that the large majority of (if not all) seriously delinquent adolescents come from families that have failed to provide some important essential ingredient.

A large number of studies relating family problems to juvenile delinquency have appeared in the literature over the past years. It is beyond the scope of this book to review them in detail. (See Geismar and Wood [1986] for a recent review of this area.) However, we should note that these studies have focused on structural variables such as family size, birth order, and broken versus intact homes (Glueck and Glueck, 1968); and functional variables such as parental affection, family deviance and pathology; family tension (Borduin and Henggler, 1982); patterns of communication (Hetherington et al., 1971; Hurbin and Madden, 1983); and poor parenting skills (Patterson, 1986).

While difficulties in each of these areas appears to correlate with antisocial behavior in children and adolescents, what is found most consistently is that the parents of many of these children are at best indifferent and at worst abusive. Redl and Wineman (1951) described the parents of the children they worked with as having little interest in maintaining contact with these children and as having basically no relationship with them.

There is evidence that problems stemming from family difficulties exhibit themselves rather early in life. Erikson et al. (1985) studied 96 preschool children from "high-risk" backgrounds. (High-risk factors included low socioeconomic and educational level of mother, chaotic living conditions, and high degree of life stresses.) They correlated the nature of the bond between mother and child with teachers and other observer ratings of the child in a preschool setting. They concluded that:

> Consistent with theoretical predictions, children who exhibited anxious/avoidant pattern of attachment in infancy were described by teachers as hostile, socially isolated, and/or disconnected (psychotic like) in the preschool setting. This presents the defensive posturing one would predict for a child with an attachment figure who is rejecting, emotionally unavailable, or perhaps depressed. (p. 149)

Bandura and Walters (1959) studied the families of 26 violently antisocial boys. They found that, compared to the control group, the dependency needs of these children were either punished or not responded to.

Their parents encouraged aggressive behavior outside the home but punished the child if he behaved aggressively at home. Further, they subjected their children to less socialization pressures and expected less of them in terms of school performance. The overall pictures of these parents is one of "hostile indifference." Similar findings were presented by McCord et al. (1961), Neopolitan (1981), Poole and Regoli, (1979), and Winnicott (1984). Lewis et al. (1981), studying the psychiatric and criminal histories of the parents of delinquents, referred to the mental health services at the family court, found that close to 15 percent of the parents had received some type of psychiatric treatment. Further, they found that 14.4 percent of the fathers of these children had a criminal history. In addition, parents were more likely to be diagnosed as schizophrenic and the fathers were often brutal in their means of disciplining the children.

Psychopathology and Delinquency

It is clear that being raised in a pathological family environment can result in less than optimal developmental adjustment. The exact form this maladjustment will take will vary among individuals. Certainly, we cannot say that all children who are raised by parents who are either uncaring and/or abusive will become delinquent. There are other variables which will determine the final outcome. Nonetheless, it is of interest to examine some of the personality characteristics of those individuals who do become seriously delinquent.

One possibility is that such a family background results in a borderline personality organization. This state describes severe disturbances of emotional life that are not neurotic but not serious enough to be called psychotic, i.e., there is an absence of such symptoms as hallucinations or serious thought disorders. Tonkin and Fine (1985) have characterized these individuals as pan neurotic, that is, presenting multiple neurotic symptoms. In addition, such individuals may have difficulty with impulse control and may express inappropriate or intense anger or lack control of anger (DSM-III, 1980). Emotional capacities that normally develop in infancy and early childhood are absent, so that there is an absence of adequate superego functioning. Other individuals in their lives are not experienced as dependable and relationships are not expected to endure. They lack what Erikson (1968) has referred to as a sense of basic trust.

These characteristics would describe the personalities of many chronic delinquents. Both Nielson (1983) and Offer et al. (1979) describe the delinquents in their studies as falling into this diagnostic category, although both suggest the presence of subtypes. Nielson's subtypes are based on the patterns of acceptance or rejection experienced by the child in the family. Offer describes not only borderline characteristics in his population of 55 institutionalized delinquents but narcissistic and impulsive types as well. Willoch (1986) discusses a narcissistic vulnerability in hyperaggressive children, suggesting that much of the child's aggressive behavior is an attempt to cope with feelings of hurt, anger, and the experience that nobody really cares about him.

In a study which compared 105 delinquent youths to a control group of non-delinquent siblings, Healy and Bonner (1936) found significantly higher levels (91%) of emotional disturbance among the delinquents than among the sibling controls (13%). Even more serious pathology is presented by Lewis (1981). She found that as many as 25 percent of the delinquents she investigated may have an underlying psychotic process. She points out that this disorder may be sporadic and masked by antisocial behavior. She found that between 10 percent and 30 percent of the delinquent children she studied were later diagnosed as psychotic adults. She noted further that retrospective studies of schizophrenics find that up to 20 percent have earlier histories of misbehavior and that incarcerated youths are "remarkably similar" to those sent to state hospitals, suffering as they do "from similar levels of neuropsychiatric disorders" and behaving in "similar antisocial, often violent ways" (p. 3). Along these lines, although not specifically related to a juvenile population, Harstone et al. (1984) noted that a significant percentage of convicted felons are transferred to state hospitals. This is in addition to those who are found not guilty by reason of insanity, incompetent to stand trial, and those adjudicated as mentally disordered sex offenders.

The value of describing seriously delinquent adolescents in this way lies in three important areas. First, it suggests a serious psychological disturbance, not just one resulting from social or socioeconomic circumstances. Secondly, we know these disorders result in part from very problematical parenting early in life. Thus, these personality descriptions are consistent with the findings relating to the families of these adolescents. Finally, it suggests directions for intervention. For example, Halpern et al. (1981) have noted that the juvenile justice system has become an important service network for disturbed youth. They suggest that it is essential that mental health screening procedures exist at entry points into the system and that there be adequate follow-up and treatment of those identified as having psychiatric problems.

We are not suggesting that all delinquents come from bad families (some just come from bad neighborhoods) or that all suffer from some form of psychopathology. However, while we may not know the full extent of mental health problems among the youthful offender population, what the literature reveals is that from a legal, correctional, and psychological perspective, the mentally disordered delinquent makes up a significant percentage of this population. We are, therefore, once again reminded of the fact that we are frequently dealing with a symptom of an underlying psychological process which needs to be addressed.

Chapter VII

BIOLOGICAL/PHYSIOLOGICAL AND GENETIC FACTORS AND AGGRESSIVE, CRIMINAL, AND DELINQUENT BEHAVIOR

BEYOND THE WORK of Franz Joseph Gall (1758-1828) and the Phrenological School, the historical roots for viewing and supporting biological, physiological, and genetic factors as the cause of crime and delinquency can be found directly and indirectly in the works of such early researchers as Lombroso, Goring, Goddard, Kretschmer, Hooton, and Sheldon.

Cesare Lombroso (1835-1909), the Italian physician and father of positivistic criminology, helped set the stage with his book *L'Uomo Delinquente (The Criminal Man)* in 1876. Like many of his contemporaries, Lombroso was greatly influenced by Darwin. He sought to explain the behavior of the serious criminal as a subhuman example of incomplete evolutionary development, similar in his mental and physical characteristics to primitive man. After measuring the skull and other anatomical parts of thousands of convicts both living and dead, Lombroso concluded that they were hereditary mutants, "born criminals," distinguished by such features of "stigmata" as a flattened nose, low, narrow forehead, hairiness, large ears, and enormous jaws.

After criticism for his selection procedures as well as for his assumption that physical appearance determines human motivation, Lombroso revised subsequent editions of his book to include social and psychological factors that were also implicated in criminal behavior. While still maintaining the hereditary link in criminal behavior, namely, his belief that there were "born criminals," Lombroso, nevertheless, revised their numbers down to one-third of the criminal population, allowing for a broader range of criminals, including those who were motivated by insanity and passion.

He even conceded that given the right conditions some of these criminals could be rehabilitated through "a healthy environment, careful training, habits of industry, the inculcation of moral and humane sentiments . . . provided . . . that no special temptation to sin comes in their path" (Lombroso-Ferrero, 1911, p. 101).

While Lombroso's theories were widely accepted in the late nineteenth and early twentieth century, they were to fall from prominence, but never to be totally ignored, as witness the research of Ernest Hooton in 1939, which appeared to affirm the view that there was such a thing as criminal stock and the fact that in more recent times researchers attempting to demonstrate a link between biological factors and criminality have sometimes been referred to as neo-Lombrosians.

The immediate cause of Lombroso's fall from prominence was the work of Charles Goring, published in 1913. Goring, an English physician, continued the work of Doctor G.B. Griffiths, Deputy Medical Officer of Parkhurst Prison, when he succeeded him in 1903. His extensive anthropometric assessment compared the measurements of 3,000 convicts and 1,000 non-criminals, the latter drawn from Cambridge and Oxford students, German army recruits, University of London professors, and the Scottish insane. His findings, published in *The English Convict: A Statistical Study*, failed to support Lombroso's belief in the "born criminal" type.

In spite of his refutation of Lombroso's thesis, Goring nevertheless maintained that criminal behavior was linked to defective intelligence and was, therefore, hereditary. He arrived at this conclusion when he discovered a higher than expected incidence of mental retardation among the criminal group in his study. While he could not accept Lombroso's belief in the "born criminal" type, he did believe that criminal behavior was a function of low intelligence. He stated, "the one vital mental constitutional factor in the etiology of crime is defective intelligence" (p. 369).

Arriving at a similar conclusion from a study of the results of intelligence tests given in a number of juvenile institutions in the United States was Henry H. Goddard, a psychologist and director of research at a training school for "feebleminded" youths. He assessed the results of these tests and found that 28 percent to 89 percent of those institutionalized delinquents were feebleminded. Based on these results, Goddard (1914) concluded that "feeblemindedness," not hereditary criminality, was the basis of criminal tendencies.

Intelligence and Delinquency

A number of studies were conducted over the next four decades which failed to support Goddard's contention. Among these studies were those of Murchison (1926), Zeleny (1933), Tulchin (1939), Shulman (1961), and Prentice and Kelly (1963). In the summary of their study Prentice and Kelly state that ". . . the true incidence of intelligence in delinquency may not be significantly different from the general population" (p. 327). In the past twenty years, however, significant support for the belief in the association between low intelligence and delinquency has been found (Caplan, 1965; Hirschi, 1969; Hirschi and Hindelang, 1977; West and Farrington, 1973; Kirkegaard-Sorensen and Mednick, 1977; Andrew, 1979).

Caplan found that "the test scores of delinquent samples tend to be about 8 IQ points less than that of the general population" (p. 131) but emphasized that the difference might be based on factors other than delinquency, e.g. socioeconomic background. Hirschi's 1969 study of the Richmond Youth project, which consisted of 17,500 students entering public junior and senior high schools, found that IQ was a more powerful predictor of delinquency than either of the two background factors of race or social class.

The studies by West and Farrington (1973) in England and Kirkegaard-Sorensen and Mednick (1977) in Denmark concluded that intelligence, or rather low intelligence, proved of value as a predictive factor among youths who later committed criminal acts. In effect, lower intelligence was found to be predictive of future delinquency. Andrew (1977), who also studied this area, found that low verbal IQ's and poor reading ability are significantly related to delinquency.

Just how IQ may become predictive of delinquency has been suggested by Hirschi and Hindelang (1977), who believe that the effect of low intelligence is indirect, operating through the youth's negative school experience. Clearly, those with low IQ's and/or poor reading skills are most likely to have trouble with their schoolwork. Further, poor achievement can influence a youth's attitude toward school and the authority it represents. Thus, the experience of failure which is associated with school can lead many to a rejection of authority in general. This rejection of authority, according to Hirschi and Hindelang, can easily lead to an antisocial and delinquent life-style.

A more recent review of the literature by Rutter and Giller (1983) found that

. . . no single explanation for the IQ-conduct disturbance can be maintained. Possibly the major link may be found to be in the temperamental features which predispose to both educational failure and antisocial behavior. However, the main evidence on this suggestion comes from ruling out other explanations rather than from direct data support. In addition, it is probable that in some cases educational failure may increase the predisposition to conduct disturbance. (p. 168)

Body Type and Delinquency

Researchers have considered not only intelligence but also body build as a determinant of crime and delinquency. Ernest Kretschmer, in his book *Physique and Character* (1925), assumed a relationship between body type and temperament. His physical measurements of psychotics led him to conclude that the schizophenics among them tended to be tall and thin, with narrow bodies, but were sometimes muscular or athletic in build. Temperamentally, they were described as "unsociable, quiet, reserved, serious, eccentric" (p. 155). The manic-depressives tended to be shorter with rounder, thickset bodies. Broad-faced and paunchy, they were (temperamentally) "sociable, good natured, friendly, genial" (p. 128). Kretschmer identified the tall, thin ones as asthenic, the muscular types as athletic, and the round types as pycknic.

While Kretschmer did not immediately apply his theory to crime and delinquency, William Sheldon, who was greatly influenced by his work, did so two decades later. Sheldon, a physical anthropologist, continued exploring the links between inherited constitution and temperament. In *Varieties of Delinquent Youth: An Introduction to Constitutional Psychiatry* (1949), Sheldon, using different measures, classifications, and terms, theorized that there were three inherited and distinct body types or somatypes that could to a greater or lesser degree be related to a specific temperamental type. He termed his body types endormorphic, mesomorphic, and ectomorphic, each corresponding to Kretschmer's earlier categories of pycknic, athletic, and asthenic.

Sheldon studied 200 youths ranging from fifteen to twenty-one years of age who were referred by parole officers, court officials, and others to a Boston social service agency. He rated and classified these youths according to the degree to which they possessed the physical characteristics of each of the somatypes, and concluded that delinquents tended to have the body type of the mesomorph. Sheldon found that temperamentally this type was more assertive, less submissive to authority, and possessing fewer inhibited motor responses than the ectomorph.

Because of the large numbers of non-delinquent mesomorphic youths and adults in all walks of non-criminal life including law enforcement, sports, and the armed forces, Sheldon's correlation could not be considered an explanation for the cause of delinquency. He was also criticized for his definition of delinquency, which was not based on violation of the law. Other criticisms were that his research methods were subjective, inasmuch as he himself rated the youths on measures of both somatype and delinquency (Sutherland, 1951).

Another major effort to explore the link between body type and criminal behavior was made by Sheldon Glueck and Eleanor Glueck (1956), who studied 1,000 youths from the Boston area, comparing 500 institutionalized delinquents and a matched group of non-delinquents on over 400 traits and factors. Their findings supported Sheldon's theory, since 60.1 percent of the delinquents were identified as mesomorphic. This was nearly twice the number found among non-delinquents (p. 8).

It should be noted that the Gluecks cautioned that similarities and differences found between delinquents and non-delinquents "integrate into a dynamic pattern which is neither exclusively biologic . . . nor . . . sociocultural, but which derives from an interplay of certain somatic, temperamental, intellectual and sociocultural forces." Regarding the etiology of delinquency, they go on to state:

> There is a natural urge for a simple explanation of the multiplicity of factors and forces involved in delinquent behavior. Such an abstraction of causal involvements is exceedingly difficult to arrive at. It would have to span the gap between heredity and environment; between the individual and his family . . . and society in general. It would have to take account of conscious and subconscious motivation. (p. 267)

Far from asserting that body type is in itself the cause of criminal behavior, the Gluecks explain that they "have suggested that some traits having an excessive affinity for a particular physique may contribute to delinquency when in combination with certain other criminogenic traits and sociocultural factors" (p. 270).

It should be noted that in a more recent study by West and Farrington (1973), no correlation was found between height-weight ratio and delinquency. Similarly, McCandless, Persons, and Roberts (1972), in their studies of 177 young males in a training school, found no association between body build and delinquency.

As can be seen from the discussion so far, there has been much controversy generated on the subject of biological, physiological, and genetic determinants of delinquency. Because much of the late nine-teenth and early twentieth century research was naive and scientifically flawed and because biogenic explanations of human behavior are con-sidered antidemocratic, hence distasteful to most social scientists, such thinking has not always been popular (Shaw, 1972). Linkages between hereditary factors and criminal behavior have been alternately pro-mulgated and refuted, with trends toward acceptance and rejection be-ing discernible at various times.

Yet in the past fifteen or twenty years, as more sophisticated method-ology has been used to investigate the genetic and biological determi-nants of criminality, the data has begun to be considered more seriously. Researchers, using sophisticated knowledge, methodology, and equip-ment unheard of by Lombroso and his early successors, have studied the effects that specific types of organic damage and physiological abnor-mality can have on behavior. While it is understood that genes by them-selves do not determine behavior, i.e. there is no gene for crime, it is true that genetic factors can influence such biochemical functions in the body as hormonal levels and enzyme action, which in turn can affect mental processes and behavior. It is recognized by modern researchers that all of this occurs within an environmental context and never in iso-lation from such interaction. With this in mind, they have assessed the effects of such conditions as a damaged limbic system, epileptic seizures, as well as other EEG abnormalities, and minimal brain dysfunction. Biogenic and biochemical research continues in these and other areas, with some interest having focused on the XYY karotype as it impacts on male criminality.

Chromosomal Abnormality and Criminal Behavior

The issue of chromosomal abnormality, particularly the effect of the XYY configuration on male offenders, has been the subject of many studies since the sixties. While a complement of 46 chromosomes, in-cluding the XY configuration, which determines male gender, is present in most males, some have an additional Y chromosome. Beginning in the mid-1960s, researchers, accepting the view that the Y chromosome produces aggressive behavior, have explored the possibility that delin-quency among males might be determined by this chromosomal abnor-mality.

Early studies supporting such a conclusion include those of Price et al. (1966), Telfer et al. (1968), and Nielson et al. (1968). The latter study of 155 criminal psychopaths in a Danish institution revealed the incidence of XYY males to be many times higher than that believed to be present in the general population. Others who also reported frequencies of XYY males in prison populations compared to the general population were Owen (1972) and Hook (1973).

The concept of chromosomal abnormality as a determinant of criminal behavior has been accepted by others, including Housely (1969), Burke (1969), and Ashley Montague (1968), who, while underscoring the interaction of environmental and biological factors, argues that the additional Y chromosome can exert "a preponderantly powerful influence in the genesis of aggressive behavior" (p. 48). There have, however, been those who have refuted this view, and their numbers appear to have increased in recent years.

Some, like Amir and Berman (1970), Roebuck and Atlas (1969), Brogoankar and Shah (1974), have commented on the skewed population sample used in the research or on other methodological flaws; others, including Gillie (1970) and Chorover (1979), have stressed that large numbers of XYY males who function normally exist in the general population. Fox (1971) has argued that institutionalized XYY males are actually less violent than their XY counterparts and that their crimes are against property rather than persons, and his findings have been supported by the work of Witken (1976). Finally, Ferrier et al. (1970) found no XYY abnormalities in their study of 103 institutionalized delinquent boys.

It is evident, then, that while a large number of researchers working primarily in the sixties and early seventies claimed to have found a linkage between chromosomal abnormality and antisocial or criminal behavior, there has been substantial work done since then which refutes this viewpoint (Craft, 1978). In a more recent controlled study by Schiavi et al. (1984), no evidence of more violent or aggressive behavior among such men could be found when compared to XY men in the general population.

Perhaps the most fascinating and compelling work that has been done, in an effort to seek a genetic connection between heredity and criminality, has been the twin studies and the adoption studies.

Twin Studies

The twin studies have explored the effects of a naturally occurring event, namely, the birth of twins (which occurs once in approximately ninety births), in an attempt to discover a genetic vulnerability to criminal behavior. Two-thirds of twin births are fraternal, or dizygotic, in nature, while identical, or monozygotic twins, occur in one-third of such births.

The fact that identical twins are genotypically identical has led researchers to view any resulting differences between them in character and/or behavioral traits as caused by environmental effects in the womb, or, after birth, in the family environment and beyond. This cannot be said to be the case with dizygotic twins, whose character traits and/or behavioral differences can more readily be attributed to both the effects of hereditary and environmental factors.

In their twin studies, researchers have made comparisons of concordance, or degree of similarity, between fraternal and identical twins. Simply stated, when both twins of a pair share the same trait, they are considered concordant with regard to that trait; when they do not share that trait, they are considered discordant with regard to that trait. The expectation has been that identical twins, sharing as they do a common genetic heritage, would exhibit greater similarity in regard to genetically determined traits than would fraternal twins.

Research findings have consistently supported this view, and much higher levels of concordance between identical twins than between fraternal twins have been reported. For example, Jencks et al. (1972), in a review of the literature, reported higher correlations on IQ scores for identical twins (0.89) than for fraternal twins (0.63). Such findings have suggested to researchers that hereditary factors are more operative than environmental ones with regard to particular traits. Further, they have led to the expectation that where environmental factors are most operative in the expression of a trait, the concordance results will be more similar between identical than fraternal twins.

Of special interest to our discussion of criminality and delinquency is Christiansen's (1977) review of nine twin studies. In eight of these he identified criminal behavior as a trait partially linked to genetic factors. The ninth study also showed a higher concordance for identical twins than for fraternal twins, but the findings were not satistically significant.

Reporting on the literature dealing with twins and criminality, Fuller and Thompson (1978) have noted that the twin research as far back as the 1930s has reported a genetic link to criminal behavior. Simply stated, where criminal behavior was concerned, concordance was found to be significantly higher among identical twins than among fraternal twins. This finding has also been supported by Ellis (1982) in his review of the literature on genetic influence and crime.

Ellis, who compared twelve of the twin studies, found that all of them indicated a greater level of concordance for monozygotic twins than for dizygotic twins. He mentions a problem, however, that has been troubling researchers for a long time, as evidenced in the work of Montagu (1941). Ellis questions whether the greater concordance found among identical twins results from them being exposed to a more similar social environment than that of fraternal twins:

> . . . because of their identical appearance, MZ twins may be more similarly treated in social exchanges than DZ twins. This more similar treatment, rather than some fairly straight-forward neurological effect of their identical genetic makeup could account for any greater behavioral similarity . . . relative to DZ twins. (p. 69)

Shaw and Roth, (1974) have also identified other problems which twin studies can be subject to, including inaccuracy in identifying twin pairs appropriately and error regarding the use of the term "criminality." In the former instance, the researchers may not always have had correct information concerning the zygosity of the twins, so that, for example, they may be classifying the same-sex fraternal twins as identical. In the case of the trait of criminality, we recognize that most crime goes unreported and that which is reported does not necessarily lead to arrest and conviction. Furthermore, when it does lead to arrest and conviction (which is the way criminality is measured), it represents only a small percentage of total criminal behavior. Inasmuch as the trait of criminality has been subject to errors in its definition and use, the classifications monozygotic and dizygotic inaccurately applied, and distinctions between genetic and environmental factors blurred (because monozygotic twins may have an unusually similar social environment), the findings of those researchers who have argued for a linkage between genetics and criminality based on twin studies, although compelling, cannot be considered without flaws or conclusive at this time.

Adoption Studies

It has been argued that clearer evidence of the effects of heredity and/or environment on behavior can be obtained from adoption studies. Part of the reason for this belief is that adoption studies, unlike twin studies, allow for a clearer distinction between genetic and environmental factors when adoption occurs at birth or shortly thereafter and when the adoptive parents are non-relatives (Cadoret et al., 1983).

While adoption research has not been confined to this area (e.g. Horn [1975] found IQ scores of adopted children to be more highly correlated with that of their biological mothers [0.32] than with that of their adoptive mothers [0.15]), it has been used extensively to explore the possible link between genetics and criminal behavior.

Among those who have conducted adoption studies in which adoptee psychopathy was associated with that of the biological parent rather than that of the adoptive parent was Crowe (1974), who studied children born to imprisoned women in Iowa who were adopted away. He identified antisocial personality disorders in six of the 46 children, whereas he found only one such child in a group of adoptees born to a similar group of non-criminal women.

Shulsinger (1980) found some evidence of what appears to be a genetic contribution to the transmission of antisocial behavior among a group of 57 Danish adoptees who were identified as psychopathic from their psychiatric and police files. He matched them with a comparable control group of 57 adoptees with no evidence of psychopathy and found that there was a greater tendency for psychopathic characteristics to exist among the biological parents, most noticeably, the fathers, of the psychopathic adoptees than among the biological parents of the non-psychopathic adoptees.

Others who have found a genetic factor implicated in antisocial behavior have been Cadoret and Cain (1980) and Hutchings and Mednick (1974). In their Copenhagen study of 5,483 adoptions, Hutchings and Mednick found that

> within the boundaries of the adoption methodology there appears to be a correlation between criminality in adoptees and criminality in their biological parents. (p. 138)

In still another expanded follow-up study of the role of genetics in the etiology of criminality, Mednick et al. (1984) examined all 14,427 male and female adoptions registered in Denmark between 1927 and 1947. They hypothesized that court convictions for biological parents would be correlated with adoptee convictions. After examining a total of 65,516 court convictions of the male adoptees and their biological and adoptive parents, they found the following: where there were no convictions for the biological or adoptive parents, 13.5 percent of the adoptees had convictions; where only the adoptive parent had been convicted,

14.7 percent of the adoptees had convictions; where only the biological parent had been convicted, the figure rose sharply to 20 percent of the adoptees who had convictions; and where both biological and adoptive parents had convictions, the rate for adoptee convictions was highest (24.5%).

It seems clear that criminal convictions in the biological parents were associated more with increases in the conviction rate of their children than either the adoptive parents or biological parents without criminal records or the adoptive parents with criminal records. When adoptees had both biological and adoptive criminal parents, the rate of their criminal convictions rose to the highest percentage. This might be explained as reflecting the combined interactive effects of both heredity vis-à-vis the adoptive parent.

Other important findings by Mednick et al. were that 4 percent of the adoptees were chronic offenders who accounted for nearly 70 percent of the convictions. Discussing his results in a later article, Mednick (1985) states that "chronic offenders were more likely than others to have biological parents with more than one conviction" (p. 60). He further attempts to buttress his argument by indicating that since it is known that more crime is committed than is charged, brought to trial or results in convictions, this undercounting lowered the chance of finding any significant results and yet such results did in fact emerge. Such findings lead Mednick et al. (1984) to conclude that

> . . . some factors transmitted by criminal parents increase the likelihood that their children will engage in criminal behavior. This claim holds especially for chronic criminality. The findings imply that biological predispositions are involved in the etiology of at least some criminal behavior. (p. 893)

As with earlier attempts to identify and separate specific biological, physiological, or genetic factors from an existing complex of multifaceted interactive environmental ones, the recent studies, while admittedly more sound and sophisticated, still leave questions open as to the relative weight which each of these variables plays in the development of antisocial behavior. It is possible that with the ever-increasing methodological sophistication that is likely to develop as a result of the major advances in genetic studies anticipated in the next few decades, more conclusive answers may be found to some of the questions regarding the issue of heredity, the environment and criminality that are not as yet answerable.

Conclusions

In drawing any overall conclusions regarding the causes of juvenile delinquency, we would, of necessity, need to be tentative and cautious. We are mindful of the fact that there are many theoretical, methodological and conceptual shortcomings which exist in the data we have presented in the preceding chapters. Nonetheless, the difficulties are not appreciably different than in trying to understand the causes of other behavior, and, as we have pointed out, the basic controversies which exist in other areas, namely, learning versus instinct, biological versus environmental determinism, and the role of intervening variables, exists here as well.

When we say that delinquent behavior is multiply determined, it does not mean that the many contributing biological, psychosocial and developmental factors operate independently to generate the behavior, but rather that these factors operate in concert, such that a causal process exists which cannot be broken down into separate factors without losing the gestalt created by their simultaneous operation. If we look for genetic, social, or psychopathological determinants as the sole explanations for delinquency, we find ourselves caught up in the same schisms of the past. On the other hand, there is sufficient evidence to suggest that each of these factors makes a contribution, but only when other conditions are met. All mesomorphs do not become delinquent, nor do all children coming from criminal parents or socially deprived neighborhoods. While many variables have been found associated with delinquency, the association becomes subject to refutation outside of the context from which they have emerged. It is not possible to fully understand the function of any determinant without understanding the context in which it operates. Kamin's (1986) comment that the answer to whether or not crime is genetically determined depends on "who chooses what evidence" does not increase our understanding of delinquent behavior but rather repeats the same argument.

For example, let us examine two apparently important variables related to delinquent behavior: genetic factors and the nature of the bonding between the mother and child during the first years of life. We have presented the results of studies which have suggested that significant variance can be attached to either of these, and yet we can demonstrate that a significant variance is NOT associated with either of them, particularly when examined in isolation. However, when they are combined, a greater amount of the total variance is accounted for but still not all of it. If we were to add a third variable, say, the nature of the social conditions under which the child was raised and experienced adolescence, presumably even a greater amount of the variance would be accounted for. Theoretically, at least, a point could be reached where all the variance could be accounted for. (See, for example, Patterson's [1986] discussion on generating performance models for antisocial boys.)

The problem lies in the fact that once we isolate and focus on any one of the variables, we lose the gestalt. We see delinquents coming from poor neighborhoods and say "poverty breeds crime." We see delinquent adolescents coming from parents who themselves have criminal histories and say the children have inherited criminal tendencies. However, each of those statements fails to grasp the essential nature of causality and the developmental nature of behavior. (This is by no means a new issue in the field, although its introduction into the area of delinquency has been unfortunately delayed. See Marx [1951] for an excellent collection of essays on theory construction in psychology.)

For example, Oyama (1981), in an article relating to genetic determinism, states:

> . . . asking whether aggression or altruism or hope or incest taboos [or criminality?] are encoded in the genes (and of course, if one is "thinking biologically," answering that indeed they are) is less productive than critically examining the concepts and the operationalizations, finding out how and when and by whom the various phenomena are exhibited, to what situational and ontogenetic variables they are responsive, and so on. (p. 579)

In other words, she is suggesting that one cannot explain any behavior as resulting from genetic mechanisms alone. She goes on to say that it is more useful to look at cells and their genetic material as information-generating devices than as information-containing devices, and that one must realize that the type of information generated will vary (presumably within certain limits) under different environmental circumstances.

In a similar vein, Bandura (1978) suggests that environmental determinism refers to the:

> . . . production of effects by events rather than in the doctrinal sense that actions are completely determined by a prior sequence of causes independent of the individual. . . . Most external influences affect behavior through intermediary cognitive process. (p. 345)

He goes on to explain that:

> From the perspective of reciprocal determinism, the common practice of searching for the ultimate environmental cause of behavior is an idle

exercise because, in an interactional process, one and the same event can be a stimulus, a response, or an environmental reinforcer, depending on where in the sequence the analysis begins. (p. 347)

Clearly, individuals do not passively respond to environmental stimuli which impinge upon them. Rather, they process and evaluate this information in a manner which leads them to respond to a similar stimulus in different ways, depending on the setting and the nature of idiosyncratic evaluations.

While Oyama is specifically addressing the issue of biological determinism and Bandura environmental determinism, both are making the point that causality cannot be understood as being generated from a single source, whether that be internal or external. It must be understood as a complex developmental and interactive process.

Ultimately, understanding the causes of delinquent behavior depends on not just isolating specific variables associated with delinquency but on understanding how and when they interact to create the behavior. This implies that future research in the area must continue to focus on the matrix of interactive factors that generate delinquent behavior.

Chapter VIII

CLASSIFICATION OF THE YOUTHFUL OFFENDER

Historical Background

TO BETTER appreciate the task of discussing classification and treatment of the youthful offender, it is important to keep in mind that these concepts did not emerge in isolation from one another.

In the past there has always been some form of offender assessment and classification in this country, but it was not until the first half of the twentieth century that a direct linkage was developed between such assessment and classification and offender treatment as we know it today. Fox (1975) indicates that in the eighteenth century the approach to offender classification and treatment was basically moral in nature, namely, that the offender was considered a sinner and the criminal act a sin; treatment, including corporal and capital punishment, was considered to be both retributive and redemptive.

As part of the growing movement in the social philosophy of the early nineteenth century, man's nature was being redefined. There emerged a belief in man's uniqueness and perfectibility, as well as in society's role in shaping human behavior. These beliefs were responsible for the offender no longer being considered a sinner and his treatment being viewed not as punitive or vengeful but rather as corrective and rehabilitative. The aim of offender treatment was that of resocialization so that the offender could be returned to society as a contributing member.

Hippchen (1975) identified this new social philosophy towards offenders as having evolved from three general historical trends, namely, "segregation, diagnosis and program planning and treatment" (p. 19).

121

To begin with, the newly emerging social philosophy justified segregating and institutionalizing prisoners more on the basis of society's right to defend and protect itself from the offender than for purposes of vengeance. There was, moreover, concern for the well-being of the prisoners themselves,

> expecially in regard to overcrowding, unsanitary conditions in the prison, the idleness of prisoners and the mixing of various types of prisoners, i.e., the young and old, persons with minor and severe offenses, the insane and the retarded. (p. 19)

Hippchen further indicates that these humanitarian concerns became the impetus for the evolution of specialized institutions where youths were separated from adults, women from men, and the mentally insane and retarded from normal offenders. In addition,

> Offenders . . . began to be segregated on the basis of the severity of the offense. Work programs were started in many prisons in order to reduce the problem of idleness, and beginning attempts were made to educate and train prisoners and give them medical care. (p. 20)

These early efforts to separate, sort, and process offenders on the basis of age, sex, mental status, and offense, along with the development of Houses of Refuge and reformatories, appear to have been part of an ongoing process of formalizing the classification and treatment of offenders. The importance of treatment and its relationship to classification was underscored, in 1915, by the efforts of William Healy, one of the first psychologists to work with delinquent youth (Gardener, 1972).

Beginning in the early 1920s and continuing over the next two decades, William Healy and his wife, Augusta Bronner, witnessed the impact of their early clinical work with delinquents as casework methods were being widely implemented in both the classification and individualized treatment of youthful offenders. With the greater involvement of mental health practitioners, the early beginnings of the child guidance movement, the eventual establishment of reception and diagnostic centers for offenders, and the growing use of the medical model with its focus on the psychogenic factors of delinquency, classification and treatment were receiving broader recognition and acceptance by those professionals working with youthful offenders.

Over the past fifty years work has been done to try to both develop and refine classification, treatment and etiology, as well as strengthen the linkages among them; however, to date this has not actually occurred.

Today, unfortunately, as a result of the diversity of agency and correctional programs that exist nationally (many precariously) and the continuing less than enthusiastic support for the rehabilitative model with offenders, we are certain to encounter more situations than not where there are no formal classification systems employed. Where they do exist, many are almost completely focused on management, security, and custody needs to the virtual exclusion of treatment in the traditional rehabilitative sense. What makes the situation more difficult is that there is still no consensus on which typology to use in the classification of youthful offenders.

One of the early researchers to assess the juvenile classification literature in relation to delinquency was Warren (1971). She provided a cross-tabulation of sixteen typologies which eventually yielded six cross-classification bands of offender subtypes, including the asocial, conformist, antisocial-manipulator, neurotic, subcultural-identifier, and situational offender. While she felt that the ability to achieve this end and find consistency in the data from several typological studies was encouraging, she maintained that it was still only one step in the process that had to be followed. She further felt that it would not be until offenders from a single population could be cross-classified from these typologies that any real progress would be made and lamented that because of the lack of consensus among the various classification systems "it was almost impossible to compare treatment programs being conducted . . ." (p. 255). Warren also indicated that with the exception of the research being done in small experimental programs, there had not been nearly enough effort expended in the development of a common taxonomy to facilitate the individualized treatment of the offender, explaining that "to date, little work has been done toward utilizing typologies for building differential treatment strategies" (p. 255).

While the interest in classification and the call for differential treatment based on classification continued, such efforts were far from being nationally adopted and/or implemented in the early 1970s. In their review of the literature as it pertains to corrections and the processing of youthful offenders, Smith et al. (1979c) cite the results of a national study conducted by Wheeler and Nichols in 1974 in which institutions in all thirty states studied indicated that they favored differential treatment, but "only 69 percent actually adopted a bonifide classification system. . . . The remaining 31 percent reported using no system or merely reading the case record to determine treatment program and where to place the youngster . . ." (Smith et al., pp. 227-228).

Echoing calls for a more adequate classification system as well as eventually recommending a new one that would reflect offender differences with implications for differential treatment is Megargee (1977a). In setting the stage for such a system, he outlined seven requirements which it must meet to be of value in applied criminal justice settings. The first six of these criteria could be found in some combination in a number of systems, but none (with the exception of a system Megargee himself developed which will be discussed elsewhere in this chapter) met all of the requirements.

According to Megargee, the system

> should be sufficiently *complete* so that most of the offenders or clients in the agency or setting can be classified. Equally important is the need for *clear operational definitions* of the various types so that each person can be classified with a minimum of ambiguity. Third, the system must be *reliable* so that two different raters will arrive at the same classification of a given individual. Fourth, it must be *valid*; it must be demonstrated that the individuals falling within a given classification actually have the attributes they are hypothesized to possess. Fifth, it should be *dynamic*, so that changes in an individual, such as improvement as a result of correctional treatment, will be reflected by a change in his or her classification. Sixth, each classification should carry with it *implications for treatment*. Finally, it should be *economical* so that large numbers of offenders can be classified with a minimal expense and personnel. (p. 108)

Palmer (1984), reiterating the need for a more effective classification system and more responsive differential treatment approaches, focuses on the need for classification to provide a more active treatment direction by helping to delineate specific treatment modalities for individual offenders. He states:

> . . . for any given individual, a treatment classification should do more than summarize and describe; it should, in effect, predict and perhaps prescribe . . . it should not just reflect . . . the main results from one's diagnostic assessment of the offender's personality, of his present situation and so on . . . [it] should suggest or perhaps prescribe principal tasks . . . areas of focus . . . and/or specified approaches which seem appropriate or even essential. (p. 257)

Clements (1985), recognizing what appears at present to be the expanding role of objective classification in corrections as opposed to subjective *ad hoc* practices of the past (which led to offender litigations based on inequities and system-wide deficiencies), describes the National Institute of Corrections' 1982 use of classification as the process by which prisoners are subdivided into groups based on a variety of considerations, which include: (1) determination of, and assignment into appropriate custody levels; (2) program placement based on inmate needs and available services — medical, mental health, vocational and educational; (3) designation to the housing placement within the institution; and (4) scheduled review of the placements to reassess inmate needs and progress. (p. 45)

It is apparent that all four aspects of the classification system are interactive so that changes in one part can effect changes in one or more of the other parts. Through the treatment program, for example, the mental health practitioner can have an impact on one or more aspects of the offender's life in the institution. For example, Wheeler and Nichols found that the length of a youthful offender's stay in an institution is affected by the type of classification system used as well as by the types of institutional treatment programs available, so that "states employing a formal classification system confined youths an average of 9.4 months; those that did not, detained them 7.6 months" (p. 227).

Current Classification Systems

Commonly used classification schemes for categorizing youthful offenders have focused on the behaviors exhibited by the youths, while others have focused on assessing the delinquents' interpersonal and world view. Despite these differences in emphasis, classification systems can and often do draw from both descriptive and dynamic foci.

In the case of the first type of classification, the two best known and widely used systems are DSM-III and the Quay System. A very widely used example of the second type is the Interpersonal Maturity Level (I-Level) classification system.

DSM-III

In the case of the first system, the process of utilizing clinical interviews for purposes of diagnosing and assessing the needs of youthful offenders dates back to the beginning of the juvenile court movement. The purposes were for psychologists and other practitioners to be able to make recommendations to the juvenile court judges concerning the youths before them. Beginning with the first edition of the *Diagnostic and Statistical Manual of Mental Disorders* (1952), which represented the first official classification manual of mental disorders, right up to the present time with the publication of DSM-III (1980), clinicians have continually sought to update, improve, and refine their approaches to evaluation, diagnosis, and classification. Those changes have been reflected in each new edition of the manual.

While the mental health practitioner's role vis-à-vis the classification of youthful offenders may vary, e.g. the practitioner may be part of a classification team effort or he/she may work alone, the use of DSM-III is said to provide those in the field with a greater ability to study, treat, and discuss the disorders whose descriptions and definitions they can more readily agree upon.

Obviously, there are many types of disorders that youths can and do at times suffer from. It is when particular maladaptive traits become characteristic of the young personality over a period of time so as to appear stable that the number of applicable classification and personality disorder categories increases. Among troubled youths it is not uncommon to see such classifications as identity disorder, oppositional disorder, avoidant disorder, even schizoid disorder. Among youthful offenders it is especially common to see the classification conduct disorder being applied, usually in conjunction with one of its four subtype categories. Conduct disorder itself is defined by DSM-III in terms of its essential feature, which is "a repetitive and persistent pattern of conduct in which either the basic rights of others or major age-appropriate societal norms or rules are violated. The conduct is more serious than the ordinary mischief and pranks of children and adults" (p. 45).

The four subtypes include the undersocialized aggressive, undersocialized non-aggressive, socialized aggressive, and socialized non-aggressive — types which are "based on the presence or absence of adequate social bonds and the presence or absence of a pattern of aggressive antisocial behavior" (p. 45). (In addition to these distinctions, descriptions of each subtype are given with discussion of associated features, age of onset, predisposing factors, family patterns, etc. Finally, diagnostic criteria are also provided for each type.)

Admitting to controversy concerning the validity of the conduct disorder subtypes, the DSM-III manual indicates that some critics would prefer distinctions among subtypes "on the basis of the variety, frequency and seriousness of the antisocial behavior rather than the type of disturbance, whereas others believe that the Undersocialized and Socialized type represent distinct disorders" (p. 45).

Although focusing on the overuse and misuse of the DSM-III classification of antisocial personality disorder as applied primarily to older offenders (over 18 years of age) and adults, Wulach (1983) demonstrates the weakness of DSM-III's operational definition and behavioral checklist, which create broader criteria and unnecessary increases of such diagnoses, and then goes on to describe another problem with this classification system:

> A second difficulty with the DSM-III childhood criteria for antisocial behavior is their failure to effectively separate chronic patterns from occasional acts that meet the diagnostic requirements. Thus, a 14-year old girl who responds to troubles at home by smoking marijuana for a semester, sleeping with several acquaintances, and performing poorly in school would satisfy the same criteria as those who have adolescent histories of multiple muggings, stabbings and narcotics abuses. (pp. 332-333)

Further, Grisso (1984) points out that because of the DSM-III's serious limitations when applied to the classification of children, the American Psychological Association has created a task force to develop a more useful form.

While these criticisms have underscored the need for further changes and refinements of the classifications, Mezzich (1982) has suggested other ways to deal with the DSM-III's shortcomings where the classification of violent youthful offenders is concerned. She recommends that the existing DSM-III multiaxial system be modified within some of the five axes and also enlarged to encompass five new axes, thereby producing a more comprehensive description of "general clinical concerns, . . . adaptive functioning and legal status" (p. 61).

Her five additions include an axis for each of the following areas: intelligence, social class, mental illness and criminality in family, chronicity and legal history, and, lastly, the magnitude of the offense.

The Quay System

Still another approach which focuses on behavior is represented by one derived from statistical analysis rather than from that based upon the observational classification system of DSM-III.

Originally researched and conceptualized by Hewitt and Jenkins (1946) and expanded upon by Quay (1964), who further refined it in 1979, the system utilizes clusters of interrelated and intercorrelated behavioral traits which are derived from ratings and then divided into categories of classification. The system was implemented at the Robert F. Kennedy Youth Center in Morgantown, West Virginia as well as at federal prisons.

To begin with, Quay helped to develop three assessment instruments to arrive at behavioral diagnosis for each youth. These instruments included a 100-item self-report true-false questionnaire, a 44-item behavioral problem checklist to be completed by a corrections counselor who has observed the youth, and a 36-item checklist for an assessment of case history data to be completed by the caseworker.

Quay, using factor analysis, was able to classify the delinquents on the basis of their highest score into one of the five following behavioral categories:

1. inadequate—immature
2. neurotic—conflicted
3. unsocialized—subcultural
4. socialized—subcultural
5. subcultural—immature

Once classified, the youths were assigned to a specially trained treatment staff, who used differential treatment methods to achieve goals established for the youths in each of the treatment categories. As explained by Gerard (1975), because the behaviorally inadequate immature youths are shy, inattentive, childish, and irresponsible, the treatment staff assigned to them would be patient and nurturing in an effort to help them reach greater maturity. The neurotic-conflicted youths, characterized as feeling depressed, anxious, inadequate, and guilt-ridden, would best be treated by sensitive, insightful staff able to draw them out while attempting to help them gain self-awareness, accept limitations, recognize their strengths, and build confidence. The unsocialized subcultural types, who are untrustworthy, aggressive manipulators in search of excitement and who can create havoc in any treatment program, require staff who are directive and firm in setting and strictly enforcing behavioral parameters, while helping such youth to become more conforming, more responsible for their behavior, and better able to build more productive interpersonal relationships.

Gerard goes on to discuss the socialized subcultural delinquents. These youths do not exhibit serious personality problems as such but are prone to become involved in gangs, accepting the values and behavior of their peers rather than of adult authority figures. Treatment for them would best be carried out by someone with a strong sense of morality who is able to exercise appropriate control and be wary of the effects of group manipulations. The goals are to help these youths choose more socially acceptable values and role models and be less dependent on delinquent peers for achieving status and satisfying their material needs. Finally, the subcultural immature youths are also involved in gangs but from a position of greater weakness than their more socialized counterparts. Such youth appear to need delinquent group affiliation to make up for feelings of inadequacy and social ineptitude. A staff member working with such youth would have to be strong yet flexible in order to help them build trusting relationships with adult figures while learning how to set limits on their behavior in order to increase their social skills and develop greater maturity (pp. 174-177).

Despite its promise, the Quay System was eventually discontinued at the Kennedy Youth Center. The reasons included charges that it created racially segregated cottage groups and staff confusion about the appropriateness and distinctiveness of the classifications. In addition, staff indicated that the Quay System actually engendered acting out among the participants, including escape attempts (Gerard, 1970, pp. 38-40).

The I-Level System

The Interpersonal Maturity Level Classification System, better known as the I-Level system, was first presented as a theoretical essay by Sullivan et al. in 1957 and was developed from the works of social and interpersonal psychologists. Regarding the underlying assumptions of the I-Level theory, Sullivan et al. state:

> The normal pattern of emotional-social development follows increasing involvement with people, objectives and social institutions. These involvements give rise to new needs, demands, and situations. Inherent in many of these new situations are problems of perceptual discrimination with regard to the relationships existing between the self and the external environment. As these discriminations are made and assimilated, a cognitive restructuring of experience and expectancy takes place. A new reference scheme is then developed; a new level of integration is achieved. . . . Each new level of integration may be regarded as the psychological analogue of an increasingly efficient optical lens. The more advanced the sequel of integration the less likelihood of perceptual distortion. The person can see himself and the world more accurately and can operate more efficiently. (pp. 373-375)

Thus, we see the I-Level system being explained as a general theory of psychosocial personality development, not just one of delinquency. Specifically, it postulates a continuum of seven developmental levels of maturity, each sequentially more demanding psychologically and interpersonally, through which individuals can move, provided they are capable of negotiating the increasing complexity found at each level.

Individuals are then classified on the basis of their level of interpersonal maturity, from I_1, the least mature level (equivalent to the behavior of a newborn child) to I_7 (an ideal of social maturity). According to Warren (1976):

> Not all individuals work their way through each stage; some may become fixed at a particular level. . . . No assumption is made that delinquents will fall at any particular stage. . . . The point is not that individuals are delinquent because they are immature, but rather that one would know something about the meaning of an individual's delinquency, as well as the nature of the intervention strategies required, if the individual's level is identified. (p. 180)

The initial research with this classification system was done by the California Youth Authority's Community Treatment Project in the early 1960s. Warren (1969) and Palmer (1973) found that most delinquents had been assigned to I-Levels 2, 3, and 4. There were nine mutually exclusive subtypes derived from the modal responses of delinquents within the I-Levels I_2, I_3, and I_4. The delinquent subtypes were classified according to the results of a semi-structured two-hour interview based on issues related to the delinquents' social values and reaction pattern to the world around them. The following classification and subtype codes resulted from this research:

	Code Name	Delinquent Subtype
I_2	Aa	Unsocialized, Assertive
	Ap	Unsocialized, Passive
I_3	Cfm	Conformist, Immature
	Cfc	Conformist, Cultural
	Mp	Manipulator
I_4	Na	Neurotic, Acting Out
	Nx	Neurotic, Anxious
	Ci	Cultural Identifier
	Se	Situational Emotional Reactor

Kornfeld et al., 1975, p. 165)

Of particular interest is the role classification plays in determining differential treatment:

The essence with the I_2s is to place the youth in a supportive environment (usually a foster home) and attempt to meet some of his unmet dependency needs while helping him to learn to perceive more accurately and respond more appropriately to the demands of society and its institutions. The treatment strategies for all I_3 subtypes involve an adult (the community agent) expressing concern for the youth by controlling his behavior. Group treatment is also used, taking advantage of the I_3's dependence of peers. . . . Treatment for the I_4 subtypes works toward reducing internal conflicts and increasing insight into personal and family dynamics which play a part in the acting-out behavior. These goals may be reached through family group therapy, individual psychotherapy, or group therapy. (California Youth Authority, p. 34)

Despite the widespread use of the I-Level classification system, it, like the other systems, had shortcomings. In his assessment of data from the Preston School, one of the institutions in which the instrument was first used, Jesness (1969, 1971) did not find evidence that either the I-Level theory or its typology (which aided in the classification and differential treatment approaches implemented at the school) reduced parole violations of delinquents. Further, some (Beker and Heyman, 1972) have questioned the interrater reliability of this classification system. There are also those who argue that since several thousand youths have been classified in this system and only a few of them placed into any of the three levels above I_4, perhaps the definitions of the maturity levels themselves are inappropriate because they fail to adequately distinguish among the youth (California Youth Authority).

Others have pointed out that since we do not have a comparable assessment of youthful non-offenders, this classification system can lead to the possibly faulty assumptions that youthful offenders are less mature than non-offenders. Finally, it has been noted that there are serious administrative and programmatic difficulties that limit its use, namely, that it creates racially segregated treatment cottages, that union agreements prevent the movement of selected staff among the various residences, thereby preventing optimal staff/offender treatment matches, and, further, that staff training requirements (a six-week period) for participating in the I-Level system are beyond the resources of most existing programs.

Classification systems are by no means limited to the representative ones discussed above. Apart from the older systems, a review of the recent literature would reveal the emergence of a wide range of classification systems, some new, some revised, which are at various stages of development and use (Robins et al., 1986; Laufer et al., 1982; Bonta and Mutiuk, 1985; Sas et al., 1985; Reitsm-Street, 1984; Annis and Chan, 1983). Among these new systems is one which has been receiving much attention and generating considerable research interest. This is the Megargee Classification System discussed at the beginning of this chapter.

The Megargee Classification System

Administering the widely used Minnesota Multiphasic Personality Inventory (MMPI), developed more than forty years ago as a paper-and-pencil, true-false, 566-item instrument that provides scores on fourteen scales (ten of which are clinical scales), along with other assessment instruments, Megargee hoped to develop a reliable personality-based classification system that would retain the advantages of the Quay and Warren systems but could be widely implemented with less cost and fewer trained personnel (1977a, p. 110). To research its applicability, he and his associates undertook a three-year longitudinal study of 5,500 male offenders, aged 18 to 27, incarcerated in the Federal Correctional Institution in Tallahassee, Florida. By administering his instruments to each offender entering the medium-security institution between November 1970 and November 1972, he was able to eventually identify ten naturally occurring, distinctive, and replicable offender groups whose within-group differences were negligible. Differences between groups were found in each of a number of areas, including personality, background, prison adjustment, and treatment needs (Mayer, 1982, p. 25).

Using non-descriptive nomenclature for each of the ten clinical categories, Megargee hoped to avoid premature labeling of each group, thereby prejudging the outcome of any group prior to the completion of the research. Once the offenders were classified, Megargee and Bohn (1977) went on to discuss treatment implications for each of the ten types, but practitioners were warned that the ten descriptions are modal stereotypes from which considerable individual variation could be expected.

Zayer (1982), who conducted a fairly comprehensive review of the research studies of Megargee's MMPI-Based Classification System, provides the following description of the ten types, along with data on the percentages found in each from the original cohort sample:

TABLE 5

Description of the Ten MMPI-Based Types

Name[1]	MMPI Profile*	%**	Description***
Item	Lacks elevations	19%	*Items* are described as the best adjusted type, free from anxiety, and interacting well with others.
Easy	Low profile with small elevations on Scales 2, 3 and 4	7%	*Easys* are also described as well adjusted, but many are underachievers who deny problems.
Baker	Low profile with small elevations on Scales 4 and 2	4%	*Bakers* are described as depressed, withdrawn and many have difficulty relating with peers and authorities. They may have alcohol problems.
Able	Moderate elevations typically on Scales 4 and 9	17%	*Ables* are described as self-confident, extroverted, manipulative and skilled interpersonal relationships. They typically show little remorse for antisocial behavior.
George	Moderate elevations typically on Scales 4 and 2	7%	*Georges* are described as submissive, adaptive yet relate well with others. They often have high levels of state anxiety.
Delta	Prominent elevation on Scale 4, "spike 4"	10%	*Deltas* are described as sensation seekers: hedonistic, amoral and manipulative. They often have problems in interpersonal relationships.
Jupiter	Meets no other group's rules. Elevated on 7, 8, and 9	3%	*Jupiters* are described as introverted, impulsive, and socially awkward.
Foxtrot	Moderate elevations on Scales 4, 9, and 8	8%	*Foxtrots* are described as hostile, immature, dishonest, and egocentric. They have poor interpersonal relationships.
Charlie	High elevations generally on Scales 8, 6, and 4	9%	*Charlies* are described as suspicious, hostile, and aggressive. They have high anxiety levels and lack ambition and egostrength.
How	Overall high elevations. At least 3 or more above 70	13%	*Hows* are described as unstable, agitated and disturbed. They seem to have a broad pattern of ineffective functioning.

[1]The types were originally given arbitrary labels rather than names because their characteristics had not yet been established. The original labels were kept so that if new characteristics emerged, the names would still be appropriate. The types are presented in order from the least deviant profile to the most deviant profile.

*The description of the profiles is based on averages. Individual profiles classified into each type may vary considerably.

**This is the percentage falling into each type in the original Tallahassee Cohort Sample.

***The descriptions presented here are based on the "average" person in each type; they may not be applicable to all inmates assigned to that group.

Among Zayer's basically encouraging findings was that the typology was generalizable with men, but she concluded that further research was necessary to determine if the same classifications exist naturally in a female population and if the instrument would prove of value with an adolescent population. One of the general problems she identified in her review of the literature was that while it is recognized that individuals change type, either improving or worsening their classification, many of the studies "have failed to collect collateral data to determine if observed changes relate to behavior changes" (p. 25).

As regards the issue of the system's applicability to adolescents, a recent study by Veneziano and Veneziano (1986) was done with 251 adjudicated male delinquents between 12 and 15 years of age. As part of an initial assessment program these youths, who were committed to a state training school, were administered the MMPI. Computer classification was then done, using both adult and adolescent norms, and it was found that the distribution of types differed from that found in Megargee's and Bohn's (1977) study of adults.

As a result, they did indicate some limitations in the paradigm. Even though ten offender types were replicated in the study, half of the categories had fewer than ten youthful offenders in them. Another concern was that 42.2 percent of this youthful offender sample fell within group "item," the best adjusted type. This is a puzzling finding, and whether it is a function of the classification paradigm or an indication that adolescent offenders are far different from the original cohort used by Megargee remains an unresolved question.

Among the possible explanations given for the great disparity was that

> The majority of incarcerated adults have been institutionalized as juveniles, yet there are considerable percentages of juvenile offenders that are never incarcerated as adults. Incarcerated adults might therefore be a select group . . . [with] demonstrated patterns of longtime difficulties, which seem likely to be reflected in higher percentages of disturbed MMPI profiles. (pp. 17-18)

Still another possible explanation is that the juvenile justice system may be dealing with many more minor offenders than does the adult system, thereby including in its sweep many more normal or better adjusted types than would be found among adult samples.

The researchers state that despite the difficulties encountered in its use with delinquents, the Megargee typology has both "etiological and service implications for adolescent offenders," and, as far as its ability to measure up to Megargee's own criteria, argue that the system, as applied to juvenile offenders, is

> (1) complete, in that 94.5 percent of the sample were classified; (2) the computerized program provides clear operational definitions of the groups; (3) the computerized program is reliable; (4) the differences obtained between the groups in the present study serve to establish the validity of the system; (5) the scheme does have implications for services; and (6) the plan is economical. (p. 21)

Explaining that adjustments can be made in the instrument, they conclude that "given the realities of a juvenile justice system overwhelmed with cases and little manpower, this classification paradigm would seem to have considerable promise" (p. 21).

In summary, it is clear that most mental health practitioners, as well as others working in the juvenile justice system, have always felt classification to be a part of the rehabilitative effort. As the first step, classification provided those in the field with information for furthering individual assessment, intervention, and treatment. Yet, the literature indicates that it has remained the subject of discussion and review, with hardly any system escaping serious challenges to its validity and/or reliability at one time or another.

Nevertheless, such systems, despite their acknowledged limitations, have served to focus the practitioner's energy and efforts on differential treatments while concurrently helping researchers to target their evaluation of the different therapeutic modalities to determine the efficacy of those treatments.

Thus, while classification helped to identify appropriate candidates for the different treatment approaches, it simultaneously generated greater concern for their treatment outcomes. In retrospect, the overall effect of the experience with the different typologies was that it led to the emergence of a growing body of knowledge, as well as challenging many researchers to develop a usable system despite earlier failures.

Chapter IX

THE PSYCHOLOGICAL TREATMENT OF THE YOUTHFUL OFFENDER

Treatment Needs

THE SPECTRUM of treatment approaches for both the adjudicated and non-adjudicated delinquent varies with the skills and background of the mental health practitioner, the type of setting in which he or she is employed, and finally the resources, goals, and philosophy of the agency or institution in which the youth and practitioner meet. While it is clear that treatment does not proceed in a vacuum and that it is essential to be able to systematically assess and distinguish among the various needs of such a heterogeneous population as youthful offenders, what is less clear is how to best accomplish this task.

In any discussion of treatment of the youthful offender it is also important to remember the context in which such treatment occurs, namely, the juvenile justice system. To a great extent the type of treatment received is largely determined by overlapping and at times conflicting legal, correctional, and psychological considerations.

Nettler (1978) states that "the criminal law is commonly considered to be useful in achieving six ends, some of which are in conflict." He then goes on to describe these treatment ends as efforts to

(1) restrain offenders, (2) deter criminals and others, (3) reform offenders, (4) revive communion symbolically, (5) achieve justice through retribution, and (6) achieve justice through restitution. (p. 48)

While the law seeks these ends, its means for carrying them out have usually been undertaken through its correctional institutions and programs. It is under the third-listed goal of correctional reform, more commonly known as rehabilitation, that we find the convergence of issues raised by law, corrections, and psychology to be most salient to our discussion of treatment. Historically, as we have seen, it has been through the avenue of offender reform that psychology and psychotherapy have entered the criminal justice arena vis-à-vis the medical model, which itself has engendered much in the way of controversy and will be discussed below.

In assessing the treatment needs of the youthful offender, it is useful to keep in mind that in 1985 these youth represented approximately 6 percent of the 25 million youth between the ages of 11 and 17 in the United States. Yet, it has been estimated by Offer (1980) that out of the total United States youth population, 25 percent could benefit significantly from intervention and treatment in four specific areas. He identifies them as mental health, education, physical health and social areas. Therefore, well over 5 million youths have need to some type of intervention and treatment in one or more of these areas.

Considering what much of the literature concerning the multiproblemed nature of the youthful offender reports, it would be expected that this population is more than proportionately represented with needs in each of the four treatment areas, with many requiring concurrent interventions in at least two or more of these areas. While the actual numbers of offending youths needing and receiving such intervention and treatment are not known, we can surmise that those requiring and receiving it are only a fraction of those who might benefit from it.

Yet, even as we move on to discuss the relationship between such youths and their therapists, it is important to remember that the great majority of adjudicated and non-adjudicated delinquents are normal, symptom-free youths whose acting out has been restricted to acts which are neither serious, nor violent, nor chronic, and whose treatment can best be handled through guidance and counseling interventions rather than the more intensive therapeutic modalities. It is equally important at this juncture to remember the lmitations of the classification systems. While the previous chapter suggested how classification systems provide the means for screening youthful offenders for differential treatment modalities, Clements (1981) cautions that any classification system is basically a labelling process with all of the limitations inherent in such a process, and that while a youth can be classified into a group, the characteristics for that group remain general for the member, so that on an individual basis we can never be certain where any member is located within the group. Clements further quotes Fowler's (1979) recommendation that great care be given to the way we use language to describe our client so that we state that "people with this profile tend to," rather than "he is," and "not overstate our ability to define and predict" (p. 26).

Before going on to discuss the different treatment approaches, we will consider some of the general issues pertaining to treatment efficacy.

Psychoanalysis, Psychotherapy and the Therapeutic Relationship

There are a number of difficulties associated with working with delinquent adolescents. First of all, they rarely appear before the therapist on a voluntary basis. Most treatment occurs within institutional or community-based programs to which the adolescents have been sent by the courts, generally after a repeated number of offenses. Hence, the adolescents find themselves in a setting in which they don't wish to be and with great restrictions on their freedom. Secondly, they may not accept the fact that they have a problem. They may blame others for their difficulties (which in some instances may be the case) or they may not perceive their behavior, as is the case with many character disorders, as problematical. Finally, even if they do recognize that they are in some difficulty, they may not wish to discuss it with an adult therapist whom they do not know and may not trust.

The psychoanalysts were the first to attempt to do psychotherapy with this group. While classical psychoanalysis is rarely applied to the treatment of delinquents, the principles on which it is based have been widely applied to working with antisocial adolescents. In fact, the early work done in this area formed the basis for other types of interventions, including group therapy (Redl and Wineman, 1957), family therapy (Healy and Bonner, 1936) and the need for classification (Friedlander, 1947) and differential treatment (Aichhorn, 1935).

However, it was clear from the outset that modification of the traditional psychoanalytic technique which relied on the cooperation of the patient, the use of free association, interpretation of unconscious material, and the analysis of a transference neurosis would have to be made. In his foreword to Aichhorn's (1935) book, Freud stated that:

> The possibility of exerting influence through psychoanalysis depends on quite definite conditions, which may be described as the "analytic situation"; it requires the formation of certain psychic structures and a special attitude toward the analyst. When these factors are lacking, as in the case of children and young delinquents and, as a rule, in criminals dominated by their instincts, the psychoanalytic method must be adapted to meet the need. (p. vii)

Similarly, Redl and Wineman (1957) point out that the psychiatric interview method cannot be effective if "treatment rapport, adequacy of communication channels, and protection of the interview from excess hyperaggressive and destructive behavior" are not guaranteed. They note that with highly aggressive adolescents the conditions necessary for effective psychotherapy cannot, by reason of the characteristics of these individuals, be met. Further, they suggest that the ability of the therapist to influence behavior outside of the therapeutic setting is "exceedingly slim" (p. 263).

Szurek (1969), in discussing the treatment of court-referred delinquents, states:

> The psychoanalytic method seems to be contraindicated for several reasons. In general psychotherapy aims to reverse the psychoneurotic process of repression, and is devised for this purpose. Its goal is to aid in transforming and integrating the repressed impulses into ego attitudes which are in harmony with such self-esteem as the patient has already integrated. But the impulsive child, in contrast to the psychoneurotically inhibited patient, suffers from lack of restraint of his impulses. (p. 80)

This is not to say that traditional psychotherapy can never be effective, but rather that the choice of such intervention must be based on the ability of the adolescent to benefit from it. Such a treatment decision would have to take into account the reasons for the delinquent behavior, the level of motivation, the adolescent's capacity to form a working alliance with the therapist, and his or her verbal abilities. Unfortunately, most serious delinquents are neither motivated, nor do they trust adults sufficiently to make an insight-oriented treatment approach helpful.

Given these difficulties, the analysts suggested that one of the most essential aspects of working with the delinquent lay in the transference, i.e. the nature of the relationship between the adolescent and the therapist. Aichhorn (1925) believed that it was the establishment of an adequate ego ideal (an internalized role model) which promoted socialized non-delinquent behavior. In this regard he stated:

> It is above all the tender feeling for the teacher that gives the pupil the incentive to do what is prescribed and not to do what is forbidden. The teacher, as a libidinally charged object for the pupil, offers traits for identification that bring about a lasting change in the structure of the ego ideal. This in turn effects a change in the behavior of the formerly dissocial child. (p. 235)

Note that Aichhorn suggested that the relationship between the therapist and the adolescent is even more critical than any insight which might be imparted. He also pointed out that the establishment of such a relationship could not easily be accomplished and that it would vary with the type of delinquent. In some instances he believed it would even be necessary to temporarily side with the adolescent's delinquent behavior and in others to take a more neutral position. Thus, he was also suggesting the need for differential treatment depending on the underlying dynamics of the individual. (Also, see Hoffer [1949] on the establishment of narcissistic transference with delinquents and Wulach [1983] on the treatment of narcissism in criminals.)

More than 50 years later, the therapeutic relationship still remains a central factor in working with delinquents. Strupp (1986), by way of explaining the mixed results of the research findings concerning treatment outcomes, indicates that part of the problem may reside in our inability to properly recognize the central position of the therapeutic relationship or properly measure its role in connection with the treatment outcome. While agreeing that therapeutic technique and skill are necessary and vital, he explains that they occur in the context of the therapeutic relationship which, when operative, facilitates the positive change more readily than when not operative.

Strupp goes on to identify those factors commonly recognized as contributing to the climate within which the therapeutic relationship develops and thrives. They include such factors as the therapist's ability to generate acceptance, warmth, respect, and empathy for his client. However, even under these circumstances, Strupp warns that there will still be those who initially can neither respond to nor benefit from the treatment experience, explaining that "Some . . . are mistrustful, antagonistic, and hostile. . . . Such attitudes are often an integral part of the patient's problem, and it becomes the therapist's task to overcome these obstacles" (p. 123). The key to overcoming such resistance, according to Strupp, is similar to that first described by Aichhorn regarding delinquent youth, namely, through establishing a therapeutic alliance with the client. Strupp refers to the therapist as building a collaborative relationship with his client.

Resistance to Therapy

While Aichhorn and then Strupp, more than sixty years later, underscore the need for developing a strong therapeutic alliance as a means for overcoming treatment resistance, Brodsky (1984) outlines some of the factors which contribute to resistance and which therapists should be mindful of. These factors are particularly salient for those treating youthful offenders. Brodsky's first concern is with the personal reaction of the therapist to the reluctant client, whose behavior leaves the therapist feeling threatened, helpless, frustrated, and angry to the point of being punitive toward the client. In effect, Brodsky argues that when in the role of therapist the needs for respect and recognition are thwarted, those needs can become exaggerated to the point where they interfere with the treatment process. He maintains that much of the difficulty arises because the therapist is not adequately prepared either by training or experience to work with involuntary clients, as most, if not all, of their experience has been with those who ostensibly seek therapy voluntarily. This is rarely the case when his client is a youthful offender.

Other issues include the guardedness with which a therapist approaches what he believes to be manipulation by such a client so that a great deal of his attention is focused on averting being used rather than on building rapport and trust between himself and his client. In addition, Brodsky discusses other salient topics such as the client's right to refuse treatment, errors in therapeutic technique, including passivity on the part of the therapist, failure to deal with problems in the therapist-client relationship, and mistakes in the timing and content of therapeutic intervention. He also considers ways to build motivation through the teaching of self-coping stress-controlling techniques and effective methods of utilizing resistance, including the therapist not permitting himself "to be set up in direct opposition" to his client.

While Brodsky's discussion focuses on many issues related to the involuntary client, of which youthful offenders can be considered a subtype, McHolland (1985) specifically addresses the phenomenon of adolescent resistance in therapy. He relates the resistance to developmental issues of the adolescent as well as the social context in which it occurs, and cautions the therapist not to create resistance where little or none exists. Where it does exist, the therapist should work to deactivate the resistance by not standing in opposition to it but, instead, recognizing that for the adolescent, resistance serves a positive and protective function that must be understood and strategically dealt with. McHolland goes on to discuss some of the basic ingredients he considers vital for therapists to include in their approach, most importantly the idea that therapists really need to like adolescents to work with them.

Other suggestions he makes include avoiding silences, allowing the adolescent, once talking, to continue without interrupting, advising, or judging, and being self-disclosing when it can be in the service of sharing one's feelings in support of the adolescent.

It is understandable that from the perspective of the youthful offender, overtures of friendliness, concern, and caring by an adult authority figure in the person of the therapist may be viewed with distrust and suspicion. If the practitioner expects such a reaction and recognizes it as basically defensive on the part of the youth, he will be better able to move beyond this initial response. If the setting in which the therapy occurs is an institutional one, then part of the explanation for the defensiveness will most assuredly be connected to the situational context. It is not uncommon for an institutional environment, with all of its pressures, to threaten an already vulnerable ego, resulting in a more protective, albeit distorted, posture, where any efforts to lower one's guard through self-examination and disclosure are resisted with much energy and vigilance. Given that delinquents, along with non-offending youth, have fluid, fragile, and forming egos, openness to treatment can be viewed by them as a weakness having very serious consequences beyond the treatment relationship in an institutional setting that they view as fraught with real and imagined dangers that threaten or appear to threaten their survival.

Thus, we recognize that the issue of resistance to self-disclosure can be viewed as a very real problem in the treatment of adolescents generally and even more so among those adjudicated delinquent. In his review of the literature, Ridley (1984) has argued that this is an especially salient problem for black clients in treatment with white therapists. While he does not discuss black youths or black delinquents in particular, his insights are indeed applicable to those populations. Ridley points to a number of difficulties, including the fact that verbal psychotherapy requires trusting and risk taking in order to achieve an uncertain objective, and that the black client is required to take those risks with a therapist whose color and social differences may appear to preclude understanding, responsiveness, or willingness to help the client. Ridley explains that "among the more commonly cited difficulties are therapists' insensitivity, stereotyping, lack of specialized training and failure to establish rapport" and urges practitioners to become mindful of the motivational factors among black clients who resist disclosure, pointing out that the motivations are "a function of numerous factors, including their unique personalities and coping styles, individual experiences with racism, and personal mental health statuses" (p. 1242).

Ridley makes a number of suggestions for coping with this problem, calling for the therapist to refine and improve his skills while achieving personal congruence and sensitivity around issues of race. He indicates that this should help the therapist focus on the uniqueness of his client, as well as his client's needs and problems. Further, he calls for the therapist to develop individualized treatment plans that truly reflect the variability that exists among black clients, as well as becoming more cognizant of how his own attitudes and behavior can unwittingly affect the black client. In Ridley's view, the effective therapist is one who has a broad repertoire of techniques and can remain flexible while applying them appropriately to specific treatment problems exhibited by the client (p. 1242).

The value and applicability of Ridley's formulations to the treatment of the black youthful offender cannot escape notice and may be particularly salient, because such a client is likely to be wary of his therapist not only because of racial differences but also because the therapist represents adult authority.

In line with the issues of trust, the therapist should take the lead early on in clarifying his obligations both to the youthful offender and the agency or institution for which he works. He should discuss the issue of confidentiality and make the youth aware, from the start, of any limitations that pertain to confidentiality so that the youth knows of the therapist's ethical responsibility to disclose information regarding behavior that might be dangerous to either the client or others. If this issue is clarified early on in the therapy, it will minimize chances for confusion and the possibility of the subsequent dissolution of the relationship.

Diagnosis

Moving on to the issue of diagnosis, Weiner (1970) highlights the importance of developing an adequate diagnosis of the youth for treatment, providing both guidelines for practitioners to follow as well as some considerations concerning sources of diagnostic data. Among the commonly recognized data, sources are those found in a youth's family, school, medical, and legal case records. They provide both a historic profile and point of departure for discussion in the clinical interview to be conducted with the youth. Weiner suggests that where the therapist suspects serious mental disturbance or where a mixed clinical picture emerges from the data, that he consider probing the youth's friendship patterns and peer group activities, as well as reviewing any history of unusual or bizarre behavior and family history of mental disturbance.

Weiner also underscores the importance of noting the youth's behavior during the clinical interview itself. He is specifically interested in the adolescent's speech pattern (for clues to any disorder in thinking), style of relating (for insight into the youth's capacity for object relatedness), appearance (to help assess levels of personality organization), and the overall level and appropriateness of affect and judgment exhibited. To round out the diagnostic picture, he cites the importance of incorporating psychological tests such as those which are particularly sensitive to personality impairments that define specific disturbances among such youth (e.g. the Rorschach Test for ascertaining latent psychosis) or those that assess intellectual functioning, perception, and attention (e.g. the WISC).

Among others who have focused on diagnosis in their work with delinquents, and in this case violent delinquents, is Lewis (1985), who underscores the need for neurological diagnosis with this population, while Ogdon (1981) provides a review of the literature concerning psychodiagnostic and projective instruments that have been used with delinquents.

The question of the efficacy of individual psychotherapy in general and in comparison to other forms of treatment has not been adequately addressed. First of all, there have been relatively few studies that have examined psychotherapy separate from a consideration of other treatments. Those that did (Massimo and Shore, 1963; Shore and Massimo, 1973) found essentially positive results using a vocationally oriented form of psychotherapy with delinquent boys. However, the small number of subjects participating in each group (10) would preclude drawing any definitive conclusions. Persons (1966) examined the effectiveness of individual and group psychotherapy with institutionalized delinquent boys and found that those receiving psychotherapy made a better adjustment both within the institution and after discharge. However, one could not partial out the effects of the group and individual therapy to know which contributed to the outcomes. Rutter and Giller (1984) concluded that intensive individual therapy is likely to prove effective only with a select population of motivated individuals. However, because of a shortage of adequate studies at this time, one cannot draw any definitive conclusions. (See Tramontana [1980] for a review of research on psychotherapy with adolescents.) Nonetheless, this would not negate many of the issues raised above regarding the importance of establishing an adequate working relationship with the adolescent regardless of the form of intervention used.

Family Therapy

In Chapter VI we pointed out that more often than not, seriously delinquent adolescents come from troubled families and that the adolescent's behavior is a reflection of, among other factors, the difficulties that exist within the adolescent's family. It is not surprising, therefore, that attempts have been made to intervene with the families of delinquents.

The idea is not a new one. Some fifty years ago Healy and Bonner (1936) suggested that working with the families of delinquents was important. They stated that

> The common sense ideal when we were working with the family was, of course, for parents to have it made plain to them that possibly some better understandings of the delinquent and themselves might accomplish much. (p. 148)

Realizing that these families often had very real life problems, Healy and Bonner provided medical, economic, and social assistance as well as psychiatric intervention. The psychiatric intervention was aimed at providing the parents with insight into the nature of their interactions with their children. Family therapy as an approach toward working with delinquents was later fostered by Ackerman (1958), Schneiderman and Evans (1975), Johnson (1975), and others.

The conceptualization of family dynamics was expanded by Munichen (1974) and Bowen (1978), who saw families as ongoing cybernetic systems, in which each member of the family is influencing and being influenced by other members of the family. Hence, the family, not just one individual member, was seen as having the problem. Despite the fact that this represented an important advance in working with families, there are few if any research studies which report the effects on recidivism rates on delinquents using just a family systems approach. Borduin et al. (1982) and Curry et al. (1984) reviewed a number of studies on family systems therapy; however, none were specifically designed to test the efficacy of this approach with delinquent adolescents.

Henggeler (1982) and his co-workers enlarged the family systems approach to working with families of delinquents to include the adolescent's school, neighborhood, and peers. The technique which is called a "family ecological systems approach" attempts to intervene in all those systems, which, in addition to the family, may have a negative impact on the adolescent. Therapists working within this modality will visit the families at home, make classroom observations, meet with teachers, etc.

Henggeler et al. (1986) compared the effects of this approach to traditional mental health services as well as a control group. Youths in the study came primarily from lower socioeconomic backgrounds and had an average of 2.1 arrests for serious offenses prior to treatment. Adolescents who received the family ecological treatment showed a significant decrease in behavior problems and demonstrated improved family interactions. However, no follow-up studies were done, nor was there any report on its impact on recidivism. Thus, while this approach appears to have merit, it has not yet been demonstrated to be an effective technique for reducing delinquency.

Another major thrust in intervening with the families of delinquents has been based on a behavioral and social learning model. Parsons and Alexander in a series of studies (Parsons and Alexander, 1973; Alexander and Parsons, 1973; Alexander, Barton, Shaw and Parsons, 1976; Klein, Alexander, Parsons, 1977) utilized short-term behavioral family therapy with the families of status offenders. They found that this technique was effective in reducing recidivism among 13- to 16-year-olds for up to 18 months and that sibling contacts with the court were reduced for up to three-and-a-half years (Klein et al., 1977). Further, they noted that recidivism rates were lower using this technique when compared to an eclectic psychodynamic approach to family therapy. Stuart (1971) and Rueger and Liberman (1984) reported on the use of "contingency contracting" with families. This involves (a) selection of target behavior for all family members, (b) rewards made contingent upon achieving goals, (c) penalties for failure to live up to the contract and (d) record keeping. Both parents and adolescents take part in the creation of the contract. Reuger and Liberman have suggested that the efficacy of such techniques is variable. They felt that the outcome is a function of the amount of control the parents have (or perhaps even care to have) over the reinforcement contingencies and is more effective when the problems are specific and behavioral in nature. Similarly, Weathers and Liberman (1975) noted that families under serious stress may be unable to maintain the necessary controls to make contingency contracting effective.

Patterson and his co-workers (see Patterson [1986] for an extended bibliography) assumed that antisocial behavior in children results from poor parental management skills. Patterson and Reid (1984) hypothesized that children may learn to coerce parents into responding through negative behavior, e.g. throwing temper tantrums, and thus negative behavior is maintained through parental reinforcement. They refer to this type of parent-child relationship as "coercion," in that it is based on aversive reinforcement compared to "reciprocity," which is based on mutual positive reinforcement between parent and child. Patterson developed a series of procedures based on social learning and operant techniques to intervene into "coercive" relationships. The program involved (a) identifying specific behaviors, (b) noting antecedents and consequences, and (c) establishing contingency contracts. Parents were given instructions in the principles of behavior modification and participated in training groups using modeling and role-playing techniques.

Patterson and Reid (1973), working with 11 families with boys aged 6 to 13, found that targeted antisocial behaviors were reduced by 47 percent up to one year after the initiation of the program. Patterson (1977) found equally positive results. It should be noted, however that most of the subjects of Patterson's work were latency-age children, and, while there is evidence that these techniques are effective in reducing aggressive and antisocial behavior in younger boys, there is no evidence regarding their impact on older adolescent delinquents. Presumably, it would be much easier for a family to gain control of a 10-year-old than a 15-year-old.

Geismar and Wood (1986) reviewed 30 behavioral and 2 non-behavioral studies of intervention with families of delinquents. The studies were also independently rated by five senior faculty members at Rutgers University as to their methodological soundness. They concluded, on the basis of the studies presented, that there was no evidence that non-behavioral therapy was effective with the problem of juvenile delinquency. On the other hand, they noted that "while behavioral interventions with families of delinquents have also not been demonstrated to be totally effective, the evidence so far is tilting the scale in their favor" (p. 145). They further stated that the non-behavioral studies tend to be less methodologically sound, a point also made by Curry et al. (1984). They felt that the most obvious short-coming of the psychodynamic therapies is their failure to measure the effects of treatment.

Nonetheless, many behavioral interventions have proven most successful when using a non-behavioral systems perspective and taking other non-behavioral variables into account. Borduin et al. (1982) concluded that the primary shortcoming of behavioral approaches is their failure to include ecological considerations in addition to family determinants of behavior. Alexander et al. (1976) found that one of the most important variables in a systems-behavioral intervention with families of

status offenders was the quality of the relationship skills of the thera
a point noted earlier by Strupp and others.

Family therapy may prove effective for working with some delinquents either on its own or in conjunction with other forms of treatment.
It is certainly no panacea. Studies on what types of delinquents, coming
from what types of families and what types of social circumstances
would best benefit from this approach have yet to be done.

Group Treatment

There are a number of reasons for the application of therapeutic group
techniques with delinquents. These include: (1) the fact that many adolescents are more readily influenced by their peers than by adults (Redl,
1945); (2) residential treatment programs, where group therapy is most frequently used, lend themselves to such an approach since they contain
ready-made groups of delinquents; and (3) given the shortage of trained
staff, it is clearly more efficient and cost effective to work with individuals
in a group as opposed to on an individual basis (Yong, 1971).

While various techniques are utilized in group approaches, there are
two basic conceptual models. In one, analytic group therapy, the focus is
on the dynamics of the individual within the group. In the other, interactive group therapy, the focus is on the group as a whole and its influence
on individual members. (We make these distinctions because they appear as such in the literature. However, as we noted below, in practice
they may be more theoretical than actual.) A fundamental assumption
made by the analytic approach is that the individual members of the
group are expressing, through delinquent behavior, an acting out of an
underlying developmental problem. This assumption is characterized
by the work of Slavson (1965) and Redl (1966), although both acknowledge the need for modification of more traditional analytic techniques in
working with delinquent adolescents. Slavson (1965) notes:

> We had to first break down the defensive armor against narcissistic in-
> jury and overwhelming anxiety and "enter into the personalities" of our
> boys before we could even attempt to take the first steps in their behav-
> ioral and psychosocial rehabilitation. (p. 98)

The goals of interactive group therapy according to Yalom (1975),
in addition to insight, include corrective family experience, altruism,
interpersonal learning, social skills training, experiences, catharsis,
existential factors (learning to take responsibility for one's behavior)
and education. However, it is of interest to note that, when asked,

adolescents found that gaining insight was least helpful to them (Corder et al., 1981).

A variation of this form of group therapy, called "guided group interaction," was developed by McCorkle (1952) and Stephenson and Scarpitti (1974). This approach assumes that the cause of delinquency lies in the delinquent's social environment. Hence, the focus of the group is to help the adolescent and the group as a whole internalize socialized values and associations, and assumes that the more "socialized" delinquent will influence the less "socialized" one.

Within these formats there are behavioral (Saranson and Ganzer, 1973; Wodarski et al., 1974) and non-behavioral approaches. However, in practice, the distinction between these approaches may blur. For example, Redl (1966), a psychoanalytic worker, discusses the role of resistance in group work with delinquents, whereas Stephenson and Scarpitti (1974) state that "the first objective of the guided group interaction must be to pierce and to undermine the delinquents defensive attitude toward delinquency" (p. 26). Further, while Julian and Kilman (1979) suggest that group treatment with delinquents could roughly be categorized into three types—therapy, behavioral rehearsal and discussion—they concluded, on the basis of a review of thirty-two studies of group therapy with delinquent adolescents, that:

> No study presented evidence that the therapists adhered to a particular treatment format. There was little consistency across the studies as to what constituted a particular treatment approach, such as group discussion. (p. 8)

Hence, the evaluation of the effectiveness or theoretical validity of one treatment approach over the other is difficult at best.

In fact, in this regard the evaluation of the effectiveness of group therapy (regardless of the theoretical approach) is apparently beset by the same problems as other treatment techniques. Specifically, no one has accounted for the ways in which the large number of subject variables (such as type and degree of pathology, IQ, nature and frequency of offense) and treatment variables (such as type of group therapy and composition of group) interact with outcomes. Nor have what constitute desired outcomes been specified, with some studies examining personality change and others recidivism rates. In addition, since group therapy techniques are most often conducted within institutional settings, one would need to partial out the effects of the therapy groups from other program interventions. Indeed, Julian and Kilman (1979) note that closed environment groups are twice as successful as open environment (non-custodial) groups, suggesting that it may be the residential treatment as a whole rather than just the group therapy per se which has been effective.

In the end there is no clear evidence that group therapy is an effective technique for reducing recidivism among delinquents as a whole. After an extensive and instructive evaluation of their own and similar programs utilizing "guided group interaction," Stephenson and Scarpitti (1974) concluded that:

> the evidence from these studies is not impressive with respect to the general efficacy of guided group interaction when compared with alternative programs of correction. (p. 189)

They did note that there may be an interaction between the type of delinquent and program success. Julian and Kilman (1979) found that of the 32 studies they reviewed, "positive results were obtained on less than one-third of all measures in outcome categories" (p. 34). While the more analytically oriented programs such as those described by Redl and Slavson reported group process in detail, they unfortunately do little if anything in the way of evaluating outcome other than anecdotally. While these results may appear discouraging at first glance, future research may suggest that certain types of delinquents may in fact respond well to particular forms of group therapy.

Behavior Modification

Behavioral and social learning approaches to the treatment of the juvenile offender are based largely on the application of classical and operant conditioning techniques (for an extensive discussion of the theory behind the application, see Kanfer and Phillips [1970] and the work of Bandura and Walters [1963] and others in the area of social learning theory). These treatment techniques have the advantage of being based on a large body of experimental research and evidence. The basic assumptions made by these theories are that: (1) all behavior is learned; (2) that learning follows from experimentally verifiable principles, e.g. learning by association, consequences, or imitation; (3) that the acquisition of maladaptive or antisocial behavior can be understood by the same principles as the acquisition of adaptive or socially acceptable behavior; (4) that the modification of antisocial behavior involves the learning of new, more acceptable and adaptable forms of behavior.

Behavior modification programs have utilized a variety of techniques such as token economies and role playing, and they have been employed in community, residential, and family settings. Typically, they will focus on specific observable "target" behaviors such as being on time, doing homework, making one's bed, or making appropriate comments in a group session. These target behaviors are assumed to be components of more global prosocial behavior. It is expected that if such component behaviors are acquired, then the individual will behave in a more acceptable manner. Thus, while reduced delinquency may be a long-range goal, programs tend not to focus on it directly. This is an important issue to which we will return later.

Perhaps one of the most commonly applied techniques is the use of a token economy. This procedure rests on the "law of effect," which states that the probability of a response occurring is a function of the consequence of that response. Therefore, the probability of a response increases if the consequences are reinforcing or positive for the individual and decreases if the consequences are punishing or negative. For example, if we wanted to increase "on-time-to-class behavior," we might reward the student with movie tickets for coming to all classes on time for a week, or punish lateness by requiring that he stay after school to wash blackboards. Since it is rarely practical to provide a direct reinforcement after each component of the target behavior, tokens are used instead. In learning theory, a token is a "secondary reinforcer," that is, one which has become associated with the "primary" or backup reinforcers, e.g. money or special privileges. For example, suppose a treatment program held 15 classes per week and we wanted to increase the rate at which the student came to those classes on time. We might first observe over the first week or so how frequently the student attended classes on time without any contingencies. This would provide us with a "base rate" from which we would evaluate the impact of our intervention. If we noted that the student attended five out of 15 classes on time, we might tell them that each time he attended a class on time he would receive a chit and that if he received eight chits during the following week these could be exchanged for a movie ticket. The chit is the "token" or secondary reinforcer. While it is not directly reinforcing, it becomes connected (by association) with the backup reinforcer, the movie ticket. The token reinforcer further has the advantage of allowing the behavior to be reinforced immediately after the behavior occurs. (In this instance, after each on-time performance.) The following week we might increase the number of "on-time" appearances required and thus increase the number of chits required to receive a movie ticket to ten, the week after to twelve, and so on until we reached the end goal of all classes attended on time.

The application of modeling, based on social learning theory to the treatment of delinquents (Bandura et al., see Chap. VI), has been reported by a number of authors (Saranson and Ganzer, 1973; Ganzer, 1973; de Lange et al., 1981; Carpenter and Sandburg, 1985). In these approaches adolescents are presented with various types of interpersonal problem situations via role playing or videotapes and then observe alternate ways of interacting within that situation. Presumably, they would wish to imitate the ones that lead to the most rewarding outcomes. They are also encouraged to discuss various outcomes and ways of interacting.

A large number of delinquency treatment programs have employed these techniques (see Blakely and Davidson, 1984). One of the more successful of these was "Achievement Place," a community-based treatment program which utilized a token economy (Phillips, 1968; Wolf et al., 1972). Boys lived with "teaching parents" in their community and attended the local schools. The "teaching parents" were trained in behavioral techniques and established a token economy system within the home. Boys were reinforced for reduced levels of aggressive speech, homework preparation, household maintenance chores, etc. In addition, with the cooperation of the local school board, a behavioral management system was established in the classroom. The boys received daily report cards from their teachers. If they received reports that indicated that they had worked in school and followed school rules, they would earn points and privileges. The authors report successfully modifying a number of target behaviors in this way. One of the long-range goals of the program was to reduce the boys' reliance on immediate token reinforcement so that more naturally occurring reinforcers such as praise might be used. Another long-range goal was to return the boy to his natural family. Davidson and Robinson (1975) report success with a similar program designed to increase prosocial and reduce delinquent behavior in 14- to 17-year-old inner-city boys. They found that graduates of the program had lower post-release arrest records and had a higher rate of returning to school or securing employment than the control group.

However, not all programs utilizing behavior modification techniques have been successful. Davidson and Wolfred (1977) report on a community-based program which utilized a token economy system as well as social learning techniques (modeling) to improve predelinquent and academic behavior in a group of adolescents. The authors found that the behavioral interventions were effective in modifying behaviors while the adolescents were in the program, but on follow up there was no improvement in terms of recidivism rate or school performance compared to that of the control group. In fact, the experimental group appeared to do worse.

This points up a problem which is common to many programs of this type. Recent reviews of the literature (Klein, 1974; Gross and Birmingham, 1980; Blakely and Davidson, 1984; Varley, 1984) suggest that while behavioral techniques may be effective in modifying target behaviors within the program, the effects frequently fail to generalize outside the program. For example, the program may increase the adolescent's punctuality time to class within the program, but, after leaving, the student may get fired from a job for chronic lateness. In addition, there is little evidence of reduced recidivism after release. Indeed, as Blakely and Davidson (1984) point out, in most evaluation studies of these programs the impact on recidivism is not even measured.

The issue of generalizability of treatment effects has been dealt with to some degree by Achievement Place type programs in which token reinforcements are gradually replaced by more "natural" reinforcements such as praise. In addition, reinforcements are administered by members of the adolescent's family and community environment rather than therapists. Klein (1975) and Agee (1979) report similar success in utilizing techniques designed to gradually fade out the use of tokens and transfer reinforcement to the adolescent's normal environment.

Nonetheless, even this may not be sufficient, since it still reflects the basic assumption underlying these programs which is that delinquents are individuals who are deficient in certain psychosocial and psychoeducational skills. However, as we have suggested in previous chapters, for many adolescents, delinquency appears to be considerably more complex a problem than skill deficiency. They come from distressed families and are mistrustful and unable to cope with the psychosocial demands of adolescence. While in some instances the absence of appropriate social behavior may reflect or be related to their delinquent behavior, one could reasonably ask whether or not it is not symptomatic of a rather chaotic intrapersonal and intrafamilial life, which inhibit not only the acquisition of the behavior but also the value systems necessary for the appreciation of these behaviors. In addition, one may lack appropriate psychosocial and psychoeducational skills without coming to the attention of law enforcement officials. That is not to say that the skill deficiency model on which behavioral approaches are based is necessarily invalid, but rather that it is unlikely that it is valid for all delinquent adolescents. Unfortunately, in these studies, one sees very little if anything about the types of delinquents with whom these approaches might be most useful. Perhaps if outcomes were correlated with those adolescents with whom the programs were and were not successful they might be more effectively applied in the future.

"Third Force" Treatments

There are a number of therapies which have been described as a "third force" in psychology, having developed as treatments in the 1950s and 1960s and functioning as alternatives to both psychoanalytic and behavioristic models of man. Philosophically and theoretically, they can be described as evolving from a humanistic-existential tradition that views growth and human potential, freedom of choice and individual responsibility as central to understanding and/or changing human behavior.

In essence, they share the belief that each individual is unique and can be consciously made aware of and meaningfully intervene in the events that shape his or her life. While they may rely to varying degrees — as do the psychoanalytic approaches — on insight for change, most do not accept the belief that behavior is largely a product of deterministic and irrational forces. Instead, they affirm a belief in human plasticity and personal growth. By focusing as they do on the healthy side of human nature, with some using peak experiences as examples of what is both ideal and possible, they generate a sense of optmism about improving the human condition.

While the individual theories, constructs, and techniques for these approaches may differ, each in its own way aims to help the individual achieve an integrated and more complete understanding of himself and his behavior while also increasing his ability to take more deliberately conscious and positive actions in his life. These common objectives, along with their emphasis on the present, the "here and now" of their therapeutic relationship, and belief in the individual's responsibility for changing his behavior, offer practitioners many advantages for working with youthful offenders.

Among the therapies included for discussion are Client-Centered Therapy, Transactional Analysis (TA), and Reality Therapy, with the latter two having been applied in complete programmatic ways with a delinquent population. Such approaches would appear to continue to hold promise for dealing with contemporary youth, selective delinquents, as well as many others, who are described by Levine (1983) as experiencing isolation, meaninglessness, normlessness and self-estrangement.

While client-centered therapy established by Rogers (1951) has not been widely used with delinquents as Transactional Analysis and Reality Therapy, this modality, with its emphasis on the need for the therapist to have positive regard for his client, might be particularly effective in the treatment of the youthful offender.

While delinquent youth are generally characterized as "bad," Rogerian therapy emphasizes the innate goodness of the individual and the belief that the therapist must enter into the relationship with his client with feelings of unconditional positive regard, respect and warmth. Such a mind-set on the part of the practitioner in itself may contribute much to facilitating positive changes in many such youth. For Rogers, the clients who are most estranged from themselves—as are many delinquents—tend to be extremely anxious, defensive, and psychologically maladjusted, all of which leads to being blocked from self-actualization and behaving psychopathically with symptoms that can be antisocial and criminal. Such blockages, Rogers believes, can be undone through a client-centered approach. It is his conviction that having positive regard for the client means that the therapist believes the client can change. Especially helpful in work with youthful offenders is the therapist's ability to attend to the positive aspects of the individual's verbalizations and behavior and carefully reflect them while giving more direct positive feedback to the client. Having such an approach can encourage the therapist to identify an individual's assets no matter how well hidden they are by negative attitudes and behavior, affording the practitioner an opening into what might otherwise be a self-sealed negative system of alienation and despair.

More commonly used in the field of rehabilitation than client-centered therapy, Transactional Analysis has been embraced by many practitioners as much for its succinct explanation of human behavior as for the ease with which its methods can be taught to others.

Eric Berne (1964), its founder, asserted that each individual personality is made up of three distinct ego states—parent, adult, and child.

These ego states react in turn to the ego states of others. Further, each of the three ego states, which is incorporated in childhood through parent-child interactions, is observable in all human transactions (units of behavior) by the distinct physical, cognitive, and emotional characteristics that are exhibited by the individual at the time of the transaction.

The parental ego state can be controlling, non-perceptive, arbitrary and rigid as well as nurturing, teaching, and warm to others. The adult ego state also reflects conditioned-response patterns, but they are essentially rational, problem solving, data processing, and devoid of affect, while the child ego state represents the feeling, thinking, intuitive, and spontaneous part of the individual's personality.

The individual exhibits only one of these ego states at any one time, switching from one to another as the situation dictates. A factor which influences the response pattern is called the "life position." It is chosen by the person in childhood and results from the type of communications concerning one's self-worth and the worth of others that is received from one's parents. These communications become incorporated in the person as "mental tapes" reflecting the feeling of either being "OK" or being "not OK." According to Berne, there are four possible "life positions":

> I'm OK — You're OK
> I'm OK — You're not OK
> I'm not OK — You're OK
> I'm not OK — You're not OK

Once a "life position" is selected, a corresponding "life script" is chosen and is acted out accordingly. Scripts calling for combativeness, deceitfulness, acting out, etc., are examples of behaviors that might be selected by a youthful offender who feels "not OK." Getting him to begin to feel "OK," thereby changing his perspective and behavior, becomes the task of the TA practitioner. He attempts to accomplish this task by conducting a "script analysis" of the delinquent's interpersonal relationships, looking for clues concerning the types of counterproductive mental "tapes" from his past that continue to be operative in the present.

What can make the treatment even more difficult for the practitioner is if the youth's life position is "I'm not OK — You're not OK," in which case there is little reason for the youth to be responsive to the therapist. Those who feel that way are perhaps the most serious and chronic of the youthful offender population. Using structural analysis, the therapist must patiently try to make his client consciously aware of his ego states and encourage him to accept a mutually agreed upon treatment contract. This contract specifies goals that have both short- and long-range consequences for behavioral change. The youth practices his newly acquired awareness in the safety of the therapeutic relationship. By bringing his "games" into the treatment and being skillfully challenged by the adult state of the therapist to respond more from his own adult state, the youthful offender begins to utilize his rational abilities more in his interactions. It is expected that there will be a gradual but continuing improvement in this direction so that the delinquent, by being more realistic, rational, and responsible, comes to view himself and eventually others as being "OK."

As regards the effectiveness of TA with a delinquent population, Jesness (1975) reported the results of a comparative study connected to the California Youth Authority. For this study, over nine hundred delinquents were randomly selected and divided into two groups, which were assigned to one of two institutions. The Close School staff was trained in transactional analysis and implemented a TA program, whereas the Holton School implemented a social learning model using the behavior modification techniques of a token economy and a parole-contingent point system. Only those youths who remained in the program for at least three months were included in the study.

Outcomes in a number of different areas were assessed, including academic achievement (reading, math, and vocabulary), levels of self-esteem, interpersonal relations misconduct, and recidivism. While participants in both programs measured higher in their achievement results, the program at the Close School produced the highest gain. TA participants also improved more in their levels of self-esteem and had more positive feelings toward treatment staff and teachers. The Holton School results exhibited somewhat greater gains in the participants' behavior ratings in such areas as communication, calmness, and independence. There were, however, no differences in the rates of recidivism, with one-third of the participants being sent back within the year and one-half within two years.

Still another therapy which relies heavily on cognitive factors in treatment is Reality Therapy. William Glasser (1965), a psychiatrist working in California, introduced Reality Therapy in the belief that emotional disturbance and delinquent behavior result from the individual's denial of the world around him. Accepting that those needing treatment suffer from an inability to satisfy basic needs, with the severity of the illness and/or maladaptive behavior reflecting the degree to which such needs go unmet, he states:

> In their unsuccessful effort to fulfill their needs, no matter what behavior they choose, all patients have a common characteristic: *they all deny the reality of the world around them.* Some break the law, denying the rules of society; some claim their neighbors are plotting against them, denying the improbability of such behavior. . . . Whether it is partial denial or a total blotting out of all reality of the chronic backward patient in the state hospital, the denial of some or all reality is common to all patients. (p. 6)

Glasser views the role of therapy as helping the individual face and overcome his denial of the world around him while aiding him in learning how to succesfully meet his needs within that reality. He views two needs as basic to all — the need to love and be loved by others and to feel worthwhile to others and to oneself. To be somewhat successful in achieving these ends helps the individual to deal with most of life's difficulties. Glasser believes that to achieve success in satisfying basic needs requires that the individual act responsibly, which he defines as having "the ability to fulfill one's needs, and to do so in a way that does not deprive others of the ability to fulfill 'their needs' " (p. 13).

Accordingly, antisocial or delinquent behavior is viewed as irresponsible, since the offending behavior violates and interferes with the rights and needs of others. For Glasser, in addition to helping the individual accept the reality of the situation and the responsibility for satisfying his needs, the therapy has a moral component, namely, that the therapist never loses sight of whether an action being considered by the client is right or wrong. By serving as a model himself, as well as helping the individual evaluate his behavior in moral terms and criticizing behavior when it is irresponsible, wrong, or not reality oriented, the therapist sustains a close and lively interest in helping the client learn to make necessary changes and to feel more competent and confident in meeting his needs appropriately.

These goals are accomplished by the therapist establishing an involved, caring relationship with his client in which he makes the client feel accepted and worthwhile, even while judging his irresponsible behaviors to be unacceptable. In time, the client comes to view his antisocial or delinquent behavior from the therapist's perspective, recognizing the negative consequences of his actions and replacing them with more realistic and responsible ways of satisfying his basic needs.

Regarding the effectiveness of reality therapy as a treatment modality at the Ventura School, a school for delinquent girls, Glasser (1965) states:

> The job of the school is difficult. Our goal is to take every girl, no matter how antagonistic she may be, and within six to eight months rehabilitate her so that, with guidance of the parole officer, she will be able to stay out of further serious trouble in the community. Naturally, we do not succeed with everyone, but do with about 80 percent of the girls. . . . Considering that on a recent count out of a total of 370 girls only 43 were returnees, we feel our program is generally successful. (p. 68)

In another study of the effectiveness of reality therapy with an offender population, MacDonald et al. (1968) report the positive outcome of an in-house study of a program utilizing Reality Therapy with both juvenile and adult sex offenders. The results indicated that less than 9 percent of the participants were rearrested.

Czunder (1985), who agrees with Glasser regarding the individual's capacity to learn to act responsibly, know right from wrong, and recognize the difference between fantasy and reality, has recently implemented a program which focuses on individual responsibility and moral behavior. Like Yochelson and Samenow (1976) and Cleckley (1964), he underscores the importance of correcting errors in thinking, believing that errors in thinking characterize the mental processes of criminals. His "cognitive moral approach" goes beyond that of Glasser, with whom he agrees that "a man is not bad because he is 'sick,' rather he is 'sick' because he is bad" (p. 65).

Czunder's treatment proceeds from the premises that the individual has as much potential for good behavior as for bad and that a primary factor which influences behavior in a negative direction is the self-centeredness exhibited by the individual. Briefly, he argues that self-centeredness is prevalent among offenders and serves to give them an uncaring attitude towards others. In addition to self-centeredness, he identified other factors that might also contribute to criminal thinking (e.g. resentment of authority, lack of guilt, and anger), which must be dealt with whenever exhibited.

Czunder's program is voluntary and participating offenders meet in groups of ten twice weekly. Group leaders control the agenda. First, the participants learn not to excuse their behavior (past or present). Next, they are brought to the point where they become fully aware of the pain and trouble they have caused others. When they have demonstrated sufficient guilt about their actions, they can go on to make a sincere commitment to change and then to demonstrate their sincerity by taking actions that are giving, caring, and considerate to others.

While this program has only recently been initiated by Czunder and is still being evaluated, the results appear to be encouraging. Only 10 percent of the offenders have voluntarily participated, but, of those, 40 percent have remained in the program and responded to treatment. Obviously, this approach is not only a cognitive moral one but one which also includes important emotional and behavioral aspects that are vital to its success. This may be yet another treatment approach that will prove successful with a very select group of amenable offenders. Since the program is voluntary and unresponsive participants are screened out, over time its chances of success should be improved.

These therapeutic approaches have not been without their detractors as much for their lack of theoretical depth and their assumptions about human motivation as for their tendency to overgeneralize about causes and cures of the many different psychological and behavioral problems their clients present. While these and other criticisms persist, efforts to research the value of these therapies continue and many practitioners are currently applying these techniques.

Other Treatment Approaches

Other methods and techniques have been employed in the treatment of youthful offenders. Of special concern to practitioners has been their belief that many of their youthful clients may not fully understand what is being communicated in the therapeutic relationship. This appears especially problematic when new and/or complex concepts are being introduced by the practitioner. Since delinquent youth are not always verbal, the therapist may often seek a more direct and less abstract means to help bridge what appears to be a communications gap in the treatment. In such circumstances common items such as a telephone, a Styrofoam cup or a camera creatively used can serve as a "prop" to help the therapist get his point across.

Harvill et al. (1984), for example, describe helping a youth understand the meaning of "taped messages" in relation to feeling "not OK" by handing him an audiotape cassette and scissors and asking him to cut out those parts of the tape containing "not OK" messages. In another example, a Styrofoam cup with holes punched in by pen was given to a youth with a history of flitting from person to person in search of self-validation and esteem. He was then asked why he might have difficulty filling the cup. The connection between the punctured cup and his own punctured sense of self-worth was quickly made apparent to the youth.

There has been a wide range of other approaches that have been implemented with some success in the treatment of delinquent youth including the following: biofeedback and video game feedback to improve self-concept and impulse control (Kappes and Thompson, 1985); transcendental meditation to reduce anxiety and impulsive behavior (Childs, 1973); vocationally oriented psychotherapy to change delinquent behavior and life-styles (Shore and Massimo, 1979); self-relaxation exercises to reduce adjustment problems of probationers (Elitzur, 1976); psychodrama to improve behavior among court-referred juvenile clinic participants (Carpenter and Sandberg, 1973); behavioral-cognitive techniques coupled with psychodrama to reduce acting-out tendencies and increase ego strength among delinquents (Carpenter and Sandberg, 1985); wilderness training to increase self-esteem and school attendance (Callahan Jr., 1985); foster family placement to help returning antisocial and delinquent youth make the transition to less restrictive community settings (Hawkins et al. 1985); and work therapy programs to reduce court contacts by probationers (Mann and Pratt, 1982).

One of the more widely recognized federally funded programs which has been replicated in a number of places around the country is Project New Pride (Charle, 1981; The Office of Juvenile Justice and Delinquency Prevention, 1985). This program, developed in Denver, Colorado and identified as a model for the treatment of hard-core youthful offenders (those with serious or violent histories and at least two prior court convictions), can be described as a community-based multiservice program. The multifaceted nature of this approach includes counseling, needs assessment, testing, alternative schooling, vocational therapy, employment, parental involvement, and ongoing follow-up services with social workers, probation officers, family, and teachers. This type of approach for "hard-core" youthful offenders appears to hold promise, as it emphasizes their special needs in a number of areas, including their need for structure, supervision, and comprehensive follow-up. The Project New Pride programs are currently being evaluated and the preliminary results suggest that they are at least as effective as some residential programs in which the financial costs are more than three times greater.

Residential Treatment

In instances where acting out and delinquency are generated by the severe psychopathological problems of youths, other treatment modalities have been implemented. An example of such an approach can be found in residential treatment programs located in hospital settings.

One that has met with some success has been described by Marohn et al. (1980). Their program, established at the Illinois State Psychiatric Institute, is designed to afford a therapeutic environment in which seriously disturbed and acting-out delinquent youth can learn through treatment to eventually reduce and control the extreme levels of anxiety and stress they experience in coping with their inner and outer conflicts. They are there essentially because they have failed to control their behavior, suffer from a lack of intrapsychic integration, and lack the external supports to maintain themselves in a less restrictive environment.

Acknowledging their debt to others, including Aichhorn (1935), Redl and Weinman (1957), Easson (1969), Bettelheim (1974), and Rinsley (1971), and building on their own experience over five years in treating these youths, Marohn et al. identify some of the considerations that have gone into meeting the needs of these delinquents as well as achieving their treatment goals.

By providing a dependable and physically safe environment and implementing a daily schedule of structural age-appropriate activities, the trained staff is able to observe the participants' behavior and make assessments that lead to the individualized treatment goals for each youth. By paying special attention to reducing much of the environmental instability and unpredictability that the youth has encountered, Marohn and his associates have set the stage for reducing the impact of external stress, thereby freeing the youth's psychological energy to focus more directly on his inner world and the personal and emotional conflicts he is experiencing. They state:

> Behaviorally disordered adolescents need an environment which helps them maintain their anxieties and feelings within a range they can tolerate. They must help examine their behavior, acknowledge it as their own and understand its effects on others. They must also be helped to name and identify the feelings they experience and also claim them as their own. Unacceptable behavior within a therapeutic milieu for delinquent adolescents needs to be understood, but not accepted, encouraged or overlooked. (p. 120)

To maintain a high level of therapeutic involvement, ongoing consideration is given to the youth's utilization of time, space, persons, and objects as diagnostic clues to his level of inner organization and possible developmental deficits as well as degree of personal growth. He is given opportunities within the therapeutic milieu to expand his horizons and increase his repertoire of skills beyond what he could achieve in the past. He soon discovers that he can "engage in productive learning, enjoy constructive activities, and explore problems in living. Therapy will in turn deal with successes and failure in these areas" (p. 20).

Much of this occurs on a daily basis through staff-patient interactions, which at times are confrontational, requiring limit setting and feedback. Staff provides external controls as needed, with the intention of supporting, through such intervention, the adolescent in testing reality and becoming more aware and introspective concerning his attitudes and behavior and how they impact on others. Initially, staff serves as the youth's "auxiliary ego and more flexible superego," and, in time, through such interventions, staff help the youth learn to control his impulses, achieve greater psychic integration, structure, and growth, all of which permit the possibility of increased utilization of verbal psychotherapy.

Programmatic components include the involvement of the youth's family where possible in the treatment milieu. In addition, other specialized interventions that are part of the design include remedial education, occupational and recreational therapy, and, when violent acting out occurs, the use of physical restraints if necessary to curb such behavior. The latter intervention is not considered punishment but rather a means of maintaining a safe and secure environment for all participants and staff. Essentially, it is another treatment intervention carried out in such a way as to maximize the therapeutic effects for the individual.

As with other effective residential treatment settings, attention is paid to anticipating possible problems and heading them off as much as possible. Much attention is also given to staff development and skill enhancement. Daily team meetings, ongoing staff supervision, participant case reviews, use of consultants on treatment issues as well as periodic self-assessments by administrative staff, and in-service staff training courses take place (p. 38). Because those who run the program believe that violently disturbed delinquent youth need the reinforcement of a well-structured and integrated program, it is made clear to participants from the beginning that there is a definite administrative hierarchy within the program. While decisions concerning the youth may be informed from a variety of sources, including the youth himself, all final decisions are made by staff.

While this discussion only begins to highlight some of the important factors which are incorporated into the residential care and inpatient treatment of disturbed delinquents, it, nevertheless, serves to exemplify, among other things, the type of staff skills, commitment, coordination, and planning that go into developing a milieu that can properly be identified as therapeutic.

Jones (1984), who surveys the literature and discusses other residential programs and techniques that have proven effective with delinquent youths exhibiting sociopathic disorders and chronic personality disorders with poor impulse control, describes the difficulty of evaluating such youth on an outpatient basis. He goes on to explore appropriate environmental, psychotherapeutic, pharmacological, and emergency management approaches within the hospital setting. Among the subjects he discusses in detail are the need to develop a therapeutic alliance, the necessary collaboration among hospital, family, and community (which must participate in providing a system of "step down" services for the youths) and the multifaceted nature of such programs for juveniles, which are usually more comprehensive than for adults, inasmuch as they also address the youth's educational, recreational, and vocational needs. Jones concludes by indicating that these programs are not only more humane but can be cost effective if we consider the high expenditures in time, money and resources for putting such youth through the criminal justice system.

One residential program which Jones mentions and that has received national recognition for its work with violent youth has been the Closed Adolescent Treatment Center (CATC) in Denver, Colorado. It is a 26-bed, maximum-security co-ed facility, but the population is mostly male, consisting of the following mix: sex offenders (50%), murderers and attempted murderers (25%), and those convicted of assorted other violent crimes (25%) (Agee and McWilliams, 1984).

Because of their stated difficulty in psychiatrically diagnosing and treating these youths, the term "aversive treatment evader" (ATE) was coined at the facility to describe them. Agee (1979) explains that the term "aversive" is used to describe the impact they have on those with whom they interact—who usually try to avoid them—and that the term "treatment evaders" refers to their history of being able to avoid or actively counter any prior rehabilitative attempts. By providing a therapeutic milieu that is strongly peer supported, using group therapy and individualized treatment goals, their well-trained residential staff who are mature and sensitive in their approach, are able to help the youths to navigate through each phase of treatment, beginning with their "early resistant" phase to their final "working through" phase of the program.

Treating what has been described as "violent," "incorrigible" and "involuntary" youth can place enormous pressures, both internal and external, on the program and its staff. Many such pressures, however, may have been lessened because of the careful program planning and design, resulting in staff-participant matching, ongoing staff supervision, an optimum staff-participant ratio (1:1), and in-service training of paraprofessionals by the professional staff. In addition, and most importantly, the ATE is informed from the very beginning that he or she will not be transferred to another institution, that in fact the CATC is the last institution to which he will be sent, and that staff are committed to an active, ongoing involvement with them in an effort to help them change. It must be noted that this message is to counter what the ATE had come to expect from institutions and staff elsewhere, namely, a series of staff and treatment separations and institutional changes, the average for these youths being eight prior institutional placements.

The program evaluation by Knott and Haiduk (1975) gave the CATC a high rating in treating these youth and meeting most of its internal and external goals. While it is evident from these programs that selected treatment approaches are indeed effective with delinquent populations, it would be mistaken to conclude that there have not been serious problems that have persisted in both the delivery of psychological services to these youth as well as an ongoing critical debate concerning the general value of those services.

In the case of the delivery of mental health services, the problems can best be highlighted by a general discussion of residential treatment programs, while a review of the evaluative research would best underscore the nature of the problems concerning treatment efficacy. Continuing our discussion of residential treatment programs, it becomes apparent that many such programs are hampered by lack of adequate funding, clear administrative responsibility, and program coordination. This is the case not only in residential facilities for the seriously disturbed and/or violent youthful offender but also in those for dependent youth with chronic psychiatric problems who are under state supervision.

The ongoing national nature of the problem has been highlighted by a recent 50-state survey of the Children's Defense Fund cited by Griffith et al. (1985), which concludes that mental health services for dependent children and adolescents are poorly coordinated and inadequately funded. Where available resources do exist, they are commonly misappropriated. Among their conclusions is that such youth are victims of "turf" wars among various agencies, or, because of a lack of consistent follow through, simply fall between the cracks, ending up with a conflicting patchwork of treatments from various institutions that for many results in more harm than good.

If this can be said to be the current status of mental health services for dependent youth, then we can begin to surmise the gross inadequacies that exist in the treatment of the violent and/or disturbed youthful-offender population.

To begin with, there have been few residential programs for such youth. While there is a wide range of residential treatment programs for delinquents, including programs with a specific focus on vocational training, academic achievement, alcohol and drug abuse, and social adjustment, as well as programs that have combined a mix of these concerns, few have focused on the violent juvenile delinquent and still fewer on the mentally or emotionally disturbed violent juvenile offender.

While, admittedly, the latter group is smaller than the media attention they receive would lead us to believe, they are, nevertheless, significant in terms of their treatment needs and the impact they can have on the juvenile justice and mental health systems. Part of the difficulty is not knowing what their full impact is, which has been discussed by Hartstone and Cocozza (1984), who in their review of this subject report that accurate data on a national level do not exist. They blame in part practitioners and behavioral science researchers who have not developed or used consistent definitions for such terms as "violent," "seriously mentally ill," or "emotionally disturbed" juvenile offenders.

While the authors indicate that a small number of states provide special facilities for treating such youth, these agencies rarely report on the degree of violence or disorder that their participants manifest, data which would be of use in gaining a clearer and broader perspective of the problem. The more typical situation that exists in most states is that the identifiable numbers of such youth who need to be in a secure facility and to receive mental health treatment are, in fact, either in a secure correctional facility receiving little or no mental health treatment or in a mental health facility that lacks either maximum security or an adequate treatment program. Part of the problem, as Hartstone and Cocozza go on to explain, is that the responsibility for administrating these programs varies from state to state, so that at times even the best-intentioned administrators may lack vital information and resources with which to develop and implement appropriate treatment programs.

While it can be seen that there have been serious problems connected to the delivery of mental health services to delinquents, there has also been a long and ongoing debate concerning the treatment value of mental health services for this population.

Treatment Efficacy

Rehabilitation and treatment programs for youthful offenders have been subject to controversy and attack almost from their very inception (Cullen and Gilbert 1982). However, few would disagree that the issue was most dramatically highlighted by the research completed by Martinson and his colleagues in 1970. They conducted an evaluation of 231 studies of offender treatment done between 1945 and 1967. Using reduced recidivism as the measure of treatment success, Martinson (1974) found that no treatment modality, from counseling to psychotherapy, from individual to group treatment, from vocational to educational training, whether in institutional or community settings, was effective. His conclusion, in brief, was that:

> With few isolated exceptions, the rehabilitative efforts that have been reported so far have had no appreciable effect on recidivism. (p. 25)

His pessimistic conclusions were soon translated in the public domain into a "nothing works" polemic against offender rehabilitation. Robert and Webb (1981), in their review of the critics' responses to Martinson et al. (1975), cited, among other objections to their findings, "methodological shortcomings" and the fact that some of the treatment programs they described as ineffective might not have been fully implemented because of lack of professional staff, insufficient funds, and other organizational restraints (p. 37).

Palmer (1975), an early and consistent critic of Martinson's (1974) often-quoted negative conclusions, argued that 48 percent of the studies summarized by Martinson yielded positive or partially positive results, which were virtually ignored in his "nothing works" conclusion. Among the positive results cited by Palmer were that amenable boys who received individual counseling had lower rates of recidivism, as did male recipients of group counseling, female recipients of group therapy and adolescent girls receiving therapy from social workers rather than psychologists and psychiatrists (pp. 133-134, 142).

In a more recent article, Palmer (1984) cited his own earlier (1978) work along with that of a recanting Martinson (1979) in concluding the following:

> In short, program results which were positive were conditional rather than all-inclusive or applicable across the board. Nevertheless, they often applied to a sizeable portion of the total target group, and the reduction in recidivism — while seldom vast — was usually substantial. (p. 252)

Others who convincingly responded to the charge that correctional rehabilitation was ineffective included Gendreau and Ross (1979), who undertook an assessment of the rehabilitation literature from 1973 to 1978. They argued that "the 'nothing works' belief reduced to its most elementary level suggests that criminal offenders are incapable of relearning or acquiring new behaviors," and asked incredulously, "Why . . . would this strange learning block be restricted to this population?" (pp. 465-466).

Their criteria used for selection of the studies to be included in the evaluation were that they have "at least a quasi-experimental design, contain a statistical analysis of the data, and report on a follow-up period of at least six months" (p. 469). Eventually, they included ninety-five correctional treatment programs that focused on the rehabilitation of antisocial behavior. Because many of the programs studied utilized more than one treatment modality, they were grouped under the following headings: "family and community intervention, contingency management, counseling, diversion, biomedical assistance and miscellaneous treatment" (p. 469). Included also were programs that dealt with related areas of alcoholism and drug abuse. It was reported that an overwhelming majority of the programs were successful in their efforts.

In their discussion as to why some programs were more successful than others at reducing recidivism, Gendreau and Ross indicated that the most successful programs did not rely on only one treatment modality and that they employed treatment derived in the main from a social learning model of behavior in which the focus was on modifying the antisocial behavior of the participants.

Seeking to avoid the mistakes of earlier programs whose limited treatment approach with offenders reduced their impact and gaining from the work of Gendreau and Ross and others, Palmer (1984) underscored the need for designing programs with a "differential treatment" modality to more appropriately reflect individual offender needs:

. . . future programs should be more closely adapted to the life circumstances and personal/interpersonal characteristics of offenders. . . .
Concentrated efforts and perhaps greater individualization are needed
in order to affect substantial change in at least serious offenders. (p.
255)

In addition to a "differential treatment" approach, the literature reveals the value of incorporating a voluntary approach wherever possible
to program participation. The importance of the youth's treatment
amenability was best underscored by Adam (1970). His work with institutionalized delinquents in California demonstrated, among other
things, that the amenable groups who received treatment by psychiatric
social workers had lower rates of recidivism than did amenables and
non-amenables who received no treatment. The worst results were with
non-amenables who were treated. Demonstrating the positive influence
of therapy on amenables, the Adam's work also points to the dangers of
involuntary treatment.

The more recent attempts to evaluate the treatment value of residential programs for delinquent youth have been those which made use
of a statistical technique known as meta-analysis (Garrett, 1985; Lipsey, 1986). This is a statistical method by which the investigator can
aggregate the results of a number of separate studies in a particular
area and, using the "effect size" (ES) measure of the difference between
the means of the treatment and control groups, can analyze them as
one set of data.

In her conclusions concerning the meta-analysis of 111 residential
treatment studies that utilized either a comparison group or pre-post test
design, Garrett found that "the results of the . . . meta-analysis are encouraging in that adjudicated delinquents were found to respond positively to treatment on many criteria. The change was modest in some
cases, substantial in others, but overwhelming in a positive direction"
(p. 306). Garrett, however, did not report any tests of statistical significance for overall mean effect sizes, whereas Lipsey, in a review of three
small-scale meta-analyses — including Garrett's study — found that, although the analyses have shortcomings, the pattern of results is relatively encouraging. In their discussion of the meta-analysis technique,
Frances and Clarkin (1981) have reported some of its general limitations
as well as identifying others who have highlighted the serious design
weaknesses of the individual treatment outcome studies that make up
the data bases of such research. Citing the questionable value of aggre-
gating studies in this way (vis-à-vis meta-analysis), they quote Kazdin

and Wilson (1978), who argue that such a "chain is no stronger than its accumulated weak links" (p. 538).

While acknowledging that meta-analysis "represents something of a lowest common denominator approach to assessing treatment efficacy" and discussing many of the acknowledged pitfalls connected to delinquency treatment research, Lipsey, nevertheless, cites improvements coming from the recent strengthening of research designs methodologies and treatment theory in such studies as well as the refinement of meta-analysis as a research technique. At present, Lipsey who is engaged in a comprehensive meta-analysis of such programs concludes:

> Again the early evidence from those research programs that combine strong treatment with strong research is very encouraging even if not yet definitive. (p. 25)

Conclusions

In examining the factors contributing to our understanding of the youthful offender and the etiology of delinquency, it becomes apparent that a range of factors, many of which are interactive, are implicated in its development. With such a variety of variables and processes involved in its development, it becomes easier to understand why an equally wide range of techniques and approaches have evolved over time to treat such troubling and troubled youth. With few exceptions, the treatments that have been proposed and implemented have had in common their attempt to build or rebuild a prosocial bond between the youth and his world. Unfortunately, this goal is not often met and frequently we do not even know why.

Over 60 years ago, Healy and Bronner (1926) made the following statement:

> It is amazing that modern civilization, with all its frank devotion to conceptions of efficiency, has not yet undertaken thoroughly critical studies of what really are the results of its dealing with delinquency and crime. Despite the tremendous equipment and expenditure for protection, detection, apprehending, for courts, jails and prisons, reformatory education, probation, little or nothing is spent to ascertain with care what is or is not accomplished. In industry, business or active science such an inquiry into results is regarded as absolutely fundamental. (p. 3)

It would seem that to a large degree this statement still holds true. Perhaps much of the confusion regarding treatment efficacy could be avoided if we asked different questions. Looking at outcome measures alone (e.g. recidivism) may be too unidimensional to truly assess the value of the program. It would make more sense to understand how a program operates and the ways in which it affects its participants than just examining the final product. In other words, we need to be able to relate program process to program goals. If we do, we will be in a better position to make those modifications necessary to make the program more effective. The attention paid to outcome alone is bound, at this point at least, to be misleading. There are a number of other factors which need to be attended to. These would include individual variables as well as treatment variables. As we have repeatedly noted, delinquency is not a unidimensional phenomena and thus cannot be responded to from a single point of view. Despite the practitioners' theoretical biases, individuals become delinquent for different reasons. Presumably, these individual differences among delinquents will interact in different ways with different treatment approaches. Understanding the nature of these interactions would allow program administrators to make the modifications so that their programs could work more effectively. As indicated earlier, there is no reason to believe that any single approach can be helpful to all adolescents.

Related to this would be an examination of: (a) the short-, mid- and long-range program goals; (b) the treatment assumptions regarding the most effective way to reach those goals; (c) the ways in which various program modalities interact (for example, how the personal characteristics of the therapist interact with the characteristics of the adolescent in any given treatment approach); (d) the degree to which treatment assumptions and plans are actually being implemented; and (e) what modifications need to be made in order to improve the program. Treatment programs need to be viewed as ongoing processes, not as final statements of what is helpful. We need to constantly look at what refinements need to be made and have a built-in process that allows for systematic evaluation and modification. While relatively few programs operate in this way, recent reviews of the literature (Blakely and Davidson, 1984; Lipsey, 1986; Patterson, 1986) indicate that progress, in fact, is being made in the area of methodology and program evaluation which hopefully will lead to useful refinements in the area of treatment.

Chapter X

THE PREDICTION AND PREVENTION
OF DELINQUENCY

IN THIS concluding chapter we will discuss some of the issues which relate to the early identification and prevention of seriously delinquent behavior. In a sense, this also constitutes a summary of earlier chapters, since the various developmental, psychosocial, and biological factors which have been presented as being related to delinquency are not surprisingly among those which are used in the early identification of delinquents. In addition, there are also other important variables that we will address here.

We are aware of the fact that there are risks associated with labeling young children as potential delinquents or first offenders as potential recidivists. Nonetheless, there may be greater risks involved for the child in not providing the necessary additional services which conceivably may allow him or her to live a more fulfilling life.

Prediction always involves probabilities, not certainties. While certain factors may be correlated to certain outcomes, the correlations are never perfect. This is as true in public health as it is in psychology. For example, in the field of public health, it is known that there is a correlation between cigarette smoking and lung cancer and heart disease. Consequently, there are public health campaigns to encourage people to stop smoking or not to start. However, not smoking does not guarantee that any given individual will not develop these diseases, nor does smoking guarantee that he will. It will, however, have an impact on smokers as a group, even though it falsely predicts that some individuals will develop cancer if they continue to smoke. To a large degree, the same issues hold true for the early identification of delinquents. To the extent that we can identify those factors in early childhood which are associated with delinquency in adolescence, we can institute remedial or preventive measures. At the same time, however, since prediction is not perfect, there will be some children who will be falsely identified as predelinquents and others who will be missed who do, in fact, become delinquent. The ratio of correct-to-incorrect identifications depends on a number of factors which we will discuss below; however, the fact is that an insufficient effort is being placed on preventative services at this time despite the fact, as we will demonstrate, that there appear to be a number of stable indicators of potential difficulties discernible in early childhood.

Early Childhood Factors

There are at least two factors which appear to make prediction possible with a reasonable degree of accuracy. One is the relative stability of certain personality characteristics from early childhood onward, and the other is the fact that seriously deliquent adolescents often share similar family backgrounds. These two issues are probably not totally unrelated.

With regard to the former, Lefkowitz et al. (1977) found that children rated as aggressive by their peers in the primary grades tend to be rated as aggressive by their peers when they were 18. Further, these individuals were three times more likely than those not so rated to have police records by age 19. In a follow-up study, Eron (1987) found that many of these same individuals remained aggressive through age 30.

> Aggression manifested during interactions with peers in early elementary school grades predicted criminal behavior, number of moving traffic violations, convictions for driving while intoxicated, aggressiveness toward spouses, and how severely the subjects punished their own children. (p. 439)

Farrington (1978), as part of the Cambridge Study in Delinquent Development, studied 411 boys from a working-class neighborhood in London. He found that 48 percent of the violent delinquents had been rated as aggressive at age 8 as compared to 21 percent of those not rated as aggressive at that time. He concluded that "teachers' ratings of aggressive behavior in class can predict future violent crime" (p. 82). While not dealing solely with early aggressive behavior, Glick (1972) found that 79.5 percent of boys who became delinquent in a sample of 301 boys had been reported by their teachers, during the first three years of school, as manifesting behavior problems in class.

Olweus (1979) reviewed and reevaluated 16 longitudinal studies of aggressive behavior in males. He found that, while the degree of stability of the measure of aggressiveness varied depending upon the subject's age when the measure was first taken and the amount of time between measures, the overall degree of stability of aggressive behavior in males was quite substantial. He concluded that this indicated that aggressive behavior may, to a large degree, exist in some individuals independently of environmental circumstances and may be understood, like intelligence, to be a relatively stable personality trait. Olweus's findings are important for two reasons. First, to the degree that such behavior is stable, it enhances the probability of making accurate predictions. Second, if his conclusions are correct, they suggest that the modification of this behavior may be quite difficult, a point substantiated by a large number of outcome studies of some treatment programs but in conflict with others such as Patterson's (1986).

Stewart (1985), reviewing the concept of aggressive conduct disorder (ACD), noted that such children tend to fight more with other children, are more quarrelsome, steal outside the home, attack adults, lie, etc. This type of behavior occurs four times more frequently in males than females and is usually noticed by parents sometime between the child's first and fifth birthday. However, he noted that there were differences between children who were brought to psychiatric clinics at an early age (before 10 years of age) and those who came later. He suggested that this might indicate that there were two developmental pathways for developing ACD: the early onset, reflecting a biological transmission from father to son, and the latter onset, resulting from a lack of adequate supervision. Stewart noted that a significant percentage of these children (up to 75%) either became antisocial as adults, developed serious psychiatric problems, or never adjusted. The latter raises an interesting issue, specifically that the final outcome of ACD or other factors associated with antisocial or problematical behavior in early childhood need not necessarily be delinquency. Such difficulties may predict other forms of social maladjustment in later life. West and Farrington (1973) followed children from high-risk backgrounds who did not become delinquent and found that many of those individuals suffered from rather marginal social existences, including isolation, unemployment and a lack of intimate relationships. Rutter and Giller (1984) noted that:

> This finding, together with the oft-repeated observation that recidivist delinquent juveniles and adults frequently show a host of other interpersonal and social problems, emphasizes that serious and persisting

delinquency is not just a matter of activities which happen to be against the law. (p. 224)

Their conclusion is neither surprising nor unique and can be found throughout the literature on the development of juvenile delinquency.

Family Factors

As we noted above, the factors associated with delinquency are also predictive of it. This seems most true in relation to family factors. We have discussed these earlier in terms of the relationship between psychosocial factors and delinquency; however, since they are highly related to prediction, it is appropriate to briefly review some of them here. [The correlation between problematic behavior and family background begins early in life. Erickson et al. (1985) found that children whose emotional needs were not consistently met as infants were more frequently described by their teachers as hostile, socially isolated, and/or disconnected in the preschool setting. They conclude that the

> quality of attachment at 12 and 18 months is a strong predictor of behavior at age 4½-5. . . . Furthermore, quality of attachment is an assessment of the quality of care and support provided in the first year of life and, as such, is also predictive of subsequent care. (p. 165)]

Further, they suggest that if the child's behavior does improve, it is as a result of changes in the quality of care to which the child was exposed.

A number of authors, including Farrington (1978), Bandura (1959), and Eron (1987), have found that harsh and sometimes inconsistent parental discipline is associated with violent delinquency in adolescence, although Eron (1987) noted that this is also dependent upon the degree to which the child identified with the father. Children who were harshly punished but were highly identified with the father were significantly less aggressive in school than those who were harshly punished but not identified with the fathers. (While it is not clear what accounts for the high vs. low level of identification, presumably it is related to a better quality of bonding between the parent and child.) Farrington (1978) found that having criminal parents before age 10, poor parental supervision, separations, daring temperament and low IQ all related positively to violent delinquency. We also ought to bear in mind Lewis et al.'s (1981) finding of a higher percentage of psychiatric disturbances and criminal histories among parents of delinquents. In addition, the studies mentioned earlier in the text have suggested a strong relationship between criminality in the biological parent and delinquency in the offspring, regardless of the criminality of the adoptive parent. Stewart et al. (1980) also found that boys with aggressive conduct disorder had a higher percentage of biological fathers who were either criminal and/or had a higher rate of psychiatric disorders than average.

Patterson's (1986) interpretation regarding the lack of requisite management skills on the part of parents in dealing with their children is also of interest. However, given the high levels of psychopathology and criminality in the parents, it would seem that management skills may just be the "tip of the iceberg." Parents who lack the capacity to love and form some empathetic bond with their children cannot be expected to do much in the way of raising them even if they do become skilled behavior modifiers.

Prediction

Given this consistency it would seem that predicting delinquency in young children ought to be a relatively straightforward and easy task. However, difficulties arise in several areas. The first of these had to do with the problem of defining delinquency. As we noted in Chapter II, this is not always a simple matter. Definitions vary from state to state and from county to county. Furthermore, the discretionary powers of the police can determine who is or is not brought into the system and thus defined as delinquent, at least in terms of official statistics. Consequently, a technique for predicting whether an individual will become delinquent by age 15 using the definition of court contact may be correct in county A but incorrect in county B, because the police in county A are more likely to bring individuals to the attention of the court. Hence, any study that is designed to predict delinquency must clearly state how delinquency is being defined, since the definition will constitute the outcome criteria for that study. However, the criteria may vary in literature from at least one police contact to 21 or more self-reported acts (Loeber and Dishion, 1983).

The criteria used for describing delinquency will also, by definition, indicate how frequently it occurs in the population, also known as the base rate. A very broad definition, e.g. any offense including a status offense, would result in apparently very high base rates of delinquency among 15-year-olds, whereas a very strict definition, e.g. conviction on two or more felonies, would result in relatively low base rates. Base rates in turn will have an impact on the effectiveness of a predictive device. It is much more difficult to accurately predict an event which is quite rare than to predict an event which has a probability of 0.50. Hence, it can be statistically demonstrated that the same technique for predicting delinquency would appear relatively more accurate in populations where the rate of delinquency comes closer to 50 percent, such as impoverished urban areas than where the rate of reported delinquency is relatively low, such as wealthy suburban areas.

		Delinquent	Non-Delinquent	
		Valid Positives	False Positives	
	Poor School Behavior	20	8	28
Teachers' Ratings				
		False Negatives	Valid Negatives	
	Good School Behavior	10	62	72
Totals		30	70	100

Predicted Values

Actual Base Rate

Figure 1.

Prediction techniques yield four possible outcomes (see Fig. 1): valid positives, i.e. correctly identifying a "predelinquent"; false positives, i.e. incorrectly identifying a "predelinquent"; false negatives, i.e. failing to identify a "predelinquent"; and valid negatives, i.e. correctly identifying a "non-predelinquent." In the example in Figure 1, the column sums represent the total numbers of eventual delinquents and non-delinquents out of a population of 100 or the base rate (30 delinquents vs. 70 nondelinquents). Using teachers' ratings of the child's behavior in the second grade as our hypothetical predictive criteria, we see that this criteria correctly labels 20 of the 30 future delinquents (valid positives) and 62 of the 70 non-delinquents (valid negatives). At the same time, it mislabels 8 of the 10 non-delinquents as pre-delinquent (false positives) and misses 10 of the 30 future delinquents (false negatives).

In evaluating the usefulness of any predictive device, one has to bear in mind the value of a correct identification as well as the costs of incorrectly labeling a child as potentially delinquent. If the latter is a problem, we could make the predictive criteria more stringent and thus perhaps reduce the rate of false positives; however, we would do so at the risk of missing a greater number of children who will become delinquent.

Perhaps, the most widely publicized prediction scales were those developed by the Gluecks (Glueck, S. and Glueck, E., 1950, 1972). The earlier version of their prediction of scale was based on five social factors, including discipline of the boy by father, supervision by mother, affection of father for the boy, affection of mother for the boy, and cohesiveness of the family. While the scale appeared to have much promise, in practice, it tended to overpredict delinquency, particularly when applied to families in which the father was absent (Craig and Glick, 1963). Craig and Glick modified the scale so that only information on the mother's discipline, affection, and family cohesiveness was used. This resulted in a lower false positive rate and more accurate prediction of delinquency. In fact, in a reanalysis of the result of this study, Loeber and Dishion (1983) found that the scale predicted approximately 80 percent better than would be expected by chance, which is quite high, since the predictions were based on ratings made when the child was 6 and the outcome measures taken when the child was 16. While the studies on prediction are too numerous to present here, other variables have proven useful in predicting delinquency. These include criminality on the part of the parent (Robins et al., 1975) and teachers' ratings of potential delinquency (Scarpitti, 1964).

Recidivism

The issues which relate to the prediction of recidivism are not appreciably different from those that relate to the prediction of delinquency in early childhood. In fact, the majority of studies which relate early childhood behavior and/or family factors to delinquency in adolescence use serious or violent delinquency as an outcome criteria. As such, they are not predicting a single delinquent act but rather a pattern of behavior. For example, Craig and Glick (1968) correlated teachers' ratings of children's behavior in the first through third grade with "serious and/or persistent" delinquency in adolescence. Further, as we have noted, delinquency tends to be underreported, so even those studies which use a single court or police contact as an outcome criterion may well be identifying individuals with a pattern of repeated antisocial behavior.

However, we may also want to be able to identify those individuals who, once they have been brought to the attention of the court or police, are likely to continue to commit crimes. In these instances, the individual is already by definition a delinquent and so measures of predicting recidivism are in a sense also measures of the success of the interventions first made in response to the behavior. For first offenses, this might include cautioning, probation, or diversion programs of some sort.

Most youths are not chronic offenders. For example, Wolfgang (1983) found that only 7.5 percent of the adolescents in his birth cohort study were responsible for 61 percent of the recorded offenses. However, as both Rutter and Giller (1984) and Loeber and Dishion (1983) note, most studies of first-time offenders indicate a reconviction rate of approximately 50 percent. Thus, conviction itself becomes a predictor of future convictions. This is particularly true if the conviction or arrest occurs during early adolescence (Ganzer and Saranson, 1973). Similarly, Osborn and West (1980) note that the reconviction rates for individuals convicted before age 14 were significantly higher than those whose first conviction occurred between 17 and 19 years of age. Further, as we have noted above, chronic recidivists tend to come from more psychologically damaged families and live a more antisocial or marginal life-style during their adolescence than do one-time offenders (Osborn and West, 1980).

Characteristics of repeat offenders are studied through treatment programs as well as by examining the characteristics of those individuals who fail to benefit from them. Hollander and Turner (1985) studied 200 incarcerated delinquents. They found that 47 percent had borderline IQs (a finding similar to Ganzer and Saranson's, 1973) and 34 percent suffered from severe personality disorders. Further, they note that almost all subjects came from backgrounds of family stress and disorganization. Brandt (1979) found that a significant percentage of boys judged to be unsuitable for a day treatment program for recidivist delinquent adolescents had histories of behavior difficulties in school prior to the fourth grade and/or scored high on the Social Maladjustment and/or Asocial Index scales of the Jesness Inventory (Jesness, 1966). Goldberg and Johnson (1980) found that the best predictor of success of 109 boys in state rehabilitation centers was the number and severity of previous offenses, i.e. the more serious and frequent the prior offenses, the greater the probability of recidivism.

Other strong predictors of recidivism include teachers' and parents' reports of stealing (Mitchell and Rosa, 1981), teachers' reports of aggressiveness between ages 13 and 15 (Mulligan et al., 1963), and serious drug abuse during the past year (Osborn, 1978). All of the above findings for recidivism are consistent with the predictors of delinquency made in early childhood. Individuals who become seriously recidivist delinquents are not behaviorally or psychologically like the rest of the population of adolescents, nor are they similar to the population of one- or two-time offenders.

Leober and Dishion (1983) conclude that:

> Composite measures of parental family management techniques tended to be most predictive of delinquency, followed by the child's problem behavior. Reports of the child stealing, lying or truancy come next followed by criminality or antisocial behavior of the family members. . . . (p. 87)

What is of interest is the remarkable consistency of the findings in this area. Children who become seriously delinquent tend to manifest behavior problems from an early age (8 or earlier), become adjudicated early in their adolescence, and have unloving, poorly skilled parents. Frequently, the parents are criminal themselves and the children typically have less than average IQ's. We know that such backgrounds typically are associated with severe forms of psychopathology of which violent delinquency is only one manifestation.

The use of predictors is not without detractors. For example, Wedge (1978) found that predictors were not always accurate, that they were frequently considered an invasion of privacy and viewed as harmful to those identified by them. However, here the problem may lie in labeling the child, particularly the young child, as "predelinquent" when in fact he or she might be better identified as a child in need of extra support and help. This is not suggested as a euphemism but rather because it may more accurately describe the psychological status and vulnerability of the preadolescent. There is nothing unusual about this. It is just good community mental health practice to identify those individuals who are in need of assistance. Nonetheless, as we will see, there is frequently a large gap between theory and practice. While we may in fact be able to identify those factors associated with future delinquency, it is obvious from criminal justice statistics that we have not been overly successful in preventing it. We will examine the reasons for this next.

Prevention

There appears to be little agreement as to whether delinquency prevention services should be targeted to youths generally, to youths in high-risk communities, to those youths that can be identified as high risk in those communities, or simply to those who have already been adjudicated delinquent and are still residing in those communities or in institutions for young offenders, in which case prevention services would be directed at reducing recidivism.

A continuing problem is that many prevention programs have lacked specificity with regard to those they serve, and when they have attempted to focus on a particular segment of the population, they have often failed to stay within their own screening guidelines. In addition, they have often neglected to base their intervention strategies on theories of delinquency causation and/or clearly specify their program goals and objectives. Consequently, whether or not they prevent delinquency, their evaluations (where available) often fail to explain the reasons for either their successes or their failures.

The degree to which many delinquency prevention programs go unevaluated or inadequately evaluated can be surmised from the work of Wright and Dixon (1977), who surveyed approximately 6,600 reports of such programs carried out between 1965 and 1974. They found only 96 reports which included any empirical data on program effects and most of these were "of low validity by scientific criteria and of low utility for decision makers" (p. 57). They concluded that as a result they could not recommend any delinquency-prevention strategy. Considering the number of prevention program studies that have been conducted over the past twenty years, with estimates running as high as 10,000 and only a small percentage of them being evaluated, it is understandable that there continue to be many enormous gaps in our knowledge concerning this subject.

In their review of the literature, Van Voorhis et al. (1983) focus not only on the lack of evaluation studies but also on a number of weaknesses encountered in the design of these prevention programs and conclude that some of these flaws are excusable, since:

> . . . the current state of crimogenic theory does not necessarily facilitate program planning. Many of the theories convey broad theoretical constructs, suggestive of numerous program strategies. Conversely, single programs are operative to numerous theories. Moreover, building a program on a single theory of delinquency implies that all offenders are alike, when in fact, due to the heterogeneous nature of the

offender population, most theories are only applicable to certain portions of the offender population. (p. 51)

Other problems inherent in such research are methodological, including the design of measures which are both valid and reliable, a problem alluded to earlier. Difficulties involved in using control groups are frequently just as insuperable as are adequate short- and long-range follow-up activities, given the attrition of many subjects whose life situations often lack sufficient stability for them to be located and included in the data base. Other difficulties often found in evaluation research of delinquency-prevention programs are those which affect evaluation research generally. Guttentag (1977) states:

> Program directors and staff in the field are indifferent or openly hostile toward the evaluation researchers who descend on them, asking what seem to be irrelevant questions. Program people are also alienated by the research armentarium that forces them either to lie or admit they are guilty of unpardonable sins such as lack of randomization, inadequate control groups, and, even worse, having permitted the program to change in ways that were not made explicit in the beginning. (p. 21)

Finally, other problems directly and indirectly related to evaluation develop when programs are forced to divert attention, energy, and resources from their mission to become embroiled in local political battles in efforts to secure sufficient funding to remain viable.

Earlier Prevention Efforts

In an effort to discuss the results of prevention programs which were in fact viable and able to incorporate the use of experimental and control groups, Berleman (1980) examined ten such programs that were in operation between 1937 and 1968 and which maintained rigorous evaluative procedures for examining programmatic outcomes. He included only those prevention programs whose participants were voluntary. While these participants had had serious antisocial propensities, they had not been adjudicated delinquent and were, therefore, considered predelinquent. As such, they were free from any mandatory compliance deriving from legal sanctions for refusal to participate in the program. Berleman did not include any studies of institutionalized delinquents whom he felt could not be categorized as having participated in a truly preventive program in the primary sense of that term.

Among the ten delinquency-prevention experiments he included in his report were the Cambridge-Somerville Youth Study, the Boston

Midcity Project, the Columbus, Ohio Youth Development Program and the Chicago Youth Development Project. These programs and all but one of the others studied by Berleman were considered ineffective: treatment produced no better results among the experimental group than did an absence of treatment among the controls. The one program that was judged to be effective was the Wincroft Youth Project. Unfortunately, this project, which was conducted in Manchester, England, had so many unusual aspects — in terms of sociocultural differences, program design and focus, staffing, and goals — that it was neither useful for purposes of comparison nor relevant to the needs and experiences of youths in the United States. In addition, Rutter and Giller (1983) reported that a one-year follow-up of the Wincroft youths revealed that "the encouraging results achieved faded with time" (p. 301).

Walker et al. (1976) have also reviewed the results of prevention programs. Tracing such efforts back to William Healy, they have described a wide range of programs and services that have been implemented from the time of Healy until the 1970s. They have included counseling programs, educational and vocational training programs, recreational diversionary and employment projects, as well as community development programs employing a multitude of personnel including therapists, caseworkers, vocational counselors, teachers, employment interviewers, and detached street workers. Among those who, along with Walker et al., have found little cause for optimism in their mixed or negative reviews have been Powers and Witmer (1951), Miller (1959), Meyer et al. (1965), Lundman et al. (1976), Wright and Dixon (1977), Newton (1978), Shorr et al. (1979), and Lishner and Hawkins (1980).

It is interesting to note that the same issues being raised today regarding the state of our knowledge concerning delinquency prevention and the continuing vulnerability of prevention programs to critical assessments for their evaluative shortcomings were raised nearly thirty years ago by Robinson (1959), who stated:

> Prevention programs do not (a) define precisely the nature of the services offered, (b) describe the customers, or (c) spell out how the effectiveness of the program will be measured. (p. 364)

Recent Developments

While the results of prevention programs have not been very promising thus far, there are a number of recent developments in the field that are encouraging, including the work of Hawkins et al. (1980), to categorize delinquency-prevention programs in an effort to bring about a more coherent approach to the problems of planning and evaluation.

In *A Typology of Cause-Focused Strategies of Delinquency Prevention,* Hawkins et al. identify 12 delinquency-prevention strategies from an extensive number of approaches, each of which derives from a presumed delinquency cause which it seeks to address and remedy by specific methods.

Among the 12 strategies to delinquency prevention, they found the following: biological/psychological strategies, psychological/mental health strategies, criminal influence reduction strategies, and role development/role enhancement strategies. In the case of psychological/ mental health strategies, for example, the assumptions are "that delinquency originates in internal psychological states viewed as inherently maladaptive or pathological. They [the cause-focused programs] seek to directly alter such states and/or environmental conditions thought to generate them." Role development/role enhancement strategies, on the other hand, "assume that delinquency stems from a lack of opportunity to be involved in legitimate roles or activities which youths perceive as personally gratifying. They [the programs] attempt to create such opportunities . . ." (pp. vii-ix). In addition to the 12 strategies that are identified, the authors also provide a framework for developing, planning, and assessing the outcomes of the prevention efforts.

In a follow-up volume entitled *Juvenile Delinquency Prevention: A Compendium of 36 Program Models,* Wall et al. (1981) review 36 prevention programs that were selected from a national sample of 512 programs as models in cause-focused delinquency-prevention planning. The authors indicate that not all of these 36 programs have been proven effective. Only two have been tested for delinquency-prevention efforts with adequate research designs, and while many of the other 34 "have shown positive results, their evaluations were not sufficiently rigorous to allow the conclusion that the programs themselves were responsible for the observed results" (p. 2).

Some might conclude that such prevention programs, which at first glance appear to yield little in the way of positive results, are not worth the effort. Others have argued that delinquency prevention might not even be considered a legitimate field of inquiry (White, 1981, pp. ix-x), let alone a distinct category of programming (Westinghouse National Issue Center, 1979, p. 1). Still others, however, have been somewhat more positive about the possible benefits of delinquency prevention.

Lipsey (1984) has argued that such programs can, in addition to producing the humane benefits implicit in the prevention of delinquency, be cost effective. Using data from the Los Angeles County delinquency-prevention program, which encompasses thirteen projects and handles more than 10,000 juveniles a year, Lipsey argues that such programs can be considered a cost-effective strategy provided that:

1. Juvenile clients selected for the programs have a high delinquency risk but have not already committed serious offenses.
2. Treatment is successful in preventing at least some future delinquent acts.
3. The financial benefits to law enforcement agencies and the juvenile justice system — because of fewer cases handled and smaller sums of money paid out to crime victims for damages and personal injuries — are significantly less than the cost of the program.

Using a formula to derive benefit-cost ratio, which he likens to a "return on investment," Lipsey found that for every dollar spent by Los Angeles County for family counseling and other services to prevent delinquency, a savings of $1.40 was generated. Making generalizations about such programs, he is cautiously optimistic, concluding that, if highly selective, they could significantly reduce the cost of juvenile justice in this country (pp. 279-297).

Meanwhile, attempts to sharpen our thinking regarding the way we define and use the term "delinquency prevention" continue. Researchers in the area include Lejins (1967), Johnson et al. (1979), Weis and Hawkins (1981), Hawkins and Wall (1980), and Van Voorhis et al. (1983).

Johnson et al. (1979) interpret and explain the following definition of delinquency prevention which appeared in a publication of the Office of Juvenile Justice and Delinquency Prevention (1977):

"Delinquency Prevention" refers to activities designed to reduce the incidence of delinquent acts and directed to youth who are not being dealt with as a result of contact with the juvenile justice system.

They argue that for programs to qualify as prevention progams they must be carefully and rigorously designed for the purpose of prevention, that their focus in terms of activity should be to reduce those acts which constitute delinquent behavior, and, finally, that such criteria do not allow for the inclusion of probation, incarceration, forms of diversion, and other activities which have brought youth into contact with the juvenile justice system (p. 24).

Regarding the latter, Johnson et al. state, "These activities are so clearly a reaction to actual or alleged delinquent acts, that they do not belong in the terrain of delinquency prevention" (p. 25). Supporting this view are Weis and Hawkins (1981), who, drawing from the work of Lejins (1967), state:

> . . . diversion and deinstitutionalization—are primarily control strategies simply because they are aimed at previously identified juvenile offenders. They are only indirectly preventive because they do not and cannot prevent initial behavior(s) which brings the juvenile into the juvenile justice system. At best, these kinds of interventions may inhibit further judicial processing but they are not "pure" prevention. (p. 2)

In a related effort to increase our precision in defining delinquency prevention, Van Voorhis et al. (1983) have reviewed the literature on the development of the public health model which has been widely used in relation to delinquency prevention. As they explain, the public health model is one which has three different preventive levels. The first is primary prevention, which is devoted to strategies aimed at eliminating any harmful conditions in the environment that might facilitate the onset of the disease in the first place. The next level is secondary prevention, which aims at screening for those who are most susceptible to developing the illness either because they live in "high-risk" environments or because they exhibit "high-risk" indicators of the disease. The third level is tertiary prevention, in which those afflicted with the illness are treated to cure them, prevent death, or prevent further physical deterioration (p. 6).

Among those who have applied this model to delinquency prevention have been Bartollas (1985) and Kralj and Allen (1982). The latter describe how specific delinquency preventions would occur at the different levels of intervention:

> The primary prevention approaches, such as Outward Bound projects, are designed to counteract harmful etiological factors before they produce ill effects. In secondary approaches (e.g., community correction centers), the goal is to identify and treat difficulties early, before they become major adjustment problems. With tertiary prevention, which can also be described as rehabilitation, the effort is to promote psychological adaptation, and reduce recidivism in those who have been adjudicated delinquent. (p. 233)

Van Voorhis et al. raise a number of questions concerning the appropriateness of the public health model as applied to deliquency prevention and are particularly critical of placing tertiary services under the rubric of prevention. Further criticism is that on the tertiary level the boundaries between prevention and treatment are blurred. Finally, from the use of this model emerges the implication that we know as much about the causes of social problems as public health officials know about the causes of medical problems, which is certainly not the case in a field such as delinquency prevention, which remains very much exploratory and experimental. As Simmons et al. (1981) state: "Current knowledge is such that the exact circumstances required to cause a child's delinquent behavior are unknown . . . there are no certain conditions that, if changed, will invariably prevent delinquent behavior . . . " (p. 5). Still another problem raised by the earlier cited results of the self-report studies is that a wide range of unreported and undetected delinquent behavior exists, which makes it very nearly impossible to expect that we can in fact screen out youths who have committed such delinquent acts for a "pure" prevention program. Therefore, to speak of such prevention in this sense is absurd. At the other end of the spectrum are those we would wish to screen into the tertiary programs. There, too, because of what studies have shown concerning the ways some youths arbitrarily become involved with the juvenile justice system, we may in fact be including under this rubric adjudicated one-time non-serious offenders with others whose chronic and violent delinquent acts would more appropriately characterize them as future career criminals in need of detention in a restrictive and secure environment.

The Public Health Model

It would indeed appear that many of the criticisms of the public health model as directly applied to delinquency prevention are valid, but the authors believe that it continues to have applicability to delinquency prevention if we reconceptualize our thinking.

The public health model of prevention of disease was adapted by Caplan (1964) and applied to the prevention of mental and emotional disorders; it was also adapted for purposes of delinquency prevention. It is the contention of the authors that, given the limitations of our current knowledge on the subject of delinquency prevention and the unresolved controversies surrounding it, we must proceed, at least for the time being, from a broader context, recognizing the relationship between mental health problems and maladjusted behavior generally and delinquency in particular. Even if this means that we cannot target prevention efforts at delinquents specifically, society would be well served if we were able to target these services at the causes of maladjusted behavior generally, as, clearly, delinquency is only one manifestation of maladaptive behavior that can occur. Furthermore, mental health problems of many types, including, for example, alcoholism and drug abuse, can eventually cause delinquency, either in the individual himself or in his children, who may become the victims of their own troubled and maladjusted parents.

While the boundaries between primary and secondary prevention may not always be clear or agreed upon, it is not within the purview of this chapter to resolve the intricacies of this complex issue, but rather to suggest strategies for delinquency prevention that, depending upon the targeted group, may at times be considered primary prevention and at other times secondary prevention. Nutrition programs, for example, for pregnant women would, if implemented with the general population, be considered primary; when implemented at lunchtime with aggressive and hyperactive children in a school setting, they would be considered secondary. Finally, such programs, when implemented in an institution for delinquent youth, would be considered tertiary prevention, a topic already discussed at length under the rubric of rehabilitation in Chapter IX.

Practical Considerations

Clearly, a key element in the prevention of delinquency on any level is the family. Prediction studies indicate the critical role played by the family in the etiology of delinquency, and the family is no less significant a factor in prevention.

The combination of negative family and developmental factors described earlier in this chapter makes such youths most vulnerable to a wide range of possible disturbances. Obviously, prompt preventive intervention, diagnosis, and treatment in the earliest stages can resolve problems that might otherwise persist and even grow into more serious conditions in adolescence and adulthood. Much of this prevention effort, however, must be undertaken within the context of the youth's family. Given the role the family plays in the etiology of maladaptive behavior, including delinquency, it is imperative that family members be considered for inclusion in all aspects of prevention.

The Family and Prevention

Responding to the generally chaotic conditions found in many delinquent homes they studied, the Gluecks (1972) underscored the importance of helping to improve family life for these children through comprehensive programs. They also recommend the establishment of more community health facilities to help educate, counsel, and guide young prospective parents regarding family planning, prenatal care and health-promoting child-rearing practices, explaining that:

> . . . a great deal of constructive effort can and should be put forth to improve family life and the guidance of children. . . . This is true of families generally, but particularly of those in which parental attitudes and practices endanger the growing personality of the child and tend to instill unwholesome and antisocial attitudes. Certainly, the great majority of delinquents when compared with the control group of nondelinquents, are shown to be the product of unwise, often cruel, parental attitudes and actions. (p. 126)

Obviously, we cannot know with certainty which child will be affected by such difficult family constellations and conditions to become delinquent; we do know, however, that these circumstances play an important role in the etiology of a wide range of disturbing maladaptive behaviors among children. This has long been recognized by the mental health profession which has engendered a vast body of literature on preventive measures. The concept of prevention in mental health has not been without controversy (Lamb and Zusman, 1982; Levine and Perkins, 1980; Glasscote, 1981), but prevention work goes on with families through intervention directed at critical times in the child's development, including the fetal stage, infancy, preschool, and school-age periods (Berlin, 1979).

Hawkins (1972) has recommended mandatory parental training at an early age in the public schools, while Clegg (1981) has advocated the implementation of STEP programs (Systematic Training for Effective Parenting) in which parents are taught common sense child-rearing principles and then serve as group leaders for other parents. Brown and Reid (1976) have described a telephone consulting service they call a "warm line" for parents having problems with children under five years of age. This service provides information, guidance, and reassurance to parents in need who are also given an opportunity to vent their feelings.

Others have discussed prevention with couples in terms of improving communication, expressing affection, and engaging in constructive fighting (Hinkle and Moore, 1971). Still others have focused on competence building and social problem solving with children and adolescents (Durlak, 1983). Patterson (1982) has reported that parents of extremely antisocial children in the Oregon Social Learning Center (discussed elsewhere) were able to learn the necessary skills to change the problem child's behavior as well as their own (p. 304).

Moving in another direction, Kairys et al. (1981) have described a program to educate college students about health issues related to child-bearing and parenting, including personal health, nutrition, physical fitness, stress management, and external risks to the developing fetus. The question of nutrition has also been raised by Schellhart (1977) and Rimland and Larson (1981), who have addressed the issue of prevention through a discussion of findings relating linkages between nutritional and ecological factors and learning and behavioral disorders, including delinquency. Such factors as maternal smoking, hypoglycemia, malnutrition, food allergies, and additives, as well as lead and other toxic metals and pollutants, are discussed, along with their conviction that some of these factors enhance the potential for antisocial and violent behavior.

The aforementioned discussion highlights only a small part of the effort that has been undertaken by mental health professionals to deal with the prevention of maladaptive behavior. It does not begin to touch upon the work that has been done with self-help groups or with such specific populations as minority members, neglected and abused children, and drug abusers, nor does it deal specifically with efforts made by mental health professionals in private non-profit youth service agencies, or religious institutions. Even so, the need for the delivery of services in this area has far outpaced available funding and resources. It is estimated that there are as many as 7.5 million children with problems severe enough to require mental health services, but less than 30 percent are receiving adequate care (Office of Technology Assessment, 1987).

According to Ciborowski ("Childhood Mental Disorders," 1987), who heads the American Mental Health Counselor Association Task Force on Children, the reasons for the disparity include federal cutbacks and a lack of a comprehensive child care system in the United States, which he describes as "the only industrial nation that doesn't have a standard childcare system" (p. 7). What we do have is haphazard and does not serve children on a regular basis, nor are there an adequate number of community-based mental health services available.

The School and Prevention

Apart from services targeted at the family and the home environment, prevention can be found in the public schools, where students spend a significant amount of time during their formative years and where their attitudes, behaviors and identity continue to be shaped (Pink, 1984; Polk, 1975).

While some (Glueck and Glueck, 1972; Little and Skarrow, 1981) have emphasized the value of utilizing the schools in preventing and attacking potential delinquent behavior and antisocial life-styles, others (Polk and Schafer, 1972; Kozol, 1968; Holt, 1967; Cohen, 1955) have argued that it is these very schools which have failed to educate vast numbers of youth and thereby engendered in them a sense of alienation, which contributes directly and indirectly to the delinquency problem. Regarding the latter, there is ample evidence of the relationship between low academic achievement in school and delinquency (Elliot and Voss, 1974; Jensen, 1976; Hawkins and Weis, 1979). Yet, as Powell (1975) suggests, schools are in a unique position to help identify potential delinquents and change their behavior. Among his suggestions are the establishment within the schools of "intervention centers" for those youth at high risk of becoming delinquent. Powell envisions such centers as being multiservice in nature, providing guidance, psychological counseling, and help with educational skills. He also makes some specific suggestions for sensitizing school administrators and teachers to the needs of students and in many ways anticipates alternative educational programs for disruptive students that are recommended by Hawkins and Wall (1980) as a means of preventing delinquency.

As Hawkins and Wall explain:

> Alternative education programs which serve disruptive youth represent a form of secondary rather than primary prevention. School based primary prevention of delinquency requires fundamental alternations (sic) in the structures and processes of schools themselves to minimize the school-related factors which contribute to delinquency. (p. v)

The secondary prevention measures they recommend include individualized instruction, rewards for academic improvement, goal-oriented emphasis on class work, small program size, optimal student-teacher ratio, caring teachers and supportive administrators who help establish a climate of respect for students and fair and constant discipline (p. vi). Some success with such programs has been reported by Foley and McConnaughy (1982) finding that students enrolled in alternative schools in New York City were well satisfied with their experiences, including their relationships with the teachers and the caring environment they found and felt that their educational needs were being met.

Clairizio (1979), concerned with preventing maladaptive behavior and improving the mental health of all students, discusses the modification of the school environment as a primary prevention technique, while Cohen et al. (1982) examine the influence of the school's physical setting, including the classroom, the possible distractions found there, and seating arrangements, on the general student population.

Others (Zimiles, 1967; Reinherz, 1982) call for greater research to be done on delinquency prevention in the schools, while Tanner and Lindgren (1971) recommend a mental health approach to classroom teaching, and Halpern (1961) discusses the role of the psychologist in the school, whom he believes is "most effective when he can help those who are in constant contact with the child to achieve a degree of maturity that enables them truly to recognize and meet the needs of the child" (p. 8).

Conclusions

Our emphasis in this text has primarily focused on the problems associated with the definitions and classification of delinquency, the developmental and psychosocial factors associated with its development and problems connected with its treatment and prevention. One fact which emerges from a review of the literature is that, while there is still much to be learned about the development of delinquency, there is quite a bit which is and has been understood for a number of years. While recent studies continue to refine our knowledge of the causes of juvenile delinquency, study after study over the past fifty years has pointed to the relationship between the role of the family, behavior problems during early childhood, low intelligence, poor school performance, childhood psychopathology, and serious antisocial behavior during adolescence.

Yet, relatively little has been done to develop effective public policies and priorities which would allow for improving the treatment and prevention of delinquency. While Rutter and Giller's (1984) conclusion that "[T]here is a considerable gap between identifying a damaging factor and knowing how to reduce its effect" (p. 324) may reflect our lack of knowledge, we should also bear in mind a statement made almost forty years ago by Lippman (1949):

> The community must share a good deal of the responsibility for our failures in doing effective work with chronic delinquent children. . . . [S]tudies demonstrated the needs for early recognition of those conditions within the home that could not help but develop dissocial behavior in children. There have never been sufficient funds for highly

trained staff who could work intensively with families . . . when pathology in the home was first recognizable. . . . In spite of proving beyond a doubt that children needed individualized care and treatment in their school work, the demands for improved school conditions have met with little adequate response to date. (pp. 162-163)

There is clearly a need to develop a national policy concerning a standard child care system guided by an ongoing process of evaluation to aid those families and children who are so clearly in need. The economic and social costs associated with delinquency are extraordinarily high. We certainly know enough at this point to make a sound, if imperfect, beginning towards developing such a policy. If we do not respond to this problem in an ongoing and consistent way, young lives will continue to be wasted and our courts and prisons will continue to be overcrowded. What, of course, is most tragic is that this has been said many times before and yet an adequate response has still not been undertaken.

REFERENCES

Aarons, Z.A. (1970). Normality and abnormality in adolescence. *Psychoanalytic Study of the Child, 25*, 309-339.

Abrahamson, D. (1952). *Who are the guilty?* New York: Rinehart.

Ackerman, N.W. (1958). *The psychodynamics of family life.* New York: Basic Books.

Adams, S. (1970). The PICO project. In N. Johnston, L. Savitz and M. Wolfgant (Eds.): *The sociology of punishment and corrections.* New York: John Wiley, pp. 548-561.

Adler, G. (1982). Recent psychoanalytic contributions to the understanding and treatment of criminal behavior. *International Journal of Offender Therapy and Comparative Criminology, 26*, 281-287.

Agee, V.L. (1979). *Treatment of the violent incorrigible adolescent.* Lexington, MA: Lexington Books.

Agee, V.L. and McWilliams, B. (1984). The role of group therapy and the therapeutic community in treating the violent juvenile offender. In R.A. Mathias, P. DeMuro and R.S. Allison (Eds.): *Violent juvenile offenders, an anthology.* San Francisco, CA: National Council on Crime and Delinquency, pp. 187-206.

Aichhorn, A. (1971). *Wayward youth.* New York: The Viking Press. (Original work published 1925.)

Aichhorn, A. (1949). Some remarks on the psychic structure and social care of a certain type of female juvenile delinquent. *Psychoanalytic Study of the Child, 3/4*: 439-448.

Akers, R.L. (1977). *Deviant behavior: A social learning approach.* 2nd Ed. Belmont: Wadsworth.

Akers, R.L., Krohn, M.O., Luzizu-Kaduce, L., and Radosevich, M. (1979): Social learning and deviant behavior: A specific test of a general theory. *American Sociological Review, 44*, 636-655.

Akiskal, H.S. and McKinney, W.T. (1975). Overview of recent research in depression: Integration of ten conceptual models into a comprehensive clinical frame. *Archives of General Psychiatry, 32*, 285-305.

Alexander, J.F. (1973). Defensive and supportive communications in normal and deviant families. *Journal of Consulting and Clinical Psychology, 40*, 223-231.

Alexander, J.F. and Persons, B.V. (1973). Short-term behavioral intervention with delinquent families: Impact in family process and recidivism. *Journal of Abnormal Psychology, 81*, 219-225.

Alexander, J., Barton, C., Schiavo, R. and Parsons, B. (1976). Systems-behavioral intervention with families of delinquents: Therapist characteristics, family behavior and outcome. *Journal of Consulting and Clinical Psychology, 44,* 656-664.

American Psychiatric Association. (1980). *Diagnostic and statistical manual of mental disorders.* 3rd Ed. Washington, D.C.: Author.

Amir, M., and Berman, Y. (1970). Chromosomal deviation and crime. *Federal Probation, 34,* 55-62.

Andrew, J.M. (1977). Delinquency: intellectual imbalance? *Criminal Justice and Behavior, 4,* 99-104.

Annis, H.M., and Chan, D. (1983). The differential treatment model: Empirical evidence from a personality typology of adult offenders. *Criminal Justice and Behavior, 10,* 159-173.

Anthony, E.J. (1969). The reactions of adults to adolescents and their behavior. In A. Essman (Ed.): *The Psychology of Adolescence.* New York: International Universities Press, 1975.

Aries, P. (1962). *Centuries of childhood: A social history of family life.* (R. Baldick, Trans.). New York: Random House.

Arnold, L.E., and Estreischer, D. (1985). *Parent-child group therapy: Building self-esteem in a cognitive-behavioral group.* Lexington, MA: Lexington Books.

Austin, R.L. (1973). Differential treatment in an institution: reexamining the Preston study. *Journal of Research in Crime and Delinquency, 14,* 177-194.

Bandura, A. (1973). *Aggression: A social learning analysis.* Englewood Cliffs, NJ: Prentice Hall.

Bandura, A. (1976). Social learning analysis of aggression. In E. Robes-Inesta and A. Bandura (Eds.): *Analysis of delinquency and aggression.* Hillsdale, WV: Lawrence Erlbaum.

Bandura, A. (1978). Learning and behavioral theories of aggression. In I. Kutash et al. (Eds.): *Violence.* San Francisco: Jossey-Bass.

Bandura, A. (1978). The self system in reciprocal determinism. *American Psychologist, 33,* 344-358.

Bandura, A. (1979). The social learning perspective: Mechanisms of aggression. In H. Toch (Ed.): *The Psychology of Crime and Criminal Justice.* New York: Holt, Rinehart and Winston, Inc.

Bandura, A., and Walters, R.H. (1959). *Adolescent Aggression.* New York: Ronald Press.

Bandura, A., and Walters, R.H. (1963). *Social learning and personality development.* New York: Holt, Rinehart and Winston, Inc.

Bartollas, C., (1985). *Juvenile delinquency.* New York: John Wiley and Sons.

Bates, J.E., Maslin, C.A., and Frankel, K.A. (1985). Attachment security, mother-child interaction and temperament as predictors of behavior-problem ratings at age three years. In I. Bretherton, and E. Waters (Eds.): *Growing points of attachment theory and research. Monographs of the Society for Research in Child Development, 50,* 167-193.

Bateson, G., Jackson, D.D., Haley, J., and Wenkland, J. (1956). Toward a theory of schizophrenia. *Behavioral Science, 1,* 251-264.

Beck, A.T., Rush, A.J., Shaw, B.F., and Emergy, G. (1979). *Cognitive therapy of depression.* New York: Guilford.

Beker, J., and Heyman, D.S. (1972). A critical appraisal of the California differential treatment typology of adolescent offenders. *Criminology: An Interdisciplinary Journal, 10,* 33-57.

Benedict, R. (1938). Continuities and discontinuities in cultural conditioning. *Psychiatry, 1,* 161-167.

Beres, D. and Obers, S.V. (1950). The effects of extreme deprivation in infancy on psychic structure in adolescence: A study in ego development. *Psychoanalytic Study of the Child, 5,* 212-235.

Bergen, M.E. (1964). Some observations of maturational factors in young children and adolescents. *Psychoanalytic Study of the Child, 19,* 275-286.

Bergin, A.E., and Lambert, M.J. (1978). The evaluation of therapeutic outcomes. In S.C. Garfield and A.E. Bergen (Eds.): *Handbook of Psychotherapy and Behavior Change.* New York: Wiley.

Berleman, W.C. (1980). *Juvenile delinquency prevention experiments: A review and analysis.* National Institute for Juvenile Justice and Delinquency Prevention. Washington, D.C.: U.S. Government Printing Office.

Berlin, I.N. (1979). Early intervention and prevention. In I.N. Berlin and L.A. Stone (Eds.): *Basic Handbook of Child Psychiatry, Vol. 4: Prevention and Current Issues.* New York: Basic Books.

Berman, S. (1984). The relationship of aggressive behavior and violence to psychic reorganization in adolescence. In E.R. Keith (Ed.): *The aggressive adolescent.* New York: The Free Press.

Berne, E. (1964). *Games people play.* New York: Grove Press.

Bettleheim, B. (1974). *A home for the heart.* New York: Alfred Knopff.

Bettelheim, B., and Sylvester, E. (1950). Delinquency and morality. *Psychoanalytic Study of the Child, 5,* 329-342.

Blackman, D.E. (1975). Ethical issues for psychologists in corrections. In J. Monahan (Ed.): *Who is the client?* Washington, D.C.: American Psychological Association, pp. 63-92.

Blakely, C.H., and Davidson, W.S. (1984). Behavioral approaches to delinquency: A review. In *Adolescent behavior disorders: Foundations and contemporary concerns.* Lexington, MA: Lexington Books.

Blos, P. (1957). Preoedipal factors in the etiology of female delinquency. *Psychoanalytic Study of the Child, 12,* 229-249.

Blos, P. (1962). *On adolescence: A psychoanalytic interpretation.* New York: Free Press of Glencoe.

Blos, P. (1965). The initial stage of male adolescence. *The Psychoanalytic Study of the Child, 20,* 145-164.

Blos, P. (1966). The concept of acting out in relation to the adolescent process. In E. Rexford (Ed.): *A developmental approach to the problems of acting out: A symposium. Monographs of the Journal of the American Academy of Child Psychiatry.* New York: International Universities Press.

Blos, P. (1967). The second individual in process. *The Psychoanalytic Study of the Child, 22,* 162-186.

Bonta, J., and Motiuk, L.L. (1985). Utilization of an interview based classification instrument: a study of correctional halfway houses. *Criminal Justice and Behavior, 12,* 333-352.

Bootzin, R.R., and Acocalla, J.R. (1984). *Abnormal psychology: Current perspective.* 4th Ed. New York: Random House.

Borduin, C.M., and Henggeler, S.W. (1982). Psychosocial development of father-absent children. In S.W. Henggeler (Ed.): *Delinquency and adolescent psychopathology.* Boston: John Wright.

Borduin, C.M., Henggeler, S.W., Hanson, C.C. and Harbin, F. (1982). Treating the family of the adolescent: A review of the empirical literature. In S.W. Henggeler (Ed.): *Delinquency and adolescent psychopathology.* Littleton, MA: John Wright.

Borganokar, D. and Shaw, S. (1974). The XYY chromosome, male or syndrome. *Progress in Medical Genetics, 10,* 135-222.

Bowen, M. (1978). *Family therapy: Clinical practice.* New York: Aronson.

Bowker (1978, November). *Menstruation and female criminality: A new look at the data.* Paper presented at the meeting of the American Society of Criminology, Dallas.

Brandt, D. (1977). Separation and identity in adolescence. *Contemporary Psychoanalyses, 13,* 507-518.

Brandt, D. (1979). Development of intake criteria in a day treatment program for delinquent boys. *Psychological Reports, 44,* 1028-1030.

Brandt, D., and Silverman, H. (1985). The impact of maternal personality on individuation during adolescence. *Psychoanalytic Psychology, 2,* 267-274.

Brantingham, P. (1979). The classical and positive schools of criminology: Two ways of thinking about crime. In F. Faust and P. Brantingham (Eds.): *Juvenile justice philosophy: Readings, cases and comments.* 2nd Ed. New York: West Publishing Company, pp. 36-47.

Breggin, P.R. (1979). *Electroshock: Its braindisabling effects.* New York: Springer.

Brendtro, L.K., and Ness, A.E. (1983). *Re-educating troubled youth: Environments for teaching and treatments.* Hawthorne, NY: Aldine.

Brodsky, S.L. (1977). Confidentiality — privacy — right to treatment — right to refuse. In *Mental health for the convicted offender, patient and prisoner.* Regional Conference, Oct. 27-29, 1976, Raleigh, North Carolina: North Carolina Department of Corrections.

Brodsky, S.L. (1984). *Psychotherapy with reluctant clients.* Unpublished paper, University of Alabama, Alabama.

Brodsky, S.L., and O'Neal Smitherman, H. (1983). *Handbook of scales for research in crime and delinquency.* New York: Plenum.

Bromberg, W. (1961). *The mold of murder.* New York: Grune and Stratton.

Bromberg, W. (1965). *Crime and the mind: A psychiatric analysis of crime and punishment.* New York: Macmillan.

Brown, S.L., and Reid, H. (1976). The warm-line — a primary preventive service for parents of young children. In H.J. Parad, H.L.P. Resnik and L.G. Parad (Eds.): *Emergency and disaster management.* Bowie, MD: Charles Press.

Burgess, R.L., and Akers, R.L. (1966). A differential association — reinforcement theory of criminal behavior. *Social problems, 14,* 128-147.

Burnham, D. (1985, June 20). Plan for crime data overhaul. *The New York Times,* p. B19.

Cadoret, R.J., and Cain, C.A. (1980). Sex differences in predictions of antisocial behavior in adoptees. *Archives of General Psychiatry, 37,* 1117-1175.

Cadoret, R.J., Cain, C.A., and Crowe, R.R. (1983). Evidence for gene-environment interaction in the development of adolescent antisocial behavior. *Behavior Genetics, 13,* 301-310.

California Youth Authority. (1968). *The community treatment project after five years.* Sacramento, California: Author.

Callahan, R. Jr. (1985). Wilderness probation: A decade later. *Juvenile and Family Court Journal, 36,* 31-35.

Caplan, G. (1964). *Principle of preventive psychiatry.* New York: Basic Books.

Carles, S. (1981). The proliferation of project New Pride. *Corrections Magazine, 7,* 28-34.

Carpenter, P., and Sandberg. S. (1973). The things inside: psychodrama and delinquent adolescents. *Psychotherapy: Theory, Research and Practice, 10,* 245-247.

Carpenter, P., and Sandberg, S. (1985). Further psychodrama with delinquent adolescents. *Adolescence, 20,* 599-604.

Chess, S., Thomas, A., and Birch, H.G. (1965). *Your child is a person,* New York: Viking Press.

Childhood mental disorders often remain undiagnosed (1987, March). *Guidepost,* p. 7.

Chilton, R., and Galvin, J. (1985). Race, crime and criminal justice. *Crime and Delinquency, 31,* 3-8.

Chorover, S.L. (1979). *From genesis to genocide.* Cambridge. MA, MIT Press.

Christiansen, K.O. (1977). A review of studies of criminality among twins. In S.A. Mednick and K.O. Christiansen (Eds.): *Biosocial bases of criminal behavior.* New York: John Wiley, pp. 44-48.

Clarizio, H.F. (1979). Primary prevention of behavioral disorders in the schools. *School Psychology Review, 8,* 434-445.

Cleckley, H. (1964). *The mask of sanity.* St. Louis: Mosby.

Clegg, J. (1981). A big prevention program on a small budget. *Advance, 31,* 7-9.

Clement, C.E., and Ervin, F.R. (1972). Historical data in evaluation of violent subjects. *Archives of General Psychology, 22,* 621-624.

Clements, C.B. (1981). The future of classification: some cautions and prospects. *Criminal Justice and Behavior, 8,* 15-38.

Clements, C.B. (1985). Towards an objective approach to offender classification, *Law and Psychology Review, 9,* 45-55.

Cohen, A.K. (1955). *Delinquent boys: The culture of the gang.* New York: Free Press.

Cohler, B.J., and Musick, J.S. (1984). *Intervention among psychiatrically impaired parents and their young children.* San Francisco: Jossey-Bass.

Coleman, J.C., Butcher, J.N. and Carson, R.C. (1984). *Abnormal psychology and modern life.* Glenview, IL: Scott Foresman.

Conger, R.D. (1976). Social control and social learning models of delinquent behavior: A synthesis. *Criminology, 14,* 17-40.

Conger, J., and Peterson, A. (1984). *Adolescence and youth.* 3rd Ed. New York: Harper and Row.

Cook, D., and Rubenfeld, S. (1960). *The nature of treatment.* In Appendix II 1960 NIMH Report to Congress on Juvenile Delinquency. 4.

Corder, B., Whiteside, L. and Haizlip, J. (1981). A study of curative factors in group psychotherapy with adolescents. *International Journal of Group Psychotherapy, 31,* 345-354.

Cowen, E. (1967). Emergment approaches to mental health problems: An overview and directions for future work. In E. Cowen, E. Gardner and M.E. Zax: *Emergent approaches to mental health problems.* New York: Appleton-Century-Crofts.

Craft, M. (1985). The current status of XYY ans XXY syndromes: A review of treatment implications, In F.H. Marsh and J. Katz (Eds.): *Biology, crime and ethics: A study of biological explanations for criminal behavior.* Cincinnati, OH: Anderson, pp. 113-122.

Craig, M.M., and Glick, S.J. (1963). Ten years experience with the Glueck Social Prediction Table. *Crime and Delinquency, 9,* 249-261.

Craig, M.M., and Glick, S.J. (1968). School behavior related to later delinquency and non-delinquency. *Criminologica, 5,* 17-27.

Crowe, R.R. (1974). An adoption of antisocial personality. *Archives General Psychiatry, 31,* 785-791.

Cullen, F.T., and Gilbert, K.E. (1982). *Reaffirming rehabilitation.* Cincinnati, OH: Anderson.

Curry, J.F., Weincrot, S.I., and Kohler, F. (1984). Family therapy with aggressive and delinquent adolescents. In C.R. Keith (Ed.): *The aggressive adolescent: Clinical perspectives.* New York: The Free Press.

Czunder, G. (1985). Changing the criminal: A theoretical proposal for change. *Federal Probation, 49,* 64-66.

Dalgard, O.S., and Kringlen, E. (1976). A Norwegian twin study of criminality. *The British Journal of Criminality, 16,* 213-232.

Dalton, K. (1960). Effect of menstruation on school girls' weekly work. *British Medical Journal, 1,* 326-328.

Dalton, K. (1960). School girls' behavior and menstruation. *British Medical Journal, 2,* 1647-1649.

Dalton, K. (1961). Menstruation and crime. *British Medical Journal, 2,* 1752-1753.

Darwin, C.R. (1964). *On the origin of species.* Cambridge, MA: Harvard University Press. (Original work published 1859.)

Darwin, C.R. (1974). *The descent of man.* Chicago: Rand McNally. (Original work published 1871.)

Davidson, W.S., and Robinson, M.J. (1975). Community psychology and behavior modification: A community based program for the prevention of delinquency. *Corrective and Social Psychiatry and the Journal of Behavior Technology Methods and Therapy, 21,* 1-12.

Davidson, W.S., and Wolfred, T.R. (1977). Evaluation of a community based modification program for prevention of delinquency: The failure of success. *Community Mental Health Journal, 13,* 296-306.

Davis, S. (1980). *Rights of juveniles: The juvenile justice system.* 2nd Ed. New York: Clark Boardman.

Davitz, J.R. (1952). The effects of previous training in post-frustration behavior. *Journal of Abnormal and Social Psychology, 47,* 309-315.

deLange, J.M., Barten, J.A., and Lunham, S.L. (1981). The wiser way: A cognitive behavioral model for group social skills training with juvenile delinquents. *Social Work with Groups, 4,* 37-48.

Dobzhansky, T. (1976). The myth of genetic predistination and of tabula rasa. *Perspectives in Biology and Medicine, 7,* 156-170.

Dollard, J. (1957). *Caste and class in a sourthern town.* Garden City, New York: Doubleday Anchor Books. (Original work published 1937.)

Dooley, D., and Catalano, R. (1980). Economic change as a cause of behavioral disorder. *Psychological Bulletin, 87,* 450-468.

Durlak, J.A. (1983). Social problem-solving as a primary prevention strategy. In R.D. Felner, L.A. Jason, J.N. Moritsugu and S.S. Farber (Eds.): *Preventive psychology: Theory, research and practice.* New York: Pergamon Press.

Easson, W.M. (1969). *The severely disturbed adolescent.* New York: International University Press.

Edelman, E.M., and Goldstein, A.P. (1981). Moral education. In A.P. Goldstein, E.G. Carr, W.S. Davisdon and P. Wehr (Eds.): *In response to aggression: Methods of control and prosocial alternatives.* New York: Pergamon Press.

Eissler, K.R. (1949). *Searchlights on delinquency.* New York: International University Press.

Eissler, K.R. (1949). Riots: Observations in a home for delinquent girls. *Psychoanalytic Study of the Child, 3/4:* 449-460.

Eissler, K.R. (1950). Ego psychological implication of the psychoanalytic treatment of delinquents. *Psychoanalytic Study of the Child, 5,* 97-121.

Eissler, K.R. (1958). Notes on problems of technique in psychoanalytic treatment of adolescents: With some remarks on perversions. *The Psychoanalytic Study of the Child, 13,* 233-254.

Elitzur, B. (1976). Self-relaxation program for acting out adolescents. *Adolescence, 11,* 569-572.

Elliot, D.S., and Ageton, S.S. (1980). Reconciling race and class differences in self-reported and official estimates of delinquency. *American Sociological Review, 45,* 95-110.

Elliot, D.S., and Voss, H.L. (1974). *Delinquency and dropout.* Lexington, MA: Lexington Books.

Ellis, A. (1962). *Reason and emotion in psychotherapy.* New York: Lyle Stuart.

Ellis, A. (1971). *Growth through reason: Verbatim cases in rational-emotive psychotherapy.* Palo Alto, CA: Science and Behavior Books.

Ellis, A. (undated). *The essence of rational psychotherapy: A comprehensive approach to treatment.* (A monograph.) New York: New York Institute for Rational Living, Inc.

Ellis, A., and Bernard M.E. (1983). *Rational-emotive approaches to the problems of childhood.* New York: Plenum.

Ellis, D.P., and Austin, P. (1971). Menstruation and aggressive behavior in correctional center for women. *Journal of Criminal Law, Criminology and Police Science, 62,* 388-395.

Ellis, L. (1984). Genetics and criminal behavior: Evidence through the end of the 1970's. *Criminology, 20,* 43-66.

Empey, L.T. (1978). *American delinquency: Its meaning and construction.* Homewood, IL: Dorsey.

Empey, L.T. (1979). The progressive legacy and the concept of childhood. In L.T. Empey (Ed.): The progressive legacy and current reforms. Charlottesville: University Press of Virginia, pp. 3-33.

Empey, L.T., and Erickson, M.L. (1972). *The Provo experiment: Evaluating community control of delinquency.* Lexington, MA: D.C. Heath.

Erikson, E.H. (1963). *Childhood and society.* New York: Norton.

Erikson, E.H. (1965). *The challenge of youth.* Garden City, NY: Doubleday Anchor Books.

Erikson, E.H. (1968). *Identity, youth and crisis.* New York: Norton.

Erikson, M.F., Sroufe, L.A. and Egeland, B. (1985). The relationship between quality of attachment and behavior problems in preschool in a high risk sample. In I. Bretherton and E. Waters (Eds.): *Growing points of attachment theory and research. Monographs of Society for Research in Child Development, 50,* 147-166.

Erskine, C. (1984). Female delinquency, feminism and psychoanalysis: An overview. In C.R. Keith (Ed.): *The aggressive adolescent.* New York: The Free Press.

Eron, L.D. (1987). The development of aggressive behavior from the perspective of a developing behaviorism. *American Psychologist, 42,* 435-442.

Esman, A.H. (1983). *The psychiatric treatment of adolescents.* New York: International Universities Press, Inc.

Eysenck, H.J. (1952). The effects of psychotherapy on evaluation. *Journal of Consulting Psychology, 16,* 319-324.

Eysenck, H.J. (1967). *The biological basis of personality.* Springfield, IL: Charles C Thomas.

Eysenck, H.J. (1973). Evaluating psychoanalysis. *New Medical Tribune.*

Eysenck, H.J. (1973). *The experimental study of Freudian theories.* London: Methuen.

Eysenck, H.J. (1975). Personality, conditioning and antisocial behavior. In Laufer and Day (Eds.): *Personality, theory, oral development and criminal behavior.* Lexington, MA: D.C. Heath.

Eysenck, H.J. (1979). *Crime and personality.* London: Routledge and Kegan Paul.

Farrington, D.D. (1978). The family backgrounds of aggressive youths. In L.A. Hergov, M. Berger and D. Schaffer (Eds.): *Aggression and antisocial behavior in childhood and adolescence.* New York: Pergamon.

Fenichel, O. (1954). Neurotic acting out. *The collected papers of Otto Fenichel, 2,* 296-304. New York: Norton.

Ferdinand, T.N. (1966). *Typologies of delinquency.* New York: Random House.

Ferrier, P.E., Ferrier, S.A. and Nielson, J. (1970). Chromosome study of a group of male juvenile delinquents. *Pediatric Research, 4,* 205.

Fineberg, B.L., Sowards, S.K., and Kettlewell, P.W. (1980). Adolescent inpatient treatment: A literature review. *Adolescence, 15I,* 913-925.

Fink, A.E. (1938). *Causes of crime: Biological theories in the United States (1800-1915).* Philadelphia: University of Pennsylvania Press.

Fisher, R.B. (1984). Predicting adolescent violence. In C.R. Keith (Ed.): *The aggressive adolescent: Clinical perspectives.* New York: The Free Press.

Flavell, J.J. (1963). *The developmental psychology of Jean Piaget.* New York: Van Nostrand.

Foley, E., and McConnaughy, S.B. (1982). *Toward school improvement: Lessons from alternative high schools.* New York: Public Education Association.

Forgays, D.G. (1983). Primary prevention of psychopathology. In M. Hersen, A.E., Kazdin and A.S. Bellack (Eds.): *The clinical psychology handbook.* New York: Pergamon.

Forssman, H. (1970). The mental implications of sex chromosome aberrations. *British Journal of Psychiatry, 117,* 353-363.

Fowler, R.D. (1979). Use of the computerized MMPI in correctional decisions. In J.N. Butcher (Ed.): *New developments in the use of the MMPI.* Duluth, MN: University of Minnesota Press.

Fox, R.G. (1971). The XYY offender: A modern myth? *Journal of Criminal Law, Criminology and Public Sciences, 62,* 59-73.

Fox, V. (1975). Changing classification organizational pattern: 1870-1970. In L.J. Hippchen (Ed.): *Correctional classification and treatment: A reader.* Cincinnati, OH: W.H. Anderson, pp. 3-12.

Frances, A., and Clarkin, J.F. (1981). Differential therapeutics: A guide to treatment selection. *Hospital and Community Psychiatry, 32,* 537-545.

Freud, A. (1949). Certain types and stages of social maladjustment. In K. Eissler (Ed.): *Searchlights on delinquency.* New York: International Universities Press.

Freud, A. (1951). Obituary: August Aichhorn. *International Journal of Psychoanalysis, 32,* 51-56.

Freud, A. (1958). Adolescence. *Psychoanalytic Study of the Child, 13,* 255-278. New York: International Universities Press.

Freud, A. (1965). *Normality and pathology in childhood: Assessment of development.* New York: International Universities Press.

Freud, A. (1970). The symptomatology of childhood: A preliminary attempt at classification. *Psychoanalytic Study of the Child, 25,* 19-41.

Freud, S. (1949). *An outline of psychoanalysis.* New York: Norton.

Freud, S. (1962). *The ego and the id.* New York: Norton.

Freud, S. (1966). Some character types met within psychoanalytic work. In *The Standard Edition, 14.* London, Hogarth Press. (Originally published in 1916.)

Friedlander, K. (1945). Formation of the antisocial character. *Psychoanalytic Study of the Child, 1,* 189-203.

Friedlander, K. (1947). *The psychoanalytic approach to juvenile delinquency.* London: Routledge and Kegan Paul.

Friedlander K. (1949). Latent delinquency and ego development. In K. Eissler (Ed.): *Searchlights on delinquency.* New York: International Universities Press.

Frieze, I.H., Parsons, J.E., Johnson, P.B., Ruble, D., and Zellman, G.L. (1978). *Women and sex roles: A social psychological perspective.* New York: Norton.

Fry, P.S. (1975). Affect and resistance to temper tantrum. *Developmental Psychology, 11,* 466-472.

Fuller, J.L., and Thompson, W.R. (1978). *Foundations of behavior genetics.* St. Louis: Mosby.

Gabrielli, W.F. Jr., and Mednick, S.A. (1984). Urban environment, genetics and crime. *Criminology, 22,* 645-652.

Ganzer, V.J. and Saranson, I.G. (1973). Variables associated with recidivism among juvenile delinquents. *Journal of Consulting and Clinical Psychology, 40,* 1-5.

Ganzer, V.J. (1974). The use of modeling techniques in rehabilitation of the juvenile offender. In J.G. Cull and R.E. Hardy (Eds.): *Behavior modification in rehabilitation settings: Applied principles.* Springfield, IL: Charles C Thomas.

Gardner, G.E. (1972). William Healy 1869-1963. *The Journal of the American Academy of Child Psychiatry, 11,* 39-54.

Garrett, C.J. (1985). Effects of residential treatment on adjudicated delinquents: A meta-analysis. *Journal of Research on Crime and Delinquency, 22,* 287-308.

Geisman, L.L., and Wood, K.M. (1986). *Family and delinquency: Resocializing the young offender.* New York: Human Sciences Press.

Gendreau, P., Madden, P., and Leipeiger, M. (1979). Norms and recidivism rates for MMPI and selected experimental scales in Canadian delinquent sample. *Canadian Journal of Behavioral Sciences,* 21-31.

Gendreau, P., and Ross, B. (1979). Effective correctional treatment: Bibliotherapy for cynics. *Crime and Delinquency, 25,* 463-489.

Gerard, R. (1970). Institutional innovations in juvenile corrections. *Federal Probation, 34,* 33-40.

Gerard, R. (1975). Classification by behavioral categories and its implications for differential treatment. In L.G. Hippchen (Ed.): *Correctional classification and treatment: A reader.* Cincinnati, OH: W.H. Anderson, pp. 94-103.

Gibbons, D.C. (1970). Differential treatment of delinquents and interpersonal maturity levels theory: A critique. *Social Service Review, 44,* 22-33.

Gilley, O. (1970). Criminals are made, not born — XYY chromosome theory exploded. *Science Journal, 6,* 8.

Ginsberg, M.D. (1976). A new perspective in prisoners' rights: the right to refuse treatment and rehabilitation. *John Marshall Journal of Practice and Procedure, 10,* 173-176.

Glasscote, R.M. (1981). Talking sense about prevention. *Hospital and Community Psychiatry, 32,* 823.

Glasser, W. (1965). *Reality therapy: A new approach to psychiatry.* New York: Harper and Row.

Glick, S.J. (1972). Identification of predelinquents among children with school behavior problems as basis for multiservice treatment program. In S. Glueck and E. Glueck (Eds.): *Identification of predelinquents.* New York: Intercontinental Medical Book Company.

Glover, E. (1944). *The diagnosis and treatment of delinquency, clinical report 1937-1941.* London: Institute for the Study and Treatment of Delinquency.

Glover, E. (1960). *The roots of crime: Selected papers on psychoanalysis.* (Vol. II). New York: International Universities Press.

Glueck, S., and Glueck, E. (1950). Unravelling juvenile delinquency. Cambridge, MA: Harvard University Press.

Glueck, S., and Glueck, E. (1956). *Physique and delinquency.* New York: Harper and Row.

Glueck, S., and Glueck, E.T. (1968). *Delinquents and nondelinquents in perspective.* Cambridge, MA: Harvard University Press.

Glueck, S., and Glueck, E. (1972). Prediction and prevention. In S. Glueck and E. Glueck (Eds.): *Identification of the predelinquent.* New York: Intercontinental Medical Book Corporation.

Goddard, H.H. (1912). *The Kallikak family: A study in the heredity of feeble-mindedness.* New York: Macmillan

Goddard, H.H. (1920). *Human efficiency levels of intelligence.* New Jersey: Princeton University Press.

Gold, M., and Petronio, R.J. (1980). Delinquent behavior in adolescence. In J. Adelson (Ed.): *Handbook of adolescent psychology.* New York: Wiley, pp. 495-535.

Gold, M., and Reimer, D.J. (1975). Changing patterns of delinquent behavior among Americans 13 through 16 years old: 1967-1972. *Crime and Delinquency Literature, 7,* 483-517.

Goldberg, R.T., and Johnson, B.D. (1980). Prediction of rehabilitation success of delinquent boys. *Journal of Offender Counseling Services and Rehabilitation, 4,* 319-329.

Goldman, N. (1963). *The differential selection of juvenile offenders for court appearance.* National Research and Information Center, National Council on Crime and Delinquency.

Goldmeier, J., Saver, R.H., and White, E.V. (1972). A halfway house for mentally ill offenders. *American Journal of Psychiatry, 134,* 45-49.

Goldstein, J. (1968). Psychoanalysis and jurisprudence: On the relevance of psychoanalytic theory to law. *Psychoanalytic Study of the Child, 23,* 459-479.

Goodard, H.H. (1914). *Feeble-mindedness.* New York: Macmillan.

Goodard, H.H. (1928). Feeble-mindedness: A question of definition. *Journal of Psycho-Asthenics, 33,* 219-227.

Goring, C. (1910). *The English convict.* London: His Majesty's Stationery Office.

Gotteoman, I., and Shields (1973). Genetic theorizing and schizophrenia, *The British Journal of Psychiatry, 122,* 15-20.

Gottsdialles, L.A., Haer, J.L., and Bates, D.E. (1972). Effect of sensory overload in psychological state: Changes in social alienation-personal disorganization and cognitive intellectual impairment. *Archives of General Psychiatry, 27,* 451-456.

Greenacre, P. (1970). Youth, growth and violence. *Psychoanalytic Study of the Child, 25,* 340-359.

Griffith, J.M., Miewarld, B.K., and Applebaum, P.S. (1985). The chronic child patient: Ensuring continuity of care. *American Journal of Orthopsychiatry, 55,* 75-87.

Grisso, T. (1981). *Juveniles' waiver of rights: legal and psychological competence.* New York: Plenum.

Grisso, T. (1984). *Forensic assessment in juvenile and family cases: The state of the art.* Keynote Address, Summer Institute of Mental Health and Law. University of Nebraska-Lincoln.

Gross, A.M., and Brigham, T.A. (1980). Behavior modification and the treatment of juvenile delinquency: A review and proposal for future research. *Corrective and Social Psychiatry and the Journal of Behavior Technology Methods and Therapy, 26,* 98-106.

Grotberg, E. (1976). *200 years of children.* Washington, D.C. Department of Health, Education and Welfare. U.S. Government Printing Office.

Guidano, J.F., and Liotti, G. (1983). *Cognitive processes and emotional disorders.* New York: Guilford Press.

Guilford, J.P. (1967). *The nature of human intelligence.* New York: McGraw-Hill.

Guttentag, M. (1977). Subjectivity and its use in evaluation research. In I. Davidoff, M. Guttentag and J. Offutt (Eds.): *Evaluating community mental health services: Principles and practices.* Rockville, MD: National Institute of Mental Health, pp. 21-30.

Hakeem, M. (1957). A critique of the psychiatric approach to the prevention of juvenile delinquency. *Social Problems, 5,* 194-206.

Haley, H.J. (1982). Correctional effectiveness: An elusive concept. *Canadian Journal of Criminology, 24,* 205-219.

Hall, G.S. (1904). *Adolescence: Its psychology and its relations to physiology, anthropology, sociology, sex, crime, religion and education.* 2 Vols. New York: Appleton.

Halpern, F. (1961). *The role of the psychologist in educational planning for the emotionally disturbed child.* Unpublished paper read at the American Psychological Association.

Halpern, W.I., Arkins, V., Mitchell, N., Freeling, N. and Healy, B. (1981). Continuity of mental care to youth in the juvenile justice network. *Hospital and Community Psychiatry, 32,* 114-117.

Hamparian, D.M., Estep, L.K., Muntean, S., Priestino, R., Swisher, R., Wallace, P. and White, J. (1982). *Youth in adult courts: Between two worlds.* Washington, D.C.: U.S. Department of Justice.

Hamparian, D.M., Schuster, R., Dinitz, S. and Conrad, J.P. (1978). *The violent few: A study of dangerous juvenile offenders.* Lexington, MA: Lexington Books.

Hankin, H.T., and Madden, D.J. (1983). Assaultive adolescents: Family decision making parameters. *Family Process, 22,* 109-118.

Hartman, H. (1958). *Ego psychology and the problem of adaptation.* New York: International Universities Press.

Hartstone, E. and Cocozza, J. (1984). Providing services to the mentally ill, violent juvenile offender. In R. Mathias, P. DeMuro and R.S. Allinson (Eds.): *Violent juvenile offenders: An anthology.* San Francisco, CA: National Council on Crime and Delinquency, pp. 157-175.

Hartstone, E., Steadman, H.J., Robbins, P.C., and Monahan, J. (1984). Identifying and treating the mentally disordered prison inmate. In L.A. Teplin (Ed.): *Mental health and criminal justice.* Beverly Hills, CA: Sage, pp. 279-296.

Harvill, R., Jacobs, E.E. and Masson, R.L. (1984). Using "props" to enhance your counseling. *Personnel and Guidance Journal, 62,* 273-275.

Hawkins, R.P. (1972). Stimulus/response: It's time we taught the young how to be good parents (and don't you wish we'd started a long time ago?) *Psychology Today, 6,* 28, 30, 36, 38-40.

Hawkins, R.P., Mendocraft, P., Trout, B.A., and Luster, W.C. (1984). Foster family-based treatment. *Journal of Criminal Child Psychology, 14,* 220-228.

Hawkins, J.D., Pastor, Jr., P.A., Bell, M. and Morrison, S. (1980). *A typology of cause-focused strategies of delinquency prevention.* National Institute for Juvenile Justice and Delinquency Prevention. Washington, D.C.: U.S. Government Printing Office.

Hawkins, J.D., and Wall, J.S. (1980). *Alternative education: Exploring delinquency prevention potential.* (NIJJDP Grant Number 77NI-99-0017) Washington, D.C.: U.S. Government Printing Office.

Hawkins, J.D. and Weis, J. (1980). The social development model: An integrated approach to delinquency prevention. In R.J. Rubel (Ed.): *Juvenile delinquency prevention: Emerging perspectives of the 1980's.* San Marcos, TX: Institute of Criminal Justice Studies, Southwest Texas State University.

Healy, W. (1920). *The individual delinquent.* Boston: Little Brown.

Healy, W. and Bronner, A.F. (1926). *Delinquency and criminals: Their making and unmaking.* New York: MacMillan.

Healy, W., and Bonner, A.F. (1936). *New light on delinquency and its treatment.* New Haven: Yale University Press.

Helfer, R.E. (1979). Childhood comes first: A crash course in childhood for adults. *Child Abuse and Neglect, 3,* 897-898.

Henderson, M. (1982). An empirical classification of convicted violent offenders. *The British Journal of Criminology, 22,* 1-20.

Henggeler, S.W. (1982). *Delinquency and adolescent psychopathology.* Littleton, MA: John Wright.

Henggeler, S.W., Vrey, J.R., and Borduin, C.M. (1982). Social class, psychopathology and family interactions. In S.W. Henggeler (Ed.): *Delinquency and adolescent psychopathology.* Boston: John Wright.

Henggeler, S.W., Rodich, J.D., Borduin, C., Harrison, C.L., Watson, S.W., and Vrey, J.R. (1986). Multisystemic treatment of juvenile offenders: Effect on adolescent behavior and family interaction. *Developmental Psychology, 22,* 132-141.

Hetherington, E.M., Stowie, R.J., and Ridberg, E.H. (1971). Patterns of family interaction and child rearing attitudes related to three dimensions of juvenile delinquency. *Journal of Abnormal Psychology, 78,* 160-176.

Hewitt, L.E., and Jenkins, R.L. (1946). *Fundamental patterns of maladjustment: The dynamics of their origin.* Springfield, IL: Michigan Child Guidance Institute.

Hindelang, M.J., Hirschi, T., and Weis, J.G. (1981). *Measuring delinquency.* Beverly Hills, CA: Sage.

Hinkle, E., and Moore, M. (1971). A student couples program. *Family Coordinator, 20,* 153-158.

Hippchen, L. (1978). *Ecologic-biochemical approaches to treatment of delinquent criminals.* New York: Van Nostrand Reinhold.

Hippchen, L. (1975). Changing trends in correctional philosophy and practice. In L.J. Hippchen (Ed.): *Correctional classification and treatment: A reader.* Cincinnati, OH: W.H. Anderson, pp. 12-24.

Hirschi, T. (1969). Causes of delinquency. Berkeley, CA: University of California Press.

Hobbs, N. (1975). *The futures of children.* San Francisco, CA: Jossey-Bass.

Hoffer, W. (1949). Deceiving the deceiver. In K.R. Eissler (Ed.), *Searchlight on delinquency.* New York: International Universities Press.

Hoffman, M.L. (1980). Moral development in adolescence. In J. Adelson (Ed.): *Handbook of adolescent psychology.* New York: Wiley.

Hollander, H.E., and Turner, F.D. (1985). Characteristics of incarcerated delinquents: Relationship between development disorders, environmental and family factors and patterns of offense and recidivism. *Journal of the American Academy of Child Psychiatry, 24,* 221-226.

Holt, J. (1967). *Why children fail.* New York: Putman.

Hook, E.B. (1973). Behavioral implication of the human XYY genotype. *Science, 179,* 139-150.

Hooton, E.A. (1939). *The American criminal: An anthropological study.* Cambridge, MA: Harvard University Press.

Horn, J.L., Loehlin, J., and Wellerman, L. (1975). Preliminary reports of Texas adoption project. *Psychological Bulletin, 82,* 623-659.

Housley, R. (1969). Criminal law: The XYY chromosome complement and criminal conduct. *Oklahoma Law Review, 22,* 287-301.

Hufstedler, S.M. (1984). Should we give up reform? *Crime and Delinquency, 30,* 415-422.

Hutchings, B. (1972). *Environmental and genetic factors in psychopathology and criminality.* Unpublished masters thesis, University of London, London.

Hutchings, B., and Mednick, S.A. (1974). Registered criminality in the adoptive and biological parents of registered male adoptees. In S.A. Mednick, F. Schulsinger, J. Higgins and B. Bell (Eds.): *Genetics, environment and psychopathology,* New York: Oxford American Elsevier, pp. 215-227.

International Prison Commission (1904). *Children's courts in the United States: Their origin, development and results.* Washington, D.C.: U.S. Government Printing Office.

Jencks, C., Smith, M., Acland, H., Bane, M.J., Cohen, D., Gintis, H., Heyns, B., and Michelson, S. (1972). *Inequality: A reassessment of the effect of family and schooling in America.* New York: Basic Books.

Jensen, G.F. (1976). Race, achievement and delinquency: A further look at delinquency in a birth cohort. *American Journal of Sociology, 82,* 379-387.

Jesness, C. (1966a). *The Jesness Inventory.* Palo Alto, CA: Consulting Psychologist Press.

Jesness, C.F. (1966b). Typology and treatment. *California Youth Authority Quarterly, 19,* 17-29.

Jesness, C.F. (1969). *The Preston typology study final report.* Sacramento, CA: California Youth Authority.

Jesness, C.F. (1971). The Preston typology study: An experiment with differential treatment in an institution. *Journal of Research in Crime and Delinquency, 8,* 38-52.

Jesness, C.F. (1974). *Sequential I-level classification manual.* Sacramento: American Institute. California Youth Authority.

Jesness, C.F. (1975). Comparative effectiveness of behavior modification and transactional analysis programs for delinquents. *Journal of Consulting and Clinical Psychology, 43,* 758-779.

Johnson, A. (1949). Sanctions for superego lacunae of adolescence. In K.P. Eissler (Ed.): *Searchlights on delinquency.* New York: New York International Universities Press.

Johnson, D.L., Simmons, J.G., and Gordon, B.C. (1983). *Temporal consistency of the Meyer-Megargee inmate typology. Criminal Justice and Behavior, 10,* 263-268.

Johnson, F. (1975). Family therapy with families have delinquent offspring. *Journal of Family Counseling, 3,* 32-37.

Jones J.D. (1984). Principles of hospital treatment of the aggressive adolescent. In C. Keith (Ed.): *Aggressive adolescents: Clinical perspectives.* New York: Free Press, pp. 359-402.

Jones, M. (1953). *The therapeutic community.* New York: Basic Books.

Julian, A., and Kilman, P.R. (1979). Group treatment of juvenile delinquents: A review of the outcome literature. *International Journal of Group Psychotherapy, 29,* 3-37.

Jurkovic, G.J. (1980). The juvenile delinquent as a moral philosopher. *Psychological Bulletin, 88,* 709-727.

Kairys, J.W., Conant, B.E. and Kairys, S.W. (1981). Great expectations: Preventive health concepts in child bearing and parenting for college students. *Journal of the American College Health Association, 29,* 299-301.

Kamin, L.V. (1986). Is crime in the genes? *Scientific American, 254,* 22-27.

Kanfer, F.H. and Phillips, V.S. (1970). *Learning foundations of behavior therapy.* New York: John Wiley.

Kaplan, H.B. (1980). *Deviant behavior in defense of the self.* New York: Academic Press.

Kappes, B.M. and Thompson, D.L. (1985). Biofeedback vs. video games: effects on impulsivit, locus of control and self-concept with incarcerated juveniles. *Journal of Clinical Psychology, 41,* 698-706.

Kashani, J.H., Horwitz, E. and Daniel, A.E. (1982). Diagnostic classification of 120 delinquent boys. *Bulletin of the American Association of Psychology and Law, 10,* 51-60.

Kazdin, A.E. and Wilson, G.T. (1978). *Evaluation of behavior therapy: Issues, evidence and research strategies.* Cambridge, MA: Ballinger.

Keith, C.R. (1984). Individual psychotherapy and psychoanalysis with aggressive adolescents: An historical review. In C.R. Keith (Ed.), *The aggressive adolescent.* New York: Free Press.

Keung Ho, Man (1978). Aggressive behavior and violence of youth: Approaches and alternatives. In A.M. Belkin (Ed.): *The criminal child.* Dubuque, IA: Kendall/ Hunt, pp. 79-87.

King, C.H. (1976). Countertransference and counterexperience in the treatment of violence prone youth. *American Journal of Orthopsychiatry, 46,* 43-53.

Kirkegaard-Sorensen, L.D., and Mednick, S.A. (1977). A prospective study of criminality: Intelligence. In S.A. Mednick and K.O. Christiansen (Eds.): *Biosocial bases of criminal behavior.* New York: Gardner.

Klaus P.A., Rand, M.R., and Taylor, B.M. (1983). The victim. In *U.S. Department of Justice Statistics Report to the Nation on Crime and Justice: The Data.* Washington, D.C.: U.S. Government Printing Office, pp. 17-27.

Klein, H.A. (1975). Behaviorally oriented treatment for juvenile offenders. *Corrective and Social Psychiatry and the Journal of Behavior Technology Methods and Therapy, 21,* 17-21.

Klein, N.C., Alexander, J.F., and Parsons, B.V. (1977). Impact of family systems intervention on recidivism and sibling delinquency: A model of primary prevention and program evaluation. *Journal of Consulting and Clinical Psychology, 45,* 469-474.

Knott, P.R., and Haiduk, R. (1975). *Evaluation of the closed adolescent treatment center: Final report to LEAA.* Unpublished manuscript.

Kohl, H. (1968). *Thirty-six children.* New York: Random House.

Kohlberg, L. (1976). Moral stages and moralization: The cognitive-developmental approach. In T. Libona (Ed.): *Moral development and behavior.* New York: Holt.

Kohlberg, L. (1979). *Measuring moral judgment.* Worcester, MA: Clark University Press.

Kornfeld, J.P., Eynon, T.G., Hetzner, W.A., Pfeiffer-Kornfeld, M.E., Bates, W., and Baumer, T. (1975). *State of the art of offender classification in the U.S.A.* Chicago, IL: IIT Research Institute, Criminal Justice Science and Technology Center.

Kozol, J. (1968). *Death at an early age.* Boston: Little Brown.

Kralj, M.M. and Allen, L. (1982). Deliquency prevention programs: models, methods and social policy. In S.W. Henggeler (Ed.): *Delinquency and adolescent psychopathology: A family-ecological systems approach.* Boston: John Wright.

Kretschmer, E. (1925). *Physique and character.* (W. Sprott, Trans.). New York: Harcourt Brace Jovanovich.

Kutush, S. (1978). Psychoanalytic Theories of Aggression. In I. Kutush et al. (Ed.): *Violence: Perspectives on murder and aggression.* New York: Jossey-Bass.

LaBarba, R.C. (1981). *Foundations of developmental psychology.* New York: Academic Press.

Laing, R.D., and Esterson, A. (1964). *Sanity, madness and the family.* London: Tavistock.

Lamb, H.R., and Zusman, J. (1982). Reply to comment. *Hospital and Community Psychiatry, 33,* 390-391.

Lampl-DeGroot, J. (1962). Ego ideal and superego. *Psychoanalytic Study of the Child, 17,* 94-106.

Lampl-DeGroot, J. (1949). Neurotics, delinquents and ideal formation. In K. Eissler (Ed.): *Searchlights on delinquency.* New York: International Universities Press.

Lamson, A. (1983). *Psychology of juvenile crime.* New York: Human Sciences Press.

Laub, J.H. (1983). Trends in serious juvenile crime. *Criminal Justice and Behavior, 10,* 672-693.

Laufer, W.S., Skoog, D.K., and Day, J.M. (1982). Personality and criminality: A review of the California psychological interview. *Journal of Clinical Psychology, 38,* 562-573.

Laufer, W.S., and Day, J.M. (1983). *Personality theory, moral development and criminal behavior.* Lexington, MA: Lexington Books.

Lefkowitz, M.M., Eron, L.D., Walder, L.O., and Huesman, L.R. (1977). *Growing up to be violent.* New York: Pergamon.

Lerman, P. (1968). Evaluative studies of institutions for delinquents: Implications for research and social policy. *Social Work, 13,* 55-64.

Lerman, P. (1970). *Delinquency and social policy.* New York: Frederick A. Praeger.

Leventhal, B.L. (1984). The neuropharmacology of violent and aggressive behavior in children and adolescents. In C.R. Keith (Ed.): *The aggressive adolescent.* New York: Free Press.

Levine, M., and Perkin, D.V. (1980). Social setting interventions and primary prevention: Comments on the report of the Task Panel on Prevention to the President's Commission on Mental Health. *American Journal of Community Psychology, 8,* 147-157.

Levine, V. (1983). Alienation as an affect in adolescence. In H. Golombek and B.D. Garfinkle (Eds.): *The adolescent and mood disturbances.* New York: International Universities Press, pp. 73-82.

Lewis, D.O. (1981). Delinquency and psychotic disorders. In D.O. Lewis (Ed.), *Vulnerability to delinquency.* New York: S.P. Medical and Scientific Books, pp. 5-20.

Lewis, D.O. (1981). Psychological vulnerabilities in perspective. In D.O. Lewis (Ed.): *Vulnerabilities to delinquency.* New York: S.P. Medical and Scientific Books. pp. 3-5.

Lewis, D.O. (1981). *Vulnerabilities to delinquency.* New York: S.P. Medical and Scientific Books.

Lewis, D.O. (1985). Special diagnostic and treatment issues concerning violent juveniles. In L.H. Roth (Ed.): *Clinical treatment of violent persons.* Rockville, Maryland: U.S. Department of Health and Human Services.

Lewis, D.O., Shanok and S.S., Balla, D.A. (1981). Parents of delinquents. In D.O. Lewis (Ed.): *Vulnerabilities to delinquency.* New York: Spectrum Publications.

Lippman, H. (1949). Difficulties encountered in the psychiatric treatment of chronic juvenile delinquents. In K.R. Eissler (Ed.), *Searchlights on Delinquency.* New York: International Universities Press.

Lipsey, M.W. (1984). Is delinquency prevention a cost effective strategy? A California perspective. *Journal of Research in Crime and Delinquency, 21,* 279-301.

Lipsey, M.W. (1986). What have we learned from evaluation of juvenile delinquency intervention? *Paper presented at the American Evaluation Association Annual Meeting, Kansas City, Missouri.*

Lipton, D., Martinson, R., and Wilks, J. (1975). *The effectiveness of correctional treatment: A survey of treatment studies.* New York: Praeger Publishers.

Lishner, D.M., and Hawkins, J.D. (1980). *Youth employment and delinquency prevention.* Office of Juvenile Justice and Delinquency Prevention, Law Enforcement Assistance Administration, U.S. Department of Justice. Washington, D.C.: U.S. Government Printing Office.

Little, J.W., and Skarrow, M. (1981). *Delinquency prevention: Selective organizational change in the schools.* Washington, D.C.: Office of Juvenile Justice and Delinquency Prevention.

Lochman, J. (1984). Psychological characteristics and assessment of aggressive adolescents. In C.R. Keith (Ed.): *The aggressive adolescent.* New York: Free Press.

Loeber, R., and Dishion, T. (1983). Early predictors of male delinquency: A review. *Psychological Bulletin, 94,* 68-99.

Lombroso, G. (1972). *Lombroso's criminal man.* Montclair, N.J.: Patterson Smith. (Original work published 1911.)

Lorenz, K. (1966). *On Aggression.* New York: Harcourt, Brace and World.

Lowenger, J. (1976). *Ego development.* San Francisco: Jossey-Bass.

Ludwig, F. (1955). *Youth and the law: Handbook on laws affecting youth.* Brooklyn: Foundation Press.

Lukin, P.R. (1981). Recidivism and changes made by delinquents during residential treatment. *Journal of Research in Crime and Delinquency, 18,* 101-112.

Lundman, R.J., McFarlane, P., and Scarpitti, F. (1976). Delinquency prevention and assessment of projects reported in the professional literature. *Crime and Delinquency, 22,* 297-308.

Lundman, R.J., and Scarpitti, F.R. (1978). Delinquency prevention: Recommendations for future projects. *Crime and Delinquency, 24,* 207-220.

MacDonald, G.J., Williams, R., and Nicholas, H. (1968). *Treatment of the sex offender.* Fort Steibacoon, Washington: Washington State Hospital.

MacNamara, D.E.J. (1977). The medical model in corrections: Requiescat in pace. *Criminology, 14,* 439-448.

Maher, A.R. (1961). The goals and families of psychotherapy: summary. In A.R. Maher (Ed.): *The goals of psychotherapy.* New York: Appleton-Century-Crofts.

Mahler, M., Pine, F., and Bergman, A. (1975). *The psychological birth of the human infant.* New York: Basic Books.

Malmquist, C.P. (1968). Conscience development. *Psychoanalytic Study of the Child, 23,* 301-331.

Malone, C.A. (1966). Children of disorganized families. In E. Rexford (Ed.): Developmental approaches to the problem of acting out: A symposium. *Monographs of the Journal of the American Academy of Child Psychiatry.* New York: International Universities Press.

Mann, C.M., and Pratt, M.D. (1982). *Building Bridges Inc.: An evaluation of work therapy program designed for juvenile probationers.* Dayton, OH: Montgomery County Juvenile Court.

Mann, C.R. (1984). *Female crime and delinquency.* Alabama: University of Alabama Press.

Marcia, J.E. (1966). Development and validation of ego identity states. *Journal of Personality and Social Psychology, 3,* 551-558.

Marcia, J.E. (1980). Identity in adolescence. In J. Adelson (Ed.): *Handbook of adolescent psychology.* New York: John Wiley.

Marcus, D. (1981). Juvenile delinquency in the bible and ancient near east. *Journal of Antiquity and Near East Studies, 13,* 31-52.

Marohn, R. (1980). The psychiatric response to delinquency. In M. Sugar (Ed.): *Responding to adolescent needs.* New York: S.P. Medical and Scientific Books.

Marohn, R.E., Dalle-Molle, D., McCarter, E., and Linn, D. (1980). *Juvenile delinquents: Psychodynamic assessment and hospital treatment.* New York: Brunner/Mazel Publishers.

Martinson, R. (1974). What works? — Questions and answers about prison reform. *The Public Interest, 10,* 22-54.

Martinson, R. (1977). Symposium on sentencing: Part II. *Hofstra Law Review, 7,* 243-258.

Marx, M.H. (1951). *Psychological theory: Contemporary readings.* New York: MacMillan.

Massimo, J., and Shore, M. (1963). The effectiveness of a comprehensive vocationally oriented psychotherapeutic program for adolescent delinquent boys. *American Journal of Orthopsychiatry, 23,* 634-642.

Masterson, J.F. (1967). *The psychiatric dilemma of adolescence.* Boston: Little Brown.

Matteson, A. (1981). Psychoendocrine aspects of male delinquency. In D.O. Lewis (Ed.): *Vulnerabilities to delinquency.* New York: Spectrum.

McCandless, B.R., Persons, W.S. III, and Roberts, A. (1972). Perceived opportunity, delinquency, race and body build among delinquent youth. *Journal of Consulting and Clinical Psychology, 38,* 281.

McCarthy, J.B. (1978). Narcissism and the self in homicidal adolescents. *The American Journal of Psychoanalysis, 38,* 19-29.

McCord, W., and McCord, J. (1969). *Origins of crime: A new evaluation of the Cambridge Sommerville Youth study.* Montclair, NJ: Patterson Smith.

McCord, W., McCord, J., and Howard, A. (1961). Familial correlates of aggression in nondelinquent male children. *Journal of Abnormal and Sociological Psychology, 62,* 79-93.

McCorkle, L.W. (1952). Group therapy in the treatment of offenders. *Federal probation, 16*, 11-27.

McCorkle, L.W., Elias, A., and Bixby, F.L. (1958). *The Highfields story: An experimental treatment project for youthful offenders.* New York: Holt.

McHolland, J.D. (1985). Strategies for dealing with resistant adolescents. *Adolescence, 20*, 344-368.

Mead, M. (1928). *Coming of age in Samoa.* New York: Morrow.

Mednick, S.A. (1985). Crime in the family: A study of adopted children and their adopted parents reveals that some criminal behavior may be rooted in genes. *Psychology Today, 19*, 58-61.

Mednick, S.A., and Christiansen, K.O. (1977). *Biosocial bases of criminal behavior.* New York: Gardner.

Mednick, S.A., Gabrielli, W.F. Jr., and Hutchings, B. (1984). Genetic influence in criminal convictions: Evidence from an adoption cohort. *Science*, 891-894.

Meehl, P.E. (1954). *Clinical versus statistical prediction: A theoretical analysis and a review of the evidence.* Minneapolis: The University of Minnesota Press.

Megargee, E.I. (1977). Directions for further research. *Criminal Justice and Behavior, 4*, 211-216.

Megargee, E.I. (1977a). The need for a new classification system. *Criminal Justice and Behavior, 4*, 107-114.

Megargee, E.I. (1984). A new classification system for criminal offenders, differences among the types on the adjective checklist. *Criminal Justice and Behavior, 11*, 349-376.

Megargee, E.I., and Bohn, M. Jr. (1977). Empirically determined characteristics of ten types. *Criminal Justice and Behavior, 4*, 149-210.

Megargee, E.I., and Dorhout, B. (1977). Revision and refinement of the classificatory rules. *Criminal Justice and Behavior, 4*, 125-148.

Meisener, W.W. (1982). The history of the psychoanalytic movement. In A.M. Jacobson and X. Parmelee: *Psychoanalysis: Critical explorations in contemporary theory and practice.* New York: Brunner/Mazel.

Mennel, R. (1973). *Thorns and thistles: Juvenile delinquents in the United States: 1825-1940.* Hanover, NH: The University Press of New England.

Menninger, K. (1958). The writing concept of mental illness. *Bulletin of the Menninger Clinic, 22*, 4-12.

Meyer, H.J., Borgatta, E.F., and Jones, W.C. (1965). *Girls at vocational high.* New York: Russell Sage.

Meyer, J. Jr., and Megargee, E.I. (1977). Initial development of the system. *Criminal Justice and Behavior, 4*, 115-124.

Mezzich, A.C. (1982). Exploring diagnostic formulations for violent delinquent adolescents: Conceptual considerations. *Bulletin of the American Association of Psychology and Law, 10*, 61-67.

Michaels, R. (1981). The right to refuse treatment: Ethical issues. *Hospital and Community Psychiatry, 32*, 251-258.

Miller, N.E. (1941). The frustration-aggression hypothesis. *Psychological Review, 48*, 337-342.

Miller, W.B. (1959). Prevention work with street corner groups. *Annals, 332*, 97-106.

Mirkin, M.P., and Koman, S.L. (1985). *Handbook of adolescents and family therapy.* New York: Gardner.

Mitchell, S., and Rosa P. (1981). Boyhood behavior problems as precursors of criminalities: A fifteen-year follow-up study. *Journal of Child Psychology and Psychiatry, 22,* 19-33.

Montagu, A. (1941). The biologist looks at crime. *Annals of the American Academy of Political and Social Science, 217,* 46-57.

Montague, A. (1968). Chromosomes and crime. *Psychology Today, 2,* 43-49.

Morton, J.H., Addison, H., Addison, R.G., Hunt, L., and Sullivan, J.J. (1953). A clinical study of premenstrual tension. *American Journal of Obstetrics and Gynecology, 65,* 1182-1191.

Mrad, D.F., Kabacoff, R., and Duckro, P. (1983). Validation of the Megargee typology in a halfway house setting. *Criminal Justice and Behavior, 10,* 252-262.

Mulligan, G., Douglas, J.W., Hammond, W.H., and Tizard, J. (1963). Delinquency and symptoms of maladjustment. *Proceedings of the Royal Society of Medicine, 56,* 1083-1086.

Munichen, S. (1974). *Families and family therapy.* Cambridge: Harvard University Press.

Murchison, C. (1926). *Criminal Intelligence.* Worcester, MA: Clark University.

Myerson, S. (1975). Adolescence and delinquency. In S. Myerson (Ed.): *Adolescence and breakdown.* London: George Allen and Unwin, Ltd.

Nass, M.L. (1966). The superego and moral development. *Psychoanalytic Study of the Child, 21,* 51-68.

National Advisory Commission on Criminal Justice Standards and Goals. (1973). *Corrections.* Washington, D.C.: U.S. Government Printing Office, Author.

National Advisory Commission on Criminal Justice Standards and Goals. (1976). *Juvenile justice and delinquency prevention: A report of the task force on juvenile justice and delinquency prevention.* Washington, D.C.: U.S. Government Printing Office, Author.

National Commission on the Causes and Prevention of Violence. (1969). *Crimes of violence.* Vol. 2. Washington, D.C.: U.S. Government Printing Office, Author.

National Institute for Juvenile Justice and Delinquency Prevention. (1975). *A comparative analysis of standards and state practices: Jurisdiction Preventing delinquency.* (Vol IV of IX). Washington, D.C.: U.S. Government Printing Office, Author.

National Task Force to Develop Standards and Goals for Juvenile Justice and Delinquency Prevention, U.S. Department of Justice. (1977). *A comparative analysis of standards and state practices.* 9 Vols. Washington, D.C.: U.S. Government Printing Office, Author.

Neapolitan, J. (1981). Parental influences on aggressive behavior: A social learning approach. *Adolescence, 16,* 831-840.

Nettler, G. (1978). *Explaining crime.* 2nd Ed. New York: McGraw-Hill.

Newton, M. (1978). Prevention of crime and delinquency. *Criminal Justice Abstracts, 10,* 245-266.

Nielson, G. (1983). *Borderline and acting out adolescents.* New York: Human Sciences Press.

Nielsen, G., Harrington, L., Sack, W., and Latham, S. (1985). A developmental study of aggression and self-destruction in adolescents who received residential treatment. *International Journal of Offender Therapy and Comparative Criminology, 29,* 211-236.

Nielsen, G., Young, D., and Latham, S. (1982). Multiple acting out adolescents: developmental correlates and response to secure treatment. *International Journal of Offender Therapy and Comparative Criminology, 26,* 195-206.

Nielsen, J., and Norland, E. (1975). Length of Y chromosome and activity in boys. *Clinical Genetics, 8,* 291-296.

Nielson, J., Tsuboi, T., Sturup, G., and Roman, D. (1968). XYY chromosomal constitution in criminal psychopaths. *The Lancet,* 576.

Noshpitz, J.D. (1984). Therapy with children. In N.S. Endler and J. McVicker Hunt (Eds.): *Personality and behavior disorders.* Vol. 2. New York: John Wiley.

Nunnally J. (1978). *Psychoanalytic Theory.* 2nd Ed. New York: McGraw-Hill.

Oates, K. (1986). *Child abuse and neglect: What happens eventually?* New York: Brunner/Mazel.

Offer, D. (1969). *The psychological world of the teenager: A study of normal adolescence.* New York: Basic Books.

Offer, D. (1980). In forward to book by M. Sugar (Ed.): *Responding to adolescent needs.* New York: S.P. Medical and Scientific Books.

Offer, D., and Offer, J.B. (1975). *From teenager to young manhood: A psychological study.* New York: Basic Books.

Offer, D., and Sabolin, M. (1966). *Normality.* New York: Basic Books.

Offer, D., Marohn, R.C., and Ostrov, E. (1979). *The psychological world of the juvenile delinquent.* New York: Basic Books, Inc.

Ogdon, D.P. (1967). *Psychodiagnostics and personality assessment: A handbook.* 2nd Ed. Los Angeles, CA: Western Psychological Services.

Ogdon, D.P. (1981). *Handbook of psychological signs, symptoms and syndromes.* Los Angeles, CA: Western Psychological Services.

Olweus, D. (1979). Stability of aggressive reaction patterns in males: A review. *Psychological Bulletin, 86,* 852-875.

Olweus, D. (1980). Familial and temperamental determinants of aggressive behavior in adolescent boys: A causal analysis. *Developmental Psychology, 16,* 644-660.

O'Malley, P.M., Bachman, J.G., and Johnston, J. (1965). Clinical evaluation of normal adolescents. *American Journal of Psychiatry, 121,* 864-872.

Osborn, S.G., and West, D.J. (1978). The effectiveness of various predictors of criminal careers. *Journal of Adolescence, 1,* 101-117.

Osborn, S.G., and West, D.J. (1980). Do young delinquents really reform? *Journal of Adolescence, 3* 99-114.

Owen, D.R. (1972). The 47 XYY male: A review. *Psychological Bulletin, 78,* 209-233.

Oyama, S. (1981). What does the phenocopy copy? *Psychological Reports, 48,* 571-581.

Palmer, T. (1973). The community treatment project in perspective: 1961-1973. *Youth Authority Quarterly, 26.*

Palmer, T. (1975). Martinson revisited. *Journal of Research in Crime and Delinquency, 12,* 133-152.

Palmer, T. (1978). *Correctional intervention and research: Current issues and future prospects.* Lexington, MA: Heath.

Palmer, T. (1984). Treatment and the role of classification: A review of basics. *Crime and Delinquency, 30,* 244-267.

Parsons, B.V., and Alexander, J.F. (1973). Short-term family intervention: A therapy outcome study. *Journal of Consulting Clinical Psychology, 41,* 195-201.

Patterson, G.R. (1974). Interventions for boys with conduct problems: Multiple settings, treatment and criteria. *Journal of Consulting and Clinical Psychology, 42,* 471-481.

Patterson, G.R. (1982). *Coercive family process.* Eugene, OR: Castalia Publishing Company.

Patterson, G.R. (1986). Performance models for antisocial boy. *American Psychologist, 41,* 432-444.

Patterson, G.R., and Reid, J. (1973). Intervention for families of aggressive boys: A replicative study. *Behavior and Therapy, 11,* 383-394.

Patterson, G.R., and Reid, J.B. (1984). Social interactional processes within the family: The study of the moment-by-moment family transactions in which human social development is imbedded. *Journal of Applied Developmental Psychology, 5,* 237-262.

Pennsylvania Governor's Justice Commission (1977). *Juvenile sections of 1977 Pennsylvania comprehensive plan,* Author.

Persons, R.W. (1966). Psychological and behavioral change in delinquents following psychotherapy. *Journal of Clinical Psychology, 22,* 337-340.

Peterson, A.C., and Tayloer, B. (1980). The biological approach to adolescence: Biological change and psychological adaptations. In J. Adelson (Ed.): *Handbook of adolescent psychology.* New York: Wiley.

Phillips, E.L. (1968). Achievement place: Token reinforcement procedures in a homestyle rehabilitation setting for "predelinquent" boys. *Journal of Applied Behavior, 1,* 213-223.

Piaget, J. (1932). *The moral judgment of the child.* 4th Ed. London: Routledge and Kegan Paul.

Piaget, J. (1969). *The psychology of the child.* New York: Basic Books.

Picketts, S. (1969). *House of refuge: origins of juvenile reform in New York State, 1815-1857.* Syracuse: Syracuse University Press.

Piliavin, I.M., and Brair, S. (1964). Police encounters with juveniles. *American Journal of Sociology, 70,* 206-214.

Pink, W.T. (1984). Schools, youth and justice. *Crime and Delinquency, 30,* 439-461.

Platt, A. (1979). The rise of the child saving movement: A study in social policy and correctional reform. In F. Faust and P. Brantingham (Eds.): *Juvenile justice philosophy: Readings, cases and comments.* 2nd Ed. New York: West Publishing Company.

Polk, K. (1975). Schools and the delinquency experience. *Criminal Justice and Behavior, 2,* 315-338.

Polk, K., and Schafer, W.E. (1972). *Schools and delinquency.* Englewood Cliffs: Prentice-Hall.

Poole, E.P., and Regoli, R.M. (1979). Parental support, delinquent friends and delinquency: A list of interaction effects. *Journal of Criminal Law and Criminology, 70,* 188-193.

Porter, J.B. (1984). Juvenile law. In R.H. Woody and Associates (Ed.), *The law and the practice of human services*. San Francisco, CA: Jossey-Bass, pp. 83-113.

Powell, W. (1975). Educational intervention as a preventive measure. *Criminal Justice and Behavior, 2,* 397-407.

Powers, E., and Witmer, H. (1951). *An experiment in the prevention of delinquency*. New York: Columbia University Press.

Prentice, M.M. (1972). Live and symbolic modeling in promoting moral judgment. *Journal of Abnormal Psychology, 80,* 157-161.

Prentice, N., and Kelly, F.J. (1963). Intelligence and delinquency: A reconsideration. *Journal of Social Psychology, 60,* 327-337.

Price, W.H., Whatmore, P.B., and McClemont, W.F. (1966). Criminal patients with XYY sex-chromosome complement. *The Lancet,* 565-566.

Prochaska, J.O. (1984). *Systems of psychotherapy: A transtheoretical analysis*. 2nd Ed. Homewood, IL: Dorsey.

Quay, H.C. (1964). Personality dimensions in delinquent boys as inferred from the factor analysis of case history data. *Child Development, 35,* 479-484.

Quay, H.C. (1965). Personality and delinquency. In H.C. Quay (Ed.): *Juvenile delinquency*. New York: Litton.

Quay, H.C. (1976). Classification. In H.C. Quay and J.S. Werry (Eds.): *Psychological disorders of childhood*. 2nd Ed. New York: Wiley.

Rabin, A.I. (1986). *Projective techniques for adolescents and children*. New York: Springer.

Reckless, W.C. (1970). Containment theory. In M. Wolfgang, S. Savitz and N. Johnson (Eds.): *The sociology of crime and delinquency*. 2nd Ed. New York: Wiley.

Reckless, W., and Dinitz, S. (1972). *The prevention of juvenile delinquency*. Columbus: Ohio State University Press.

Reckles, W.C., and Smith, M. (1932). *Juvenile delinquency*. New York: McGraw-Hill.

Redl, F. (1945). The psychology of gang formation and the treatment of juvenile delinquents. *Psychoanalytic Study of the Child, 1,* 367-377.

Redl, F. (1951). Ego disturbances. *American Journal of Orthopsychiatry, 21,* 273-279.

Redl, F. (1959). Strategy and technique of the life space interview. *American Journal of Orthopsychiatry, 29,* 1-18.

Redl, F. (1966). *When we deal with children: Selected writings*. New York: The Free Press.

Redl, F., and Toch, H. (1979). The psychoanalytic perspective. In H. Toch (Ed.): *The psychology of crime and criminal justice*. New York: Rinehart and Winston.

Redl, F., and Wineman, D. (1951). *Children who hate*. Glencoe, IL: The Free Press.

Redl, F., and Wineman, D. (1957). *The aggressive child*. Glencoe, IL: The Free Press.

Reiner, B.S., and Kaufman, I. (1959). *Character disorders in parents of delinquents*. New York: Family Service Association of America.

Reinherz, H.Z. (1982). Primary prevention of emotional disorders in school settings. In H.C. Schulberg and M. Killilea (Eds.): *The modern practice of community mental health*. San Francisco: Jossey-Bass.

Reitsma-Street, M. (1984). Differential treatment of young offenders: A review of the conceptual level matching model. *Canadian Journal of Criminology, 26,* 119-215.

Rendleman, D. (1979). Parens patriae: From chancery to the juvenile court. In F. Faust and P. Brantingham (Eds.): *Juvenile justice philosophy, readings, cases and comments*. 2nd Ed. New York: West.

Rexford, E. (1966a). A developmental concept of the problems of acting out. In E. Rexford (Ed.): *Developmental approaches to the problems of acting out: A symposium.* New York: International Universities Press.

Rexford, E.N. (1966b). A survey of the literature. In E.N. Rexford: *A developmental approach to problems of acting out: A symposium.* New York: International Universities Press, pp. 173-219.

Rexford, E.N., and van Anerongen, S. (1957). The influence of unresolved maternal conflicts upon impulsive acting out in young children. *Journal of American Orthopsychiatry, 27,* 75-85.

Ridley, C.R. (1984). Clinical treatment of the nondisclosing black client: A therapeutic paradox. *American Psychologist, 39,* 1234-1244.

Rimland, B., and Larson, G.E. (1985). Nutritional and ecological approaches to the reduction of criminality, delinquency and violence. In R.A. Weisheit and R.G. Culberton (Eds.): *Juvenile delinquency: A justice perspective.* Prospect Heights, IL: Waveland Press, Inc.

Rinsley, D.B. (1967). The adolescent in residential treatment: Some critical reflection. *Adolescence, 2,* 83-95.

Rinsley, D. (1971). Theory and practice of intensive residential treatment of adolescents. *Adolescent Psychiatry, 1,* 479-509.

Robbins, L.N. (1966). *Deviant children grown-up.* Baltimore: Williams and Williams.

Robins, L.N., West, P.A., and Herjanic, B.L. (1975). Arrests and delinquency in two generations: A study of black urban families and their children. *Journal of Child Psychology and Psychiatry, 16,* 125-140.

Robins A., Anasseril, E.D., Reid, J.C., and Harr, B.E. (1986). The Missouri classification system applied to female offenders; Reliability and validity issues. *Corrective and Social Psychiatry* and *Journal of Behavior Technology Methods and Therapy, 32,* 21-38.

Robinson, S. (1959). How effective are current juvenile delinquency prevention programs? *Journal of Negro Education,* 351-365.

Roberg, R.R., and Webb, V. (1981). *Critical issues in corrections: problems, trends and prospects.* New York: West.

Roebuck, J., and Atlas, R.H. (1969). Chromosomes and the criminal. *Journal of Social Therapy, 15,* 103-117.

Rogers, C. (1951). *Client centered therapy.* Boston: Houghton Mifflin.

Rogers, C. (1961). *On becoming a person.* Boston: Houghton Mifflin.

Rosenhan, D.L. (1975). The contextual nature of psychiatric diagnosis. *Journal of Abnormal Psychology, 84,* 442-452.

Rosenhan, D.C. (1979). On being sane in insane places. *Science, 179,* 250-258.

Rosenheim, M.K. (1976). *Pursuing justice for the child.* Chicago: The University of Chicago Press.

Rosenthal, D. (1970). *Genetic theory and abnormal behavior.* New York: McGraw-Hill.

Ross, R.R., and Gendreau, P. (1980). *Effective correctional treatment.* Toronto: Butterworth.

Rothman, D. (1979). The progressive legacy: Development of American attitudes toward delinquency. In L.T. Empey (Ed.): *Juvenile justice: The progressive legacy and current reforms.* Charlottesville: University Press of Virginia.

Ruben, M. (1957). Delinquency: A defense against loss of objects and reality. *Psychoanalytic Study of the Child, 12,* 335-355.

Rueger, D.B., and Liberman, R.P. (1984). Behavioral family therapy for delinquent and substance-abusing adolescents. *Journal of Drug Issues, 14,* 403-418.

Rutherford, R.B. Jr. (1978). Establishing behavioral contracts with delinquent adolescents. In A.M. Belkin (Ed.): *The criminal child.* Dubuque, Iowa: Kendal/ Hunt, pp. 88-96.

Rutter, M., and Giller, H. (1983). *Juvenile delinquency: Trends and perspectives.* New York: Guilford.

Samenow, S.E. (1984). *Inside the criminal mind.* New York: Time Books.

Sanders, W.B. (1970). *Juvenile offenders for a thousand years: Selected readings from Anglo-Saxon times to 1900.* Chapel Hill: The University of North Carolina Press.

Sandler, J. (1960). On the concept of superego. *Psychoanalytic Study of the Child, 15,* 128-162.

Saranson, I.G., and Ganzer, V.I. (1973). Modeling and group discussion in the rehabilitation of juvenile delinquents. *Journal of Counseling, 20,* 442-449.

Sas, L., Jaffe, P., and Reddon, J. (1984). Unravelling the needs of dangerous young offenders: A clinical-rational and empirical approach to classification. *Canadian Journal of Criminology, 27,* 88-96.

Scarpitti, F.R. (1964). Can teachers predict delinquency? *The Elementary School Journal, 65,* 130-136.

Schauss, A.G. (1980). *Diet, crime and delinquency.* Berkeley, CA: Parker House.

Schellhardt, T.D. (1977). Can chocolate turn you into a criminal? Some experts say so. *Journal of the International Academy of Preventive Medicine, 4,* 86-89.

Schiavi, R.C., Theilgraad, A., Owen, D.R., and White, D. (1984). Sex chromosome anomalies, hormones and aggressivity. *Archives of General Psychiatry, 41,* 93-99.

Schmideberg, M. (1956). Delinquent acts as perversions and fetishes. *International Journal of Psychoanalysis, 37.*

Schneiderman, G., and Evans, H. (1975). An approach to families of acting-out adolescents: A case study. Adolescence, 10, 495-498.

Schulsinger, F. (1980). Biological psychopathology. *Annual Review of Psychology, 31,* 583-606.

Schur, E.M. (1973). *Radical non-intervention: Rethinking the delinquency problem.* Englewood Cliffs, NJ: Prentice-Hall.

Scott, W.O. (1977). *Pre-1900 disposition of 601-type cases.* Unpublished paper. Davis, California.

Sellin, T. (1930). The house of correction for boys in Hospice of St. Michael in Rome. *Journal of the American Institute of Criminal Law and Criminology, 20,* 533-553.

Shah, S. (1977). Dangerousness: Some definitional, conceptual and public policy issues. In B. Sales (Ed.), *Perspectives in law and psychology.* Vol. 1. New York: Plenum, pp. 91-119.

Shannon, L.W. (1976). *Predicting adult careers from juvenile careers.* Unpublished manuscript. Iowa City, University of Iowa, Urban Community Research Center.

Shannon, L.W. (1977). Assessing the relationship of adult criminal careers to juvenile careers—A summary. (Microfiche, NCJ, 77737.)

Shaw, S.A. (1972). Recent developments in human genetics and their implications to problems of social deviance. *National Foundation Birth Defects, 8,* 42-82.

Shaw, S.A., and Roth, L.H. (1974). Biological and psychophysiological factors in criminality. In D. Glasser (Ed.): *Handbook of criminology.* New York: Rand McNally College Publishing Company, pp. 101-173.

Sheck, D.C., Emerich, R., and El Assal, M. (1973). Adolescents' perception of parent-child relations and development of internal-external central orientation. *Journal of Marriage and the Family, 35,* 643-654.

Sheldon, W.H. (1949). *Varieties of delinquent youth: An introduction to constitutional psychiatry.* New York: Harper and Row.

Sheldon, W.H. (with the collaboration of S.S. Stevens) (1942). *The varieties of temperament: A psychology of constitutional differences.* New York: Harper.

Shore, M., and Massimo, J. (1973). After ten years: A follow-up study of comprehensive vocationally oriented psychotherapy. *American Journal of Orthopsychiatry, 43,* 128-132.

Shore M.F., and Massimo, J.L. (1979). Fifteen years after treatment: A follow-up study of comprehensive vocational-oriented psychotherapy. *American Journal of Orthopsychiatry, 49,* 240-245.

Shore, M.F., Massing, J.L., Kiseilewski, J., and Manar, J.K. (1966). Object relations, changes resulting from successful psychotherapy with adolescent delinquents and their relationships to academic performance. *Journal of American Academy of Child Psychiatry, 5,* 93-104.

Shorr, D.N., English, D.E., and Janvier, R.L. (1979). *An assessment of evaluations of school-based delinquency prevention programs.* Office of Juvenile Justice and Delinquency Prevention, Law Enforcement Assistance Administration, Washington, D.C.: U.S. Government Printing Office.

Shulman, H.M. (1951). "Intelligence and delinquency." *Journal of Criminal Law and Criminology, 41,* 763-781.

Sielski, L.M. (1979). Understanding body language. *The Personnel and Guidance Journal, 57,* 238-242.

Simmons, J.G., Johnson, D.L., Gouvier, W.D., and Muzyczka, M.J. (1981). The Myer-Megargee inmate typology: dynamic or unstable? *Criminal Justice and Behavior, 8,* 49-54.

Simmons, C.L., Kannensohn, M.D., Foster, J.D., Johnson, A., Murphy, W.C., and White, J.L. (1981). *Major issues in juvenile justice information and training: Grants in aid of local delinquency prevention and control services.* (Project MIJJIT: Grant Number 78-JN-AX-0038) Columbus, OH: Academy of Contemporary Problems.

Skogan, W.G. (1976). *Sample surveys of victims of crime.* Cambridge, MA: Ballinger.

Slavson, S.R. (1965). *Reclaiming the delinquent.* New York: Free Press.

Slitt, W. (1977). The XYY chromosone abnormality and criminal behavior. Connecticut Law Review, 3, 484-510.

Smith, A.B., and Berlin, L. (1981). *Treating the criminal offender.* 2nd Ed. Englewood Cliffs: Prentice-Hall.

Smith, C.P., Alexander, P.S., Halatyn, T.V., and Roberts, C.F. (1979b). *A national assessment of serious juvenile crime and the juvenile justice system: The need for a rational response (Vol. II). Definitions, characteristics of incidents and individuals, and relationship to substance abuse.* (NIJJDP Grant Numbers 77-NI-99-0009 and 77JN-99-0008). Washington, D.C.: U.S. Government Printing Office.

Smith, C.P., Berkman, D., Fraser, W.M., and Sutton, J. (1979a). *A preliminary national assessment of status offenders and the juvenile justice system: Role conflicts, constraints and information gaps.* NIJJDP Grant Numbers 77 NI-99-0009 and 77JN-99-0008). Washington, D.C.: U.S. Government Printing Office.

Smith, C.P., Black, T.E., and Weir, A.W. (1979c). *A national assessment of case disposition and classification in the juvenile justice system: Inconsistent labeling Vol. III.* (NIJJDP Grant Numbers 77NI-99-0009 and 71JN-99-0008). Washington, D.C.: U.S. Government Printing Office.

Smith, C.P., Black, T. Edwin, and Campbell, F.R. (1979d). *Reports of the National Juvenile Justice Assessment Centers. A national assessment of case disposition and classification in the juvenile justice system: Inconsistent labeling* (Vol. I.). *Process description and summary.* Washington, D.C.: U.S. Government Printing Office.

Snyder, S.H., Banergee, S.P., Yamamura, H.I., and Greenberg, D. (1974). Drugs, neurotransmitters and schizophrenia. *Science, 184,* 1243-1253.

Society for the Reformation of Juvenile Delinquents (1970). The founding of the New York house of refuge. In P. Lerman (Ed.): *Delinquency and social policy.* New York: Praeger.

Sohm, R. (1970). *The institutes: A textbook of the history and system of Roman private law.* 3rd Ed. (J. Ledlie, Trans.) New York: Augustes Mikelly Publishers.

Spiegel, L. (1951). A review of contributions to a psychoanalytic theory of adolescence: Individual aspects. *Psychoanalytic Study of the Child, 6,* 375-393.

Spiegel, L.A. (1958). Comments on the psychoanalytic psychology of adolescence. *Psychoanalytic Study of the Child, 13,* 296-308.

Sprinthall, N.A., and Collins, W.A. (1984). *Adolescent psychology: A developmental view.* Reading, MA: Addison-Wesley.

Steadman, H.J., Monahan, J., Hartstone, E., Davis, S.K., and Robbins, P.C. (1982). Mentally disordered offenders; A national survey of patients and facilities. *Law and Human Behavior, 6,* 198-219.

Steele, B.F. (1976). Violence in the family. In R. Helfer and C.H. Kempe (Eds.): *Child abuse and neglect: The family and community.* Cambridge: Ballinger.

Steele, B.F., and Pollock, C.B. (1968). A psychiatric study of parents who abuse infants and small children. In R.E. Helfer and C.H. Kempe (Eds.): *The battered child.* Chicago: University of Chicago, pp. 103-147.

Stephenson, R.M., and Scarpitti, F.R. (1974). *Group interaction as therapy: The use of the small group in corrections.* Westport, CO: Greenwood Press.

Stewart, J., and Resnick, J.H. (1970). Verbal conditioning and dependence in delinquents. *Journal of Abnormal Psychology, 76,* 375-377.

Stewart, M.A., deBlois, C.S., and Cummings, C. (1980). Psychiatric disorders in the parents of hyperactive boys and those with conduct disorders. *Journal of Child Psychology and Psychiatry, 21,* 283-292.

Stewart, M.A. (1985). Aggressive conduct disorder: A brief review. *Aggressive Behavior, 11,* 323-331.

Stone, L.J., and Church, J. (1957). *Childhood and adolescence.* New York: Random House.

Stott, M.W.R., and Olczak, P.V. (1978). Relating personality characteristics to juvenile offense categories: Differences between status offenders and juvenile offenders. *Journal of Clinical Psychology, 34,* 80-84.

Strasburg, P.A. (1978). *Violent delinquents.* New York: Monarch.

Strupp, H.H. (1986). Psychotherapy: Research, practice, and public policy (how to avoid dead ends). *American Psychologist, 41,* 120-130.

Sullivan, C., Grant, M.Q., and Grant, J.D. (1957). The development of interpersonal maturity: Applications to delinquency. *Psychiatry: Journal of the Study of Interpersonal Processes, 20,* 373-385.

Sutherland, E.H. (1947). *Principles of criminology.* 4th Ed. Philadelphia: Lippincott.

Sutherland, E.H. (1952). Critique of Sheldon's varieties of delinquent youth. *American Sociological Review,* 10-13.

Sutherland, E.H., and Creesey, D.R. (1970). *Criminology.* 8th Ed. Philadelphia: Lippincott.

Szasz, T. (1961). *The myth of mental illness.* New York: Hoeber (Harper and Row).

Szasz, T.S. (1963). *Law, liberty and psychiatry.* New York: Macmillan.

Szasz, T. (1965). *Psychiatric justice.* New York: Macmillan.

Szurek, S.A. (1969). Some impressions from clinical experience with delinquents. In S.A. Szurek and I.N. Berlen (Eds.): *The antisocial child: His family and his community.* Palo Alto, CA: Science and Behavior Books.

Tanner, J.M. (1972). Sequence, tempo and individual variation in growth and development of boys and girls aged twelve to sixteen. In J. Kugan and R. Coles (Eds.): *Twelve to sixteen: Early adolescence.* New York: Norton.

Tanner, L.N. and Lindgren, H.C. (1971). *Classroom teaching and learning: A mental health approach.* New York: Holt, Rinehart and Winston.

Teasdale, T.W., Sorensen, T.I.A., and Owen, D.R. (1984). Social class in adopted and nonadopted siblings. *Behavior Genetics, 14,* 587-593.

Tedisaki, J.T., Smith, R.B., and Brown, R.C. (1974). A reinterpretation of research on aggression. *Psychological Bulletin, 81,* 540-562.

Teitelbaum, L.E., and Harris, L.J. (1977). Some historical perspectives in governmental regulation of children and parents. In L.E. Teitelbaum and A.R. Gough (Eds.): *Beyond control: Status offenders in the juvenile court.* Cambridge: Ballinger.

Telfer, M.A., Baker, D., Clark, G.R., and Richardson, C.E. (1968). Incidence of gross chromosomal errors among tall criminal American males. *Science,* 1249-1250.

Temeslin, M.K. (1970). Diagnostic bias in community mental health. *Community Mental Health, 6,* 110-117.

Teplin, L.A. (1984). *Mental health and criminal justice.* Beverly Hills: Sage.

Thrasher, F. (1936). *The gang.* Chicago: University of Chicago Press.

Tittly, C., Villenez, W., and Smith, D. (1978). The myth of social class and criminality: An empirical assessment of the empirical evidence. *American Sociological Review, 43,* 643-656.

Toch, H. (1980). *Therapeutic communities in corrections.* New York: Praeger.

Tolmach, J. (1985). There ain't nobody on my side: A new day treatment program for black urban youth. *Journal of Clinical Child Psychology, 14,* 214-219.

Tonkin, M., and Fine, H.J. (1985). Narcissism and borderline states: Kernberg, Kohut and psychotherapy. *Psychoanalytic Psychology, 2,* 221-239.

Tramontana, M. (1980). Critical review of research psychotherapy outcome with adolescents: 1967-1977. *Psychological Bulletin, 88,* 429-450.

Tulchin, S.H. (1939). *Intelligence and crime: A study of penitentiary and reformatory offenders.* Chicago: University of Chicago Press.

Under reporting of crime. (1985, Dec. 2). *New York Times,* p. B15.

U.S. Department of Commerce, Bureau of the Census (1985). *Estimates of the population of the United States by age, sex, and race: 1980-1984.* (Series P-25, No. 965). Washington, D.C.: U.S. Government Printing Office.

U.S. Department of Justice (1980). *Juvenile justice, before and after the onset of delinquency. United States discussion paper for the sixth United Nations Congress on the prevention of crime and the treatment of offenders.* Washington, D.C.: Superintendent of Documents.

U.S. Department of Justice, Federal Bureau of Investigations (1984). *Uniform Crime Reports.* Washington, D.C.: U.S. Government Printing Office. (Tables 28, 30, 35, 37).

U.S. Department of Justice, (Office of Juvenile Justice and Delinquency Prevention). (1985). *Project New Pride.* Washington, D.C.: U.S. Government Printing Office.

Vachss, A., and Bakal, Y. (1979). *The life style violent juvenile.* Lexington, MA: Lexington Books.

Vandenbos, G.R., and Pino, C.D. (1980). Research on the outcome of psychotherapy. In G.R. Vandenbos (Ed.): *Psychotherapy: Practice, research, policy.* Beverly Hills, CA: Sage.

Vaneziano, C., and Vaneziano, L. (1986). Classification of adolescent offenders with the MMPI: An extension and cross-validation of the Megargee typology. *International Journal of Offender Therapy and Comparative Criminology, 30,* 4-23.

Van Voorhis, P., Grosser, R.C., Kastan, J., and Meservey, F.B. (1983). *Prevention programs for youth: An examination of the state of the art.* (DCJS #2987). New York State Council on Children and Families, Division of Criminal Justice Services.

Varackevher, A., and Muir, B. (1975). Acting out, rebellion and violence. In S. Myerson (Ed.): *Adolescence and breakdown.* London: George Allen and Unwin, Ltd.

Varley, W.H. (1984). Behavior modification approaches to the aggressive adolescent. In C.H. Keith (Ed.): *The Aggressive Adolescent: Clinical Perspectives.* New York: Free Press.

Wall, J.S., Hawkins J.D., Lishner, D., and Fraser, M. (1981). *Juvenile delinquency prevention. A compendium of 36 program models.* National Institute for Juvenile Justice and Delinquency.Prevention. Washington, D.C.: U.S. Government Printing Office.

Walter, R.H., Leat, M., and Mezei, L. (1963). Response inhibition and distribution through empathetic learning. *Canadian Journal of Psychology, 17,* 235-243.

Warren, M.Q. (1969). The case for the differential treatment of delinquents. *Annals of the American Academy of Political and Social Science, 381,* 47-59.

Warren, M.Q. (1971). Classification of offenders as an aid to efficient management and effective treatment. *Journal of Criminal Law and Police Science, 62,* 239-258.

Warren, M.Q. (1976). Intervention with juvenile delinquents. In M.K. Rosenheim (Ed.): *Pursuing Justice for the Child.* Chicago: The University of Chicago Press.

Warren, M.Q. (1977). Correctional treatment and coercion: The differential effectiveness perspective. *Criminal Justice and Behavior, 4,* 355-376.

Waton, J.B., and Raynor, R. (1920). Conditional emotional reactions. Journal of Experimental Psychology, 3, 1-14.

Weatherly, D. (1964). Self-perceived rate of physical maturation and personality in late adolescence. *Child Development, 15,* 1197-1210.

Weathers, L., and Liberman, R.P. (1975). Contingency contracting with families of delinquent adolescents. *Behavior Therapy, 6,* 356-366.

Wedge, R. (1978). *A review of the literature on the early identification of delinquent-prone children.* Sacramento, CA: California Youth Authority.

Weeks, K.A. (1958). *Youthful offenders at Highfields: An evaluation of the effects of short-term treatment of delinquent boys.* Ann Arbor, MI: University of Michigan Press.

Weiner, I.B. (1970). *Psychological disturbance in adolescence.* New York: Wiley.

Weiner, I.B. (1982). *Child and adolescent psychopathology.* New York: Wiley.

Weis, J.G., and Hawkins, J.D. (1981). *Preventing delinquency: The social developmental approach.* Seattle: U.S. Department of Justice, Center for Law and Justice, University of Washington.

Weisheit, R.A., and Culbertson, R.G. (1985). *Juvenile delinquency: A justice perspective.* Prospect Heights, IL: Waveland.

Weissman, S., Diers, A., and Bemesderfer, S. (1974). Psychiatric services in a youth corrections unit. *Hospital and Community Psychiatry, 25,* 602-605.

West, D.J., and Farrington, D.P. (1973). *Who becomes delinquent?* London: Heinemann.

Wheeler, G., and Nichols, K.D. (1974). *A statistical inquiry into length of stay and revolving door: The case for modified fixed sentence for the juvenile offender, research series, number one.* Columbus: Ohio Youth Commission, Division of Research Planning and Development.

White, J.L. (1981). Preface. In C.L. Simmons, M.D. Kannensohn, J.D. Foster, A. Johnson, W.C. Murphy and J.L. White (Eds.): *Major issues in juvenile justice information and training: Grants in aid of local delinquency prevention and control services.* National Institute of Juvenile Justice and Delinquency Prevention. Washington, D.C.: U.S. Government Printing Office.

Wicks-Nelson, R., and Israel, A.C. (1984). *Behavior disorders of childhood.* Englewood Cliffs, NJ: Prentice-Hall.

Willock, B. (1986). Narcissistic vulnerability in the hyperaggressive child: The disregarded, unloved and uncared for self. *Psychoanalytic Psychology, 3,* 54-80.

Wilson, J.Q., and Herrnstein, R.J. (1985). *Crime and human nature.* New York: Simon and Schuster.

Winnicott, D.W. (1958). The antisocial tendency. In *Collected papers.* New York: Basic Books.

Winnicott, D.W. (1965). Psychoanalysis and the sense of guilt. In D.W. Winnicott (Ed.): *The maturational process and the facilitating environment.* New York: International Universities Press.

Winnicott, D.W. (1973). Delinquency as a sign of hope. *Adolescent Psychiatry, 2,* 364-373.

Winnicott, D.W. (1984). *Deprivation and delinquency.* London: Tavistock.

Witkin, H.A., Mednick, S.A., Schulsinger, F., Bakkestrom, E., Christiansen, K.O., Goodenough, D.R., Hirschhorn, K., Lundsteen, F., Owens, D.R., Phillips, J., Rubin, D.B. and Stocking, M. (1976). XYY and XXY men: Criminality and aggression. *Science, 193*, 547-555.

Wodaroki, J.S., Feldman, R.A., and Flax, N. (1974). Group therapy and antisocial children. *Small Group Behavior, 5*, 182-210.

Wolf, M.M., Phillips, E.L., and Fixsen, D.L. (1972). The teaching family: A new model for the treatment of deviant child behavior in the community. In S. Bijou and E. Rikes — Inesta (Eds.): *Behavior modification: Issues and extensions.* New York: Academic Press.

Wolfgang, M.E. (1983). Delinquency in two birth cohorts. *American Behavioral Scientist, 27*, 75-86.

Wolfgang, M.E., and Ferracuti, F. (1967). *The substitute of violence.* London: Tavistock.

Wolfgang, M.E., Figlio, R.M., and Sellin, T.C. (1972). *Delinquency in a birth cohort.* Chicago: University Press.

Wolpe, J., Salter, A., and Reyna, L.J. (1964). *The conditioning therapies: The challenge in psychotherapy.* New York: Holt, Rinehart and Winston.

Wright, L., Schaefer, A.B., and Solomono, G. (1979). *Encyclopedia of pediatric psychology.* Baltimore: University Park Press.

Wright, W.E., and Dixon, M.C. (1977). Community prevention and treatment of juvenile delinquency: A review and evaluation. *Journal of Research in Crime and Delinquency, 14*, 35-67.

Wulach, J.S. (1983). Diagnosing the DSM-III antisocial personality disorder. *Professional Psychology: Research and Practice, 14*, 330-340.

Wulach, J. (1983). August Aichhorn's legacy: The treatment of narcissism in criminals. *International Journal of Offender Therapy and Comparative Criminology, 27*, 226-233.

Yalom, D. (1975). *The theory and practice of group therapy.* New York: Basic Books.

Yates, A. (1981). Narcissistic traits in certain abused children. *American Journal of Orthopsychiatry, 51*, 55-62.

Yochelson, S., and Samenson, S.E. (1976). *The criminal personality.* Vols. I and II. New York: Aronson.

Yong, J.N. (1971). Advantages of group therapy in relation to individual therapy for juvenile delinquents. *Corrective Psychiatry Journal of Social Therapy, 17*, 34-39.

Zager, L.D. (1982). *A critical review of derivation procedures and recent investigations of its generalizability and dynamic features.* FCI Research Reports, U.S. Department of Justice, Federal Prison System.

Zeleny, L.D. (1983). Feeblemindedness and criminal conduct. *American Journal of Sociology, 38*, 564-576.

Zimiles, H. (1967). Preventive aspects of school experience. In E.L. Cowen, E.A. Gardner and M. Zax (Eds.): *Emergent approaches to mental health problems.* New York: Appleton-Century-Crofts.

Zimring, F. (1970). The serious juvenile offender: Notes on an unknown quantity. In U.S. Department of Justice, *The serious juvenile offender.* Minneapolis, Minnesota: Office of Juvenile Justice and Delinquency Prevention.

AUTHOR INDEX

227

SUBJECT INDEX